UNTAMED SPIRIT II

LIVING A DREAM

DORIS MARON

iUniverse, Inc.
New York Bloomington

Untamed Spirit II
Living a Dream

iUniverse books may be ordered through booksellers or by contacting:

iUniverse
1663 Liberty Drive
Bloomington, IN 47403
www.iuniverse.com
1-800-Authors (1-800-288-4677)

ISBN: 978-1-4502-3277-7 (sc)
ISBN: 978-1-4502-3278-4 (ebook)

Printed in the United States of America

iUniverse rev. date: 06/11/2010

Contents

Foreword

I was there on that rainy summer day in Emily Murphy Park on the Edmonton (Alberta) riverbank, when friends said goodbye and "Good Luck" to Doris Maron.

Many of us envied her; none of us would be brave enough or determined enough to undertake an adventure of this magnitude.

In the following three years she rode her "Magna" through forty-four countries on six continents, covering over 120,000 kilometers.

There were difficulties posed by weather, bad roads, pro-bureaucratic border crossings and sometimes, bad water and food. But the overriding impression Doris returned with, was, that ordinary people all over the world are wonderfully friendly and helpful. Fellow adventurers she met along the way, whether on motorcycles, bicycles or on foot were all cut out of the same cloth.

This strong woman, riding all alone, found the way to get to know the "real world",— something you can never do by flying to all the tourist hot-spots around the globe.

Reading this book will help you understand.

Rudi Zacsko Sr.

Acknowledgments

Many people have encouraged me to write about my experiences traveling as a single female around the globe. The list is unending and I thank each and every one of you.

The first person I must thank is Colleen McFarland. Colleen was my biggest supporter when I was planning my journey and her support continued throughout my travels. Colleen, you cannot imagine how much your e-mails meant to me when I was alone in foreign countries— Thank you. Thank you to Rudi Zacsko Sr. for writing the foreword for my book and for all the friendly advice about places previously traveled on your motorcycling journeys. Thank you to the staff at iUniverse for your recommendations, advice and patience.

Thank you to all my friends in the motorcycling community who encouraged me to write and helped build my confidence. Thank you to all my friends outside of the motorcycling community for your support and interest in my story. Last but not least, thank you to my family for standing by me and for not writing me off as a *vagabond*. A special thank you to my children and grandchildren. I hope these stories will give you courage and inspiration to follow your dreams.

I wish to say a very special thanks to all the wonderful people I met during my travels; those who were so gracious with their hospitality, those I traveled with briefly, those who helped me in so many ways, and those who were just there to add to my experiences.

I add, with great gratitude and appreciation, a special thanks to all my readers. Your feedback on my first book (*Untamed Spirit—Around the World on a Motorcycle*) and your inquiries on the status of my second book (*Untamed Spirit II—Living a Dream*) held me to the commitment.

Thank you.

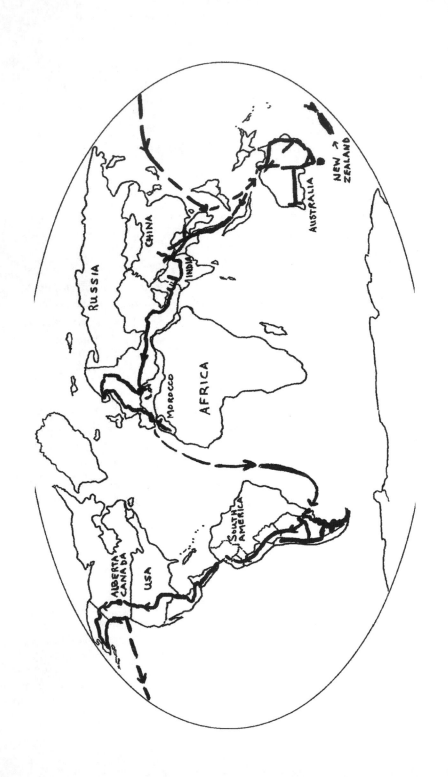

Introduction

I had a dream to travel the world. Or was it a passion that, over the years of my life, grew to be a burning desire? However it came to be, I knew I must eventually follow it.

In 1989, at forty-one years of age, I took the motorcycle safety-training course and bought my first motorcycle. This was the beginning of my travels throughout North America. Over the next eleven years I traveled by motorcycle into most of the states in America and all ten provinces across Canada. These journeys ranged from weekend getaways to multiple-week trips.

In year 2000 I joined two fellow riders and traveled from the Pacific to the Atlantic and back, riding east across the United States and west across Canada. What an adventure! We were on the road for seven weeks—not nearly long enough to see all that I wanted to see.

My passion for traveling only became greater during those days as I could see the years passing by. When I returned from my "cross-Canada/USA" adventure, I began to think about going around the world. I spoke to friends within the motorcycling community about my idea, in hopes of enticing someone to join me. This did not materialize. The commitment was far too great. But I knew that if I waited much longer, I would soon be too old for such an adventure. I feared waking up one morning and saying, "I wish I had … "

Ideas began to evolve into plans. Everything was falling into place.

All too soon the date for my departure arrived and I set out on the biggest journey of my lifetime. On August 4, 2001, at the age of fifty-three, I left Edmonton, Alberta and headed for Alaska. The disaster of September 11, 2001 (9/11) almost stopped me, but I knew that if I quit now, I would never start again.

After Alaska I shipped my bike to Australia where I was reunited with my youngest son who moved there more than two years earlier. I toured most of Australia, flew to New Zealand, came back to Australia, and then moved on to Singapore. From Singapore I rode to Malaysia. Here I met and traveled for two weeks with Martin and Jen, a couple from the Netherlands who were riding BMWs.

From Malaysia I entered Thailand, riding north through the narrow peninsula to Bangkok. I stayed in Bangkok for seven months, teaching English as a second language. My work was part-time, allowing ample opportunity to explore Cambodia, Laos, and the northern parts of Thailand.

My first book, *Untamed Spirit—Around the World on a Motorcycle*, explored these first nineteen months of my journey. I am picking up the story here, with *Untamed Spirit II—Living a Dream*. It is March 4, 2003. I have been on the road for one year and seven months. Next stop … Kathmandu, Nepal.

Chapter 1

Nepal

Today is Tuesday, March 4, 2003. My flight to Nepal leaves Bangkok airport at 2:15 PM. After eight months in Thailand I am anxious to resume my travels. I still have half the world to see and I have already been away from home for nineteen months. This journey will definitely take longer than two years.

I feel excited about going to the exotic city of Kathmandu, seeing the Himalayan Mountains, and possibly entering Tibet. I have heard great things about Nepal. At this point in time, however, the Canadian Embassy is not recommending travel in Nepal. It was approximately a year ago that King Birendra and some of his immediate family were assassinated. I have made contact with other travelers and it seems they have not had any problems, so I will continue on this route.

My flight is an hour late leaving Bangkok so it is late afternoon when we touch down at the Tribhuvan Airport in Kathmandu. In spite of the short runways, our landing is so smooth I don't even feel the wheels make contact with the ground. Coming through Customs is a breeze. I pay thirty dollars US for a sixty-day visa and proceed out of the building.

Taxi drivers, pushing their services, immediately bombard me. I politely refuse and look for a payphone to call the *Servas* family I contacted by e-mail in December. Servas is a worldwide, non-profit organization of travelers hosting travelers. I joined while in New Zealand, and have met many wonderful people and stayed in their homes. Dr. Gyanendra Shestra has invited me to stay in his home and has instructed one of his family members to pick me up at the airport.

The payphones do not accept change and I am without a phone card, unable to make a call. To my surprise one of the taxi drivers notices my predicament and offers to lend me his card. I reach Gyanendra's daughter, Shreetu. She says she will be right there to get me. She explains that I must get out of the airport to the front gates, as people cannot drive through without an airline ticket. The gate is down a steep hill and quite a distance from here. With my mass of luggage I must use a taxi. Now I know why the driver was so generous with his card.

When we arrive at the house I meet Mrs. Shestra and their eldest son Dhariz. Their younger son and Dr. Shestra are away at a convention and will not be home for a couple of days. Shreetu and her mother show me around the house and to the room I will be staying in. The house is 150 years old and has been handed down for generations. It is constructed of cement and is tall and narrow, rising up four stories, like a small apartment building. The stairs are very narrow and steep. On the first floor is the doctor's office, reception room, casting room, and a squat toilet with a wash-up room directly across the hall. Dr. Shestra is a well-known orthopedic doctor in Nepal. We continue up the narrow staircase to the second floor where there is a small bathroom with a squat toilet and shower, but no sink. Shreetu explains that the rest of this floor is the living quarters for other family members, but the bathroom is for the whole house. On the third level are three bedrooms and a living room for Dr. Shestra's family. On the fourth floor are the kitchen, two bedrooms, a prayer room, and a square cement trough with a tap. Here is where the maid does the dishes and the family members brush their teeth and wash their hands and faces. This is not an elaborate home. The cement walls are dull and lack color, evoking a cold and dreary feeling. It shows its age and is in much need of upgrading and maintenance.

Shreetu is a lovely young woman, about nineteen years of age, who attends college. She gives up her bedroom on the fourth level and moves into the smaller one across the hall. I protest, telling the family I am quite happy with the smaller room, but they will not hear of it. I have time to settle in and relax before meeting another cousin and his family. Everyone speaks fairly good English except for Mrs. Shestra, who understands, but speaks very little of it.

The evening temperature is cool in Nepal and I have to dig out my fleecy jacket. The windows are left open to allow the fresh air in, and I wonder why no one else is cold. I have been in balmy Thailand for so long that my body will have to adjust to the cooler climate.

Mrs. Shestra makes dinner but does not eat at the table with Shreetu, Dhariz, and myself. Nepalese custom is for the wife to eat later. After dinner I wash up and settle in for the night. It has been a long and tiring day.

Gyanendra calls that night and instructs his son, Dhariz, to assist me in getting my bike out of customs the next day. I am ever so grateful as it will be an immense help to have someone interpret for me.

The next morning I hop on the back of Dhariz's 100cc motorcycle and ride to air cargo. We stop at a bank machine before going to the airport so I can get some Nepal rupees. A security guard, with a rifle propped against his shoulder, stands outside the booth that is only large enough to hold one person. One Canadian dollar is equal to approximately fifty rupees so I draw out the equivalent of two hundred dollars. I tuck it into my money belt and leave, feeling extremely self-conscious about carrying that much cash on me.

We arrive at the cargo sheds before they open and wait for about twenty minutes. Finally a well-dressed man approaches us and gets the ball rolling. First he sends us back to the airport to retrieve the shipping papers. Upon entering the big gates to the airport we are met by five soldiers wielding rifles on their shoulders. I show my waybill and they wave us through to proceed up the hill. Once my waybill is verified against their shipping documents, we are instructed to return to the air cargo lot.

The customs officer who is serving us speaks English, but as we proceed he continually talks to Dhariz in Nepali rather than address me. I believe he is negotiating a price for his services. In less than an hour my oversize crate is delivered to the dock by a forklift. After the numbers are checked against my documents and I pay the customs agent one thousand rupees (about twenty Canadian dollars), I am allowed to dismantle the crate. Immediately, several dockworkers offer to help. They even offer to take the crate away.

"They will use the wood," Dhariz explains. "It is worth about two thousand rupees."

This is wonderful. In Australia I had to pay them to dispose of the crate.

My helpers remain watching as I reassemble the bike and wheel it down the dock ramp. Dhariz has taken my jerry can and gone to buy fuel. We are not allowed to bring it inside the cargo compound so we must push the bike across the huge yard and outside the gates. With gas now in the bike, I follow my friend through this manic traffic to a map store, and then back to his home. I can see that driving here is going to be more hectic than in Bangkok. I think I will be doing a lot of walking.

The next morning Shreetu walks with me to "New Road"—a popular shopping area. I desperately need a pair of hiking boots and this is a good place to start, as dozens of shops line the street. I try on several boots and finally find a pair that fit and will be sufficient for hiking and riding.

Shreetu has left for a class and I continue on to Durbar Square. The buildings are fascinating—temples, Buddhist shrines, and statues built several centuries ago. I enter the Temple of Kumari, which houses *The Living Goddess of Nepal*. She is a child chosen at a very young age, born Buddhist, and believed to have the spirit of Kumara in her. When she has her first menstrual cycle she is no longer the Goddess. A new child is then chosen, who is believed to hold the Spirit of Kumara. Kumara, meaning "always a youth", is believed to be one of God's sons and holds the knowledge of the pathway to Heaven. Once each year the King of Nepal seeks the Kumari's blessing.

The Goddess appears at the window in the courtyard at set hours during the day. My timing is perfect. I am only in the courtyard a few minutes before she makes her presence. She is a beautiful child, and my heart aches for her as I wonder what kind of life she has. Is she missing out on her childhood?

A guide latches onto me in the courtyard, wanting to show me around. I manage to shake him off and continue on my own. An hour later, as I sit at the top of Maju Deval Temple, enjoying the view from the center of the square, the same man approaches me again. He is very persistent and presents a strong case. I finally relent and accept his offer to be my guide.

Tanu is a wonderful guide, explaining the roles of various statues as he shows me through the temples. There are three major Gods: Lord Shiva the destroyer, Lord Brahma (Buddha) the creator, and Lord Vishnu the preserver. The stories are intriguing and I find myself curious to learn more.

From Durbar Square we hike up to the Swayambhunath Stupa, more commonly known as the Monkey Temple. The nickname is fitting, as this seems to be a favorite spot for monkeys to hang out. The Stupa sits high on a hill overlooking the Kathmandu valley, providing a spectacular sight of the city below—or should I say, "It would be a spectacular sight except for the smog that hangs heavily over the city below." Kathmandu is nestled in a valley surrounded by mountains that trap the pollution and prevent it from blowing away, thus creating a constant smog cover.

I pay my guide and thank him for the wonderful tour, then retrace my steps to Durbar Square. My feet ache so I sit for a time on the steps of Maju Deval before going in search of Freak Street. In the early 1960's Freak Street was a hippy hangout. Today it is still a popular street lined with good restaurants. I pick one and stop for lunch. The menu is varied with a fair selection of western food, so I enjoy a sandwich and fries before walking back to the Shestra home.

I have been at the Shestras' for three days when Gyanendra (the doctor, husband and father) returns home. Early in the morning he takes me to meet Mr. Bibendra, the National Secretary for Servas Nepal. Mr. Bibendra is very helpful with travel information and encourages me to contact Servas hosts as I travel in his country. I appreciate his input and accept the directory listing the hosts in Nepal.

When we return home Dr. Shestra shows me around his shop. He has a patient this morning and invites me to sit in while he fits a man with an artificial leg. He also does a lot of volunteer work at the children's hospital, providing free artificial limbs for child amputees. He is an honorable man and a highly respected doctor.

With his patient taken care of, Gyanendra leads me out through the back of the house and shows me the shop where employees build artificial limbs, corrective shoes, and whatever else his patients might need. From here we go to the second floor and exit out the back to another workshop where women are sewing kidney belts, arm slings, braces, et cetera. Dr. Shestra asks if I wear a kidney belt (a wide padded belt protecting the lower back) when I ride my motorcycle. When I say no, he instructs one of the women to make one for me.

"You must wear a kidney belt when you are riding that much," he says. He asks one of the seamstresses for a tape, measures my waist and hips, and a few minutes later I have a custom-made kidney belt. Wow, how wonderful is that!

From this workshop on the second floor we take an outside staircase up two flights to the rooftop at the back of the house. Here is where the laundry is washed and hung to dry on a line that runs the length of the flat roof. Every bit of usable space has a purpose.

Later that evening I hop on the back of Dr. Shestra's little motorcycle for a tour around the city. We ride to Paton's Durbar Square, the Golden Temple (which is actually black), the homes of family and friends, and to Thamel, in the heart of Kathmandu.

Thamel, the tourist center of Kathmandu, is crowded with people. Many guesthouses, backpacker's hostels, restaurants, and shops line the narrow streets. The buildings are tall, making the streets seem even narrower. Shopping is abundant with some excellent bargains to be had.

It is after 10:00 PM by the time we return home and I'm exhausted. I wonder if my hosts always keep such late hours. Dr. Shestra says, "I get up at 5:00 every morning, go to the family temple for prayers, do yoga, meditate, and bathe before breakfast at 8:00." Just the thought of it makes me tired. Maybe they rest in the afternoon so they are able to maintain this pace.

The houses in Nepal are all made from brick and cement. There is no central heating even though the weather in winter is quite cold. Portable heaters are used to heat the home, but this time of year is not cold enough to justify that. In the morning the Shestras open all the windows and wear heavy clothes to stay warm. The women wear shawls and blankets wrapped around their heads and shoulders. Boy, what I would give for a nice wool blanket. This is quite a contrast to the weather in Thailand, where temperatures were over 30 degrees Celsius. Here in Nepal, by 10:00 AM it warms up enough to wear a t-shirt and stays very pleasant until about five or six in the evening.

On March 8 Gyanendra takes me sightseeing—he on his little 100cc Honda with me following on my 750cc Honda Magna. We go to the Pashupatinath Temple where the Hindu people cremate their *expired*. The term "dead" is not used here. Non-Hindus are not allowed in this temple so we continue toward the river where Buddhist cremations are taking place. We cross the bridge to the other side of the river and watch.

Gyanendra explains the activities. "There is no ceremony," he says.

"The family has grieved before the cremation takes place. The ideal situation for a person to expire is to come, or be brought down to the river and die with their feet in the water."

Six to ten people perform the duties of the cremation. First, large pieces of wood are placed in orderly crosshatch formation on top of one of the many pedestals that line the riverbank. The body, wrapped 'mummy style' in bright orange cloth, is carried out and placed on the cement beside the pedestal. Four men pick up the body and, while chanting, carry it around the pedestal three times before placing it on the wood platform. Two men remove the orange wrap, exposing a white wrap. One man pours water over the face and head while two others pile straw bundles neatly over the entire body, and stuff more straw into spaces at the bottom of the wood. One man lights a long stick and touches it first to the straw at the head, and then to the straw at the base. The cremation has begun. When the wood has burned down to an ash, everything is pushed into the river. It is common to see men bathe in the river after a cremation, as this water is considered sacred.

From here we ride to the Boudha Stupa—the temple of worship for a considerable population of Tibetans who fled Tibet during the Chinese invasion of 1959. It is the largest Stupa in Nepal and one of the largest in the world. It looks exactly like the Swayambhunath Stupa (Monkey Temple).

It is now four days since I arrived at the Shestra home and time to move on. The Poudal family in Bishal Nagar, a sub-division of Kathmandu, has requested that I stay with them. Mr. Poudal is a Servas host and also owns the Yeti Trekking Company.

After lunch I pack my things and say goodbye to my wonderful hosts. They insist I eat with them again, even though we had lunch just an hour ago. Dr. Shestra presents me with a gift—the face of a Goddess made from pewter. It is a gift I will cherish forever.

My bike is packed and I am about to leave when Dr. Shestra decides he should ride with me to Bishal Nagar. How kind of him. In this hectic traffic I will accept all the help I can get. Mr. Poudal meets us at the top of the hill near his home and thanks Dr. Shestra for accompanying me. I ride down a dirt street to a gated mansion where Mr. Poudal instructs me to park my bike in the yard next door. This yard and home, surrounded by a high fence and locked gate, belongs to

Mr. Poudal's mother. He explains that my bike will be safer here since the gate in his yard is left unlocked for receiving trekking clients.

The Poudal home is grand! My host leads me up a long, wide, polished marble staircase to my room on the second floor. The double locked doors at the top of the stairs open to a beautiful large foyer with a small table and two chairs. My bedroom is the first room at the beginning of a long hallway. The next room is a large sitting room and the bathroom is at the end. The hallway makes a right turn to more rooms occupied by the family. The staircase continues up to the third and fourth floors with locked double doors to similar foyers on each landing. The family living room is on the third floor, and the fourth floor houses the kitchen and dining area with a rooftop patio overlooking Kathmandu to the east.

I am fortunate to have made this contact. Mr. Poudal arranges a safari in Chitwan National Park and a fourteen-day trek of the Jomosom track in the Annapurna Himalayas for me. The total cost of the seventeen-day package, including a guide for the trek, is 26,500 Nepal rupees (530 Canadian dollars).

I have two days to prepare for my next adventure. Mr. Poudal walks with me to a shopping center nearby, then to the Thamel area where I buy last-minute items for my trek. We have walked many blocks and Mr. Poudal is tired, so he hires a taxi to take us to a restaurant. At one point the taxi pulls over to the side of the road and stops. Before I can ask why, my host explains that when a cat crosses the road in front of you, it signifies bad luck. To counteract the bad luck you must wait until someone walks across the road or another vehicle drives past. The driver only waits a few seconds before it is *safe* to continue. He stops at a new hotel sitting high on a hill, with grounds still under construction. The view of Kathmandu is awesome from here—except for the pollution that hangs overhead. Mr. Poudal instructs the taxi driver to wait while we go in for lunch. This family is obviously amongst the wealthier population.

The following evening I am invited to accompany the family to an event celebrating the birth of a child. During our walk to the party I meet Mrs. Poudal for the first time. She is quiet and does not make an attempt to speak to me. Soon we arrive at the party where guests are gathered in a large open courtyard. Mr. Poudal introduces me to family members and friends and tells them briefly about my trip around the world. At first the women seem to hold back and do not speak to me.

Maybe they feel threatened. As the evening wears on they relax and include me in their conversations. The meal is a huge potluck buffet prepared by the women in attendance—not much different from back home, except for the type of food. At this function the women and men eat together, unlike the tradition in homes and formal gatherings.

I learn that Mr. Poudal also does some great volunteer work. He built a school in one of the rural mountain villages and runs it with his own money. One hundred and sixty students now attend. He solicits volunteers to teach, and sometimes goes out to teach a class or two himself. He also sends a doctor out periodically to perform examinations on all the people in the village. Besides this he does other community volunteer work. Today he makes this profound comment, "when we die we don't have anything, and it is my desire to leave something behind"—*What a wise and generous soul.*

It is late when we return from the party and I appreciate that I packed my backpack earlier. Tomorrow I leave for my jungle safari and then a two-week trek in the Annapurna Himalayas. I hope I am fit enough. The trek reaches an elevation of almost four thousand meters.

Driving in Kathmandu is crazier than in Bangkok. The only difference is that the locals do not drive as fast because the roads are full of bumps and holes. But people just drive wherever they want. One day I thought I was going the wrong way on a one-way street because all the vehicles coming towards me filled the road. Then I saw a couple of cars turn into the street going in the same direction as me and somehow they made it. Vehicles and bikes successfully wind their way around each other. It is a crazy system but it seems to work. I wonder what it will be like when I get out of the city.

Early the next morning I make my way, with great difficulty, out of Kathmandu. The street consists of holes, rocks, and broken pavement. I begin to wonder if this is the right road leading to Pokhara, so decide to stop and ask. "Yes, keep going that way" a storeowner says, pointing in the direction I was going.

For an hour I struggle through the road mess and traffic, often following big trucks and buses belching black smoke from their exhausts. I hope to be out of the city soon and escape these vehicles. The road climbs and follows along the side of the mountains surrounding Kathmandu. Most of the mountainsides are terraced with small flat platforms for gardens, farming, and homes. It looks quite beautiful but I try to visualize how spectacular it was before the trees were cut down. It seems there is road construction happening in several places along this highway and I travel most of the morning in slow-moving traffic and polluted air. I was so looking forward to some clean mountain air.

It is not until I leave this highway and head south towards Chitwan National Park that I finally breathe some clean air. Rains have washed out some parts of the road and riding is slow. It is noon before I reach the Jungle Lagoon Safari Lodge, after stopping several times to ask for directions. I get settled into my room and have a short nap before joining a walking tour through Tharu Village with the lodge owner, Gyander.

The villagers greet us as we walk. Gyander is well known here and residents display friendship and respect. Houses are made of bamboo and covered with a mud plaster. Each year another layer of plaster is added to the walls—very efficient. The roofs are made of thatch and the floor is dirt. Every morning the villagers spread a layer of mud made from clay and cow dung over the floor. My host tells me that cows are sacred and the dung helps kill insects. Cow piss is used for healing wounds on humans—they tell me it is like an antiseptic.

The next morning I get up early, ready for a trek into the jungle with my young guide, Rahj. We hike about twenty minutes to a dock where we meet two women from Saskatchewan and share a canoe for the half-hour ride down the river. We spot a crocodile on the far bank and watch as he slips quietly into the water. *I hope he is swimming in the other direction!*

We reach our destination and begin our trek. The jungle here is not extremely thick, but thick enough that I would not want to be out here alone. We see a rhino and keep our distance. A deer runs through the high grass and is only visible as it leaps across the opening in the trees. Monkeys are plentiful and swing from branch to branch, while birds of many varieties sing in the treetops. We do not see a tiger but I am not disappointed. Somehow I feel a bit nervous at the thought of getting too close to one while walking.

On our way back to the lodge my guide crosses the river on a fallen tree that rests about a meter above the water. Before I have a chance to protest, he is on the other side. I call out to him, "Do I have to cross here?"

"Yes," he states, very matter of fact.

"Is this the only way across?" I ask.

"We can go around, but we will walk another hour longer," he replies.

"Okay, but if I have to walk across that log, you must come back for my camera and take a picture of me."

Rahj grins and comes back across the log, sprinting as if he were on a wide sidewalk. He takes my camera and returns to the other side. It looks so easy. I should be able to do this. I get my footing on the log and gingerly stand up, gaining my balance. As I walk the log Rahj coaches me, telling me to look ahead. This takes me back to my youth when my younger sister, and brothers and I would walk the log fence rails on the farm. What fun we had. My balance was a lot better back in those days, though. Thank goodness this crossing is not too long and I make it without falling in. I think about that crocodile we saw earlier today—maybe that is what keeps me from falling.

After lunch I join a group of tourists on an elephant safari into the jungle. I am teamed up with John and Kate, a father and daughter from Australia, and one other person who does not speak English. The four of us share a square box-like saddle that is strapped to the back of the elephant. John is a big man and takes up more than his share of space. The fit is snug and rather uncomfortable, to say the least. Two hours in this saddle and body squeeze is more than enough. However, the view from this height is wonderful and we see several rhinos including a mom and baby. Even the baby is huge!

Our guide tells us that the elephant rules the jungle. We are treated to a demonstration when the elephant I am riding boots a very large rhino off the path with his trunk. We go past tree houses built high in the branches that are used for watching wildlife. One can rent these and spend the night out here in the jungle. I'm not brave enough for that so I will give it a miss. As we ride back to the lodge in an open jeep it starts to pour rain. Being one of the first dropped off, I don't get too wet but some of the others are sure to be soaked in minutes.

Today has been a fabulous adventure and I would love to stay longer, but tomorrow I must leave for Pokhara. At 8:00 PM it is still pouring rain and I begin to wonder if I will make it out of here on these roads.

I pack up and leave after breakfast. The roads are wet but hard packed, making riding tolerable. I follow Gyander's directions, but when I come to the river I am faced with a temporary bridge just wide enough to handle a motorcycle or bicycle. I stop my bike and walk half way across the bridge to determine its safety. It looks pretty shaky but I have no other choice—the main bridge was washed out with the heavy rains of the past few days.

I cross slowly and on the other side must climb a steep sandy bank to reach the road. There is no point in stopping. I keep the throttle steady, increasing power as I near the top and ride safely onto level ground. From here the road improves and I enjoy the mountain scenery on my four-hour ride to Pokhara. I am high in the mountains but there is no snow and the temperature is comfortable for riding.

In Pokhara I find the Royal Guesthouse and begin sorting my backpack. I try to keep the weight down for my trek into the Annapurna Himalayas. I will leave my bike, locked and covered, in the courtyard of the guesthouse. Benjh, the proprietor, assures me that it will be safe. My guide, Dawa Tamang, arrives later in the evening, and we have a chance to get acquainted before our two weeks together. Dawa is a short man with wavy black hair, dark skin, and a pleasant smile. I guess him to be about forty-five years old and can see he is in good shape. He is a family man and takes on guiding for a second income. I am totally dependent on him out here and have to trust that Yeti Trekking has assigned a reliable person.

Early the next morning I do forty-five minutes of yoga before meeting Dawa. The exercises and stretches are important if I am to complete this trek. Dawa and I negotiate a price for a taxi to take us to Naya Pul, the beginning of the trail. The sun is shining and it is a beautiful clear day. Dawa points out the peaks of Annapurna South, Annapurna 1, 2 and 4, and many other peaks visible this morning. It takes an hour to reach our starting point where I pay the taxi driver five hundred and fifty rupees before strapping on my backpack. I cannot help but notice that Dawa's pack is about one-third the size of mine.

It is 9:00 AM when we begin our hike up the mountain trail through small villages and past homes situated on the terraced mountainsides. We climb, descend, and then climb again, stopping only for short snack breaks and lunch. We reach Tikedungha around 4:30 and stop for the day. We have increased in elevation from one thousand meters to 1,525 (approximately 5,000 feet). My room at the Chandra Guesthouse is fifty rupees, which is about one Canadian dollar. It is nothing fancy. The building is constructed of cement or rock blocks and has two levels of rooms consisting of two to four single beds each. My room is on the second level with two single beds, an old dresser, and a table light. The bathroom and shower are downstairs on the ground level. I have brought my sleeping bag, tied to the bottom of my backpack, and am thankful for its warmth when the temperature drops considerably after sundown.

There is not a lot to do in these small mountain villages. I meet Mark, a trekker from England, and we swap stories of our first day on the trail. I feel very good and my muscles don't ache, so I'm confident I will be fine. Mark is a lot younger than me, in excellent shape, and only doing a four-day hike. Mark's guide tells us that the second day is the hardest. Tomorrow we will see ...

I awaken at 6:00 next morning and try to meditate, but cannot seem to quiet my mind for any length of time. I am anxious to get going. It is 8:00 by the time we finish breakfast and hit the trail. The temperature is cool and I wear my lined nylon jacket over a long sleeved t-shirt. It is a steep climb for the first two hours, and then the ground flattens out for a stretch before rising once again. This pattern continues throughout the day on a trail of dirt, gravel, and rock. Large flat rock slabs create narrow paths and steps running through the villages. We meet several donkey caravans trudging up and down hauling goods between settlements. I marvel at the surefootedness of the donkeys as they clamber over rocks, boulders, and sharp inclines and declines.

The last hour seems to be a continual climb and I begin to wonder when Dawa will call it a day. At 3:00 in the afternoon we reach Ghorapani and climb another hour to the top of the village to find the Moonlight Hotel. We have increased in elevation from 1,525 to 2,750 meters. Today is the hardest day of the Jomosom Trek and I made it!

There is a fire burning in a barrel heater in the lodge where six other trekkers from Germany and Australia are enjoying a warm drink. I drop my pack in my room and take out the clothes I need to wash. Dawa directs me to a tap outside in the middle of the yard, where I wash my clothes in freezing cold water. I bring them into the lodge and hang them on lines strung over the barrel heater. There is time to warm up around the fire and chat with other guests before dinner, then an early exit to bed.

On day three we start again at 8:00 AM and hike on a steady downhill trail. I am doing great until about 11:30 when my knees begin to feel the strain. I do some stretches when we stop for lunch and try to relieve the pain. Back on the trail the pain escalates. Dawa carves a walking stick for me, and I hobble along feeling (and probably looking) like an invalid. As we make our way through a small village, children run out with their hands outstretched for money or gifts. Three children continue to follow me past the village, chattering and grabbing at my backpack. I want to scream at them, "Leave me alone. Can't you see I'm a cripple?" Of course I don't, but the pain is so severe now that it has put me in a foul mood. I finish the last two hours of the day sidestepping my way down rocks and cliffs. At the sight of the next donkey caravan, I tell Dawa he might have to hire one of those to carry me out of here. He looks concerned.

We stop early (3:00 PM) today, arriving at Tatopani just as the rain starts. We have dropped in elevation from 2,750 to 1,190 meters. After we check into the lodge Dawa takes me down to the natural hot springs and tells me a soak in the pool will help my knees. I do not have a bathing suit with me so I roll up my pant legs and sit with my feet and legs soaking in the hot water. The pool is quiet but soon I am joined by others who strip out of their clothes and slip into the water. Now I realize why Dawa looked at me strangely when I said I did not have a bathing suit.

On my way back to the Dhalagri Lodge I walk through a garden of mandarin orange and lemon trees. The fruit is enormous and I ask the desk clerk if I may pick some. He tells me that picking is not allowed but I can buy some from him. I purchase a few oranges and enjoy them immensely.

The rain stops sometime during the night and the sun is shining when we leave at 7:40 next morning. It is a gorgeous day but by mid-morning I feel myself slowing down. I tread cautiously on the descents so my knees do not give out. We stop at Ghasa and have lunch at the National Guesthouse rooftop restaurant. As I sit on the patio drinking lemon tea, I look out at the white peaks of mountains surrounding me and realize that I am deep in the Annapurna Himalayas of Nepal—breathtaking and exhilarating!

We have not hiked far after lunch when Dawa offers to take my pack. I protest, but he can see I am having trouble and insists that I give it to him. I offer to carry his small pack but he will not hear of it. He straps it to my large one. What a difference this makes. I can walk faster and my knees do not hurt quite so much. I feel guilty watching Dawa carrying both packs, so several times I ask him to let me take the small one. He refuses to give it up. If I did not hurt so badly I would insist.

Today, besides the usual donkey caravans, we pass two porters carrying large wooden crates on their backs. The crates extend from their butts to several centimeters over their heads and weigh thirty to forty kilograms. A strap secures it around the waist and another wide strap extending from the bottom of the load is supported around the man's forehead. Both men carry walking sticks and wear flip-flops on their feet. I wonder how they can possibly walk over the rock and stones without proper footwear.

Dawa says, "They are used to that. They do it every day and would find boots uncomfortable."

We follow the Kali Gandaki Valley, which continues all the way to Jomosom and is the world's deepest gorge running between Annapurna I and Dhaulagiri Mountains. By the time we reach Ghasa we are at 2,120 meters. This is our stop for today.

Day five should be short. We reach Larjung, the scheduled stop, at noon; and decide to continue on to Marpha, doing two days in one. We began at 7:25 this morning and end the day at 3:30. We are at an altitude of 2,680 meters. My right knee seems to be stronger and is not hurting so much, but my left knee is still a problem, especially on the downward stretches.

The villages are interesting with their stone walks and brick buildings forming long narrow alleyways. Today we see men and women pounding on rocks, making bricks for a house under construction. In one village we spot women bathing behind a chest-high rock wall. The sun is shining but the temperature is quite cool for an outdoor bath. As we climb higher the temperature drops and the wind whistles around the mountains, stinging my eyes and cheeks.

We stay at the Paradise Lodge tonight. The cost for accommodation each night has been fifty rupees, but this lodge is classier than most and charges two hundred and fifty (five dollars Canadian). At least the walls aren't as thin as some we have stayed in, and light from adjoining room does not shine through the cracks. I meet people from Canada, Germany, Ireland, England, and an author from Bermuda named Andrew. He has published seven travel books. I have a very interesting chat with him and welcome his tidbits of advice.

On day six we hit the trail at 7:25 for a short trek. Walking is difficult as we battle the rocks along the riverbed. The wind has picked up and I must cover my head to protect my ears from the cold. We make a stop in Jomosom where Dawa goes to the clinic to purchase muscle rub and tensor bandages for my knees. I rub in the salve and wrap them snuggly, before continuing. I welcome the early stop today—my legs and feet ache.

From Ghasa to Jomosom, the Thakalis inhabit the villages. Many are rich by Nepali standards and own businesses in Pokhara and Kathmandu. Jomosom is the last village of Thakali people; farther north live the Tibetans.

We pass long donkey caravans hauling supplies to Mustang. The Tibetans move from Kali Gandaki valley to Mustang for the summer months. We reach Kagbeni, an elevation of 2,810 meters, at noon, and stop for the day. Kagbeni is a Tibetan village and as close as we get to Mustang without paying a permit fee of seven hundred dollars US.

I am glad that we have stopped. The wind is howling and by 3:00 PM rain is coming steadily down. We can see snow falling farther up the mountains, and by 6:00 it is snowing hard in Kagbeni. Tomorrow may be a hard trek.

I get up at 5:30, do some stretching exercises, pack my bag, and go down to the kitchen. I am excited about getting on the trail. Today is day seven and we will reach our destination of Muktinath, at three thousand, eight hundred meters. I revel in the quiet of the morning and take pictures of the fresh snow on the ground before other trekkers appear. As we prepare to leave, the proprietor of the Guest House places a long white scarf around each of our necks for good luck.

The trail takes us immediately on an incline. It is tough going first thing in the morning and it helps immensely that my knees are wrapped. The morning is peaceful and walking through the fresh snow high in the mountains lends a special magic. The sun is shining and by 9:00 AM the snow is melting, making the track slippery in sections. We stop for tea at Khingar, and Dawa visits with the women cleaning hot chili peppers and pounding grain in a tall, narrow clay bowl. The villagers along the trek know the guides and welcome them when they come through. Dawa seems to be well liked.

We continue to climb and the wind whistles around my ears. The next village we come to is Jharkot, at three thousand, five hundred meters. Grey and brown rock brick buildings line the top of a mountain ridge high above the tree line. From a distance it looks like a medieval village. We steadily trek uphill, bringing us to Ranipauwa at 3,710 meters. The air is thinner up here, making breathing more difficult.

This is one of the reasons why our last two days of trekking have been shorter. As we reach the higher altitudes it is a good idea to stay a night to let your body adjust before continuing higher. A slight headache is the only effect this altitude has on me. I drink plenty of water, which I am told helps prevent altitude sickness and headaches.

We check into our rooms at the Hotel Dreamhome in Ranipauwa before noon. Dawa takes me to meet the owners and we find them both sewing. The woman sits on a short wooden stool using a hand treadle sewing machine and her husband sits on the floor sewing by hand. They appear to be quite elderly, but I suspect this climate and hard lifestyle ages people quickly.

After lunch we walk up to Muktinath, or Chumig Gyatsa—as it is known by its local name. The Central Gompa is a pilgrimage center for both Tibetan Buddhists and Hindus and has been shared by both religions for hundreds of years. The Vishnu Temple of Jwala Mayi, the goddess of fire, shelters a spring and natural gas jets that provide Muktinath's famous *eternal flame*. Here they celebrate the four major elements of the universe: earth, air, water, and fire.

I notice an amazing thing as I gaze around me—the sides of the mountains are bare except for this sacred village of Muktinath where trees are scattered on the hillside amongst the temples and other structures. Flat stone rocks create a stairway leading through the leafless trees to the buildings. Prayer flags strung between trees flap in the wind and add some color to the otherwise grey, brown, and white surroundings. I experience a feeling of empowerment. We have now reached an altitude of almost 3,800 meters (over 12,300 feet). *I have made it!*

On my way back to our hotel I browse through the tables of handmade crafts and purchase a colorful striped scarf and headband. Local people sell their crafts to the tourists to make some money. It is hard to know what else they do to survive up here, but they appear to be very resourceful.

Back at the hotel I sit out on the patio, relaxing in the sun, and watching this slow-paced world go by. I see a man working his field far below with a one-blade plow attached to a wooden pole and harnessed to a team of water buffalo. In another direction a hills man is herding his yaks across the mountains. I feel a sense of serenity.

We're up again at 5:00 AM. This is not difficult to do when you go to bed at eight or nine. We have breakfast and are ready to begin our trek at 7:15. Before leaving the hotel this morning the proprietor drapes a yellow silk scarf around each of our necks. The morning is sunny and there is no wind. We hike mostly downhill with only a few steep descents. My left knee feels the stress of the steep sections, but the tensor bands are doing their job. By 10:30 AM the wind begins again and by 11:00 it is blowing hard in our faces, slowing our pace. As we cross the rocks of the riverbed we meet a holy man dressed in long white robes, walking barefoot. I am so in awe of him I have to stop and watch. He moves as though he were stepping on carpet! Is it really mind over matter? Dawa explains that he is called "Baba" or "Sadhu" and is making a pilgrimage to Muktinath to worship Lord Shiva. Some of the Sadhus wear brightly colored robes and some wear flip-flops or sandals on their feet. Not all walk barefoot, as this man does.

We arrive at Marpha at 2:20 PM and after a short rest walk up to the Gompha high in the rocks overlooking the village. I get some great pictures of the tops of the village houses, courtyards, and pens. Wood is neatly piled along the top edges of the roofs, where it is stored for winter use. Our walk through the village takes us into long narrow alleyways, no more than a meter wide, flanked with rock brick walls and doors opening onto the flat rock sidewalks.

Today, March 22, (March 21 in the United States) President George W. Bush ordered an attack on Iraq. The headlines in a Nepal paper read: "Fifteen British soldiers lost their lives in the invasion of Iraq. Hundreds of Iraqi's also lost their lives." One more day into the attack the headlines read: "Twelve US soldiers and six pilots killed in Iraq … Unknown number of soldiers taken captive." My, what a senseless act!

Over the next couple of days we meet other hikers who are in worse shape than I. I make special note of four young women we overtake on the trail. They have stopped because of blisters, sore feet, and aching muscles. I feel proud that at age 54 I have outlasted them. In fact I am feeling stronger each day. We meet some children as we pass through one village and I give them my trail mix. Dawa tells me not to give the bag to just one of them because they will not share; so I pour nuts into their little outstretched hands. One girl is so tiny I have to resist the temptation to give her the whole bag.

The fourth day into our homeward trek is mostly uphill. We ascend from 1,190 meters to 2,750. We meet two teenage girls walking to school. They are each dressed in pink pants with a pink skirt that comes to the knees, a blue sweater, and a nice green scarf wrapped around the head and tossed over the shoulders—very colorful. They skip up the rock stairs effortlessly. One girl jumps up on the rock wall and walks the ledge to the end. I smile as I think, *that is exactly what I would have done at her age.* They take this uphill trail every day for more than an hour to attend school. I imagine they skip down in the afternoon in half that time. Like many of the children I have come across, these two are very small for their age. The ones I guess to be eight or nine are actually twelve or thirteen.

This part of the walk is very pretty but the steep incline slows me down. Dawa is far ahead of me and I stop a few times to take pictures—a good excuse for a short break.

On March 25 I write in my journal: "More lives lost in this senseless war for power and money."

We trek through sheep valley, between Ghandruk and Tolka, where farmers allow their sheep to graze on the hills until summer, at which time they are moved farther up the mountain slopes. The hills and valleys are covered with rhododendron trees in full bloom. The view is a solid mass of vibrant pink blossoms. Dawa tells me that March is the best month to see them; soon the flowers will be gone.

My strength is improving every day and my legs and knees no longer ache. On March 27, day fourteen of my trek, we have dropped down to 1,130 meters upon arrival at Phedi. We find a taxi for three hundred rupees and head back to Pokhara. The taxi is a wreck; belching blue smoke into the back seat so bad I have to keep my face out the window. Even that does not help. The car only works in first and second gear, and almost fails to make it up a couple of hills. In Pokhara the driver nearly hits a cyclist, but at the last minute veers off to the right and over a grass boulevard, narrowly missing him. I am ever so glad when we arrive so I can get out of this death trap.

I say goodbye to Dawa before he catches a bus back to Kathmandu and to his family. It is still early so I shower and explore Pokhara. There are some wonderful little restaurants and I enjoy a sandwich on a patio with stunning views of Phewa Tal Lake and the Varahi Temple.

The temple is built on a little island in the lake, directly out from the shore where the prince lives in the Royal Palace. Nepal is still feeling the effects of the 2001 assassination of King Birendra and several members of his family. There is much controversy over who is responsible, and the Nepali people have their own suspicions. In Pokhara people openly accuse the king's brother, yet investigative reports and newspaper articles attribute the murder to the king's son Prince Dependra. Still other groups suspect the Maoist Communist Party of Nepal. Will the truth ever be known? The Royal Palace in Kathmandu is still heavily guarded. Army and police officers march up and down the sidewalks bordering the high, cement fences that surround the Palace Square.

Back at the Guesthouse I have tea with the proprietor. First I tell him I do not like the price he is charging for my room. As I walked around town earlier, I saw several signs advertising one hundred to two hundred rupees for a room. Benjh is quick to negotiate and we agree on one hundred and fifty rupees. As we visit he asks about my family—am I married, do I have children, how do they feel about me traveling alone, what kind of work do I do …?

I tell him I am divorced, and he replies that divorce is scorned upon in Nepal. "If I do not like my wife, I cannot divorce her. People point and say, "Why he want to divorce her?" Marriages are still arranged by the parents, but Benjh and his wife Maree met in college and fell in love. Maree's family disowned her because she married someone of a lower caste. Even though Benjh is a successful businessman, this is not acceptable. His wife does not visit her parents and they rarely visit her.

I tell him I have three children—two boys and one girl. He replies excitedly, "Oh, that is a perfect family in Nepal. We all hope to have two boys and one girl. Two sons so that if something should happen to one, there is still another to carry on the family name. That is very important. And one daughter, because in Nepal we have a festival where the daughter is very important."

I ask Benjh what he knows about the murder of the king and his family in Kathmandu.

"Here in Pokhara people say most definitely the new king is responsible. If you ask any child on the street they will tell you we don't like a murderer for a king," he says.

Benjh continues to tell me about the new prince who lives in the Grand Palace in Pokhara. "This prince is a nasty man. He has been known to grab a beautiful woman off the street and take her to the palace for two or three days, then turn her out. If she is a single woman, not so bad, the family can cover it up and lie about where she was. But if she is a married woman, her reputation is ruined. If it was my wife I could not accept that she was with another man, so she would have to lie and say she was at her parents or at her friends."

"But what about the woman's feelings?" I ask. "Imagine how horrible all this would be for her!"

"My wife cannot go anywhere without my permission. That is the Nepali custom."

I want to say, "But if you love her, would you not have compassion for her, would you not see that it is not her fault?" But I know the answer without asking the question—That is the Nepali custom.

Although I am shocked by Benjh's reaction, I remind myself that these traditions are long bred into the minds of these people. The fact that he and his wife defied tradition by marrying out of their caste is a hopeful sign that things are slowly changing.

The next morning I pack my bike and ride southwest toward Tansen on the Siddhartha Highway that connects Pokhara to Butwal. The sky is cloudy and it rains off and on as I travel on the narrow paved road that winds along the edge of the mountains. Views of the treed valley far below and the mountains rising up all around me are spectacular. I would like to stop for pictures but the road is extremely narrow and the edge drops hundreds of meters into the valley. I keep my attention on the often broken up pavement and tight curves, honking my horn as I round blind corners. This road is not for the weak of heart and mind.

While in Nepal I contacted Servas host Mangal Shrestha, as recommended by Mr. Bibendra. Mangal is a retired teacher and welcomes me to stay in his home in Tansen, just forty kilometers north of Butwal. When I arrive in Tansen I search out a phone and call Mr. Shrestha. It seems I am in the busiest part of town. With the sketchy directions he gives me, I have to stop several times to ask for help from people on the street before arriving at my destination.

My host is a slightly built, short, jovial man. His home is part of a long block of four-storey brick buildings, with small family-run stores at ground level facing the street. Living quarters are in the back of the store and in the upper levels. Mr. Shrestha is renovating their home at the moment and offers me a bed in the sitting room on the third floor.

Three of Mangal's sisters also live here. One is married and lives in one section of the attached building; two have never married and occupy rooms on the second floor. Mrs. Shrestha is away at the moment visiting their eldest son, and Mr. Shrestha is sleeping on a cot in the back of their variety store and phone service. The toilet is on ground level. I go down two flights of stairs, out the door and into another door of the attached building, to find a squat toilet. There is no sink or shower. I wash under a tap protruding from a water barrel stationed outside the door.

The next morning after breakfast Mangal takes me to see the historical sights of Tansen. We walk to Durbar Square, entering through the huge historic gates that open to the Tansen Palace. We visit Hindu and Buddhist temples, markets, and bazaars. When we come across a group of women in the park, Mangal goes over and speaks with them. He discovers that these women have dared to challenge tradition by opening their own bank accounts. They meet regularly for support, and to help each other make deposits. I am moved and feel great pride for these women. It must be very difficult to break from long-standing customs. Mr. Shrestha praises them for their courage and tells them to continue their mission.

I leave Tansen in the early morning to find Lumbini, the birthplace of Lord Buddha who was born in 623 B.C. I continue south of Tansen to Butwal where I get caught up in horrendous traffic of cars, trucks, buses, rickshaws, motorcycles, bicycles, cows, people, and anything else that moves. It takes awhile, but I finally get through the madness and make it to Lumbini. I spend the afternoon walking through the sites and riding to a new area where temples representing other Asian countries are being built. This is a pilgrimage site for many Buddhists around the world and is being developed for tourism. It is situated in the southwest of Nepal just a few kilometers from the India border.

Now if I had planned this properly I would be crossing the border into Uttar Pradesh, India tomorrow; but I still want to try and get into Tibet before leaving Nepal, so I will head back to Kathmandu instead.

I arrive back in Kathmandu on April 1 and check into a guesthouse instead of calling on Servas hosts. I call Mr. Poudal about picking up the things I left at his home while I was out trekking, and he insists that I stay in his guesthouse near the airport. I think I would rather stay in the Thamel area where most of the backpackers are, but I agree to take a look at his place tomorrow.

In the morning I pick up my things at Mr. Poudal's and ride over to his guesthouse. It's a fair distance from Thamel but not unreasonable. It is quiet and very secure, so I decide to stay. I call Mr. Poudal and he tells me I may stay for free. I cannot accept that and we finally agree on one hundred and fifty rupees.

Next morning I ride into Thamel, park my bike and go for breakfast, before searching out an Internet café. When I have completed all my tasks, I go in search of a tour agency to gather information about riding to Lhasa, Tibet. I chat with the owner of Eco Treks, who was recommended by Gyander at Chitwan National Park. He tells me that to get my bike into China I need to hire a guide and a truck with a driver. That will cost a lot of money. The Chinese government does not allow foreigners to drive anywhere they wish. He suggests that I take a bus tour if I want to see Tibet. I take a look at his packages and decide to book an eight-day bus tour from Kathmandu to Lhasa for 590 dollars US.

With that taken care of I explore more of the streets of Thamel. Vendors push their products in my face, shoe shine boys try to sell a shine (even though I am wearing runners), and a young boy about eight years old follows me for blocks, begging for money for a meal for his sister. Signs are posted all over telling tourists not to encourage the beggars. I wonder if this boy is legit, or if he has learned the ropes of the begging scam. The men here have a disgusting habit of "horking" (loudly clearing their throats and spitting). I soon tire of all this and return to my bike to head back to the guesthouse.

A few blocks from the guesthouse I have an accident. I am riding very cautiously when I notice three women in long colorful saris on the sidewalk ahead. A moment later one of the women, dressed in red, turns and steps off the sidewalk directly into my path. I hit the brakes hard and go down with a bang! As I pick myself up off the road, "F*#*!," involuntarily explodes from my mouth. I should not have used such foul language but I am angry. The woman is half-lying on the ground in front of my bike. She looks up at me with huge, scared, round eyes, picks herself up off the ground, and scurries to the other side of the road. I know I did not hit her, so I'm not sure why she fell.

I have to get the bike up and off the road. I look around and it seems that the world has stopped—people are motionless on the sidewalk and traffic is at a standstill. Everyone is staring at me. I spot a couple of fellows on the sidewalk and gesture for them to come help me pick up the bike. Luck is with me as one of the men points to a bike shop just a few meters back. He helps me wheel the bike over to the curb. The windshield is broken, the right brake and floorboard are bent, the mirror is pushed out of place, and there are a few scratches on the chrome. But this is all the damage I can see.

The man who helped wheel my bike to the shop immediately begins straightening parts. I begin to feel pain in my right leg and decide to take a look. Pulling up my pant leg, I notice that my right shin is badly gashed, bleeding, and swollen like a balloon. Another fellow standing by the bike motions across the road to a Chemist Shop (a common term here for pharmacy). He helps me cross through traffic, takes me right to the shop, and waits. The clerk comes around from behind the counter and examines my leg. She then brings out a bottle of iodine to clean my wound, which is about six centimeters long and four centimeters wide. The iodine stings like hell but I grit my teeth and bear it. When she has it all cleaned up, she rubs ointment on it and wraps it with gauze. I buy an antibiotic, disinfectant, ointment, and gauze from her for 240 rupees. When I pay for my purchases, the old fellow who escorted me across the street holds out his hand and says "Twenty rupees." I cannot believe it! Oh well, he did help. I give him twenty rupees and he takes me back to the bike shop.

My bike is being hammered back into shape. I pick out the plexiglass pieces that have broken out from the lower part of the windshield. There is a crack on both sides near the chrome cross bar, but I think it will hold together. In a short time the man working on my bike is finished and I ask, "How much do I owe you?"

"Nothing," he says shaking his head from side to side.

I am very grateful and insist that he take something. Finally he takes one hundred rupees. His kindness more than makes up for those few people who take advantage.

When I arrive back at the guesthouse I talk to the manager about storing my bike while I am on my Tibet tour. He assures me that it will be no problem and makes room in a storage garage attached to the house. "It will be safe here," he says.

The following morning I awaken not feeling well. This can't be! I leave tomorrow for Tibet. *I can't be sick!* By mid-morning I am throwing up violently and have difficulty picking my head up off the pillow. I call the manager and ask him to please send someone out for bottled water. I am so weak I cannot stay in an upright position for more that five or ten minutes. I *must* pack my bag today because I leave at five in the morning for Eco Treks. One of the staff brings me toast and tea, but I cannot eat anything. I sip on the tea and sleep most of the day. Somehow, between short naps, I manage to get my bag packed. By evening I manage to eat a slice of toast.

I am not sure what happened. Maybe my body went into shock from the accident. That is the only explanation I can come up with. In spite of feeling weak and tired, I look forward to my excursion to Tibet. I would not miss this for anything.

Chapter 2

Tibet (China)

At five o'clock in the morning on Saturday, April 5, I take a taxi to Eco Treks in the Thamel area. My leg still hurts, I'm limping, and I feel tired and weak from yesterday's ordeal; but I cannot miss this tour. I am the first to arrive, and wait half an hour for the others. There are ten tourists on the bus that will take us north to the Chinese border. This highway from Kathmandu to Lhasa is known as the Friendship Highway. Police and army check posts are set up periodically along the route. We go through one of each after breakfast. An army officer, with his rifle in hand, steps onto the bus, says good morning, smiles, looks around, and exits. At 10:50 we finally arrive at the Nepal border gate, then the Chinese border. I really want to say, "Tibet border" but it is officially called China.

It takes two hours to finally get through both border gates, and then we drive seven kilometers to Chinese customs only to wait another hour. Our guide handles all the paperwork. Eco Treks compiled our passport and personal information and the authorities must check each one of us. My companions consist of two German women, Edda and Uda, who are forty-four and fifty-two; a twenty-eight year old couple from the Netherlands, (Drs.) Lisala and Remco; Tina and Dar from Denmark, twenty-six, who each have a partner back home; a couple, Andre and Monica—he is forty-nine and from the USA and Monica is twenty-three, from Romania; Orika, twenty, from Germany; and myself, the oldest in the group at age fifty-four.

Once we all clear customs we walk two hundred meters up a hill to board another bus with a new Chinese guide and driver. Our original guide and driver have been replaced. We only drive a short distance when our driver, Chen, stops at Zhngmu where we check into a hotel for the night. Our guide, Joe (that must be a nickname), tells us we will stay here for the night because Chen needs to find a repair for the bus. This is only our first day and already we are off schedule. It is still early so I stroll through the town and check out a few shops before dinner with the group, and then head off to bed. A karaoke bar across the street keeps me awake long into the night and the next morning my roommate and I sleep in. At 7:55 AM someone from our tour group bangs on our door and tells us the bus is leaving in five minutes.

Within two hours our bus is overheating. Chen pulls over to the side of this narrow road. He opens the engine cover next to his seat and unscrews the radiator cap, which immediately blows and hits the ceiling with a bang.

After an hour of mechanical work and adding cold water to the radiator, our driver cannot find the cap. We all begin a search, first inside the bus, then outside on the ground. No luck! Much time passes before Chen finally finds the cap, somewhere on the engine. When we continue we are now three and a half hours behind schedule. Our next stop on the itinerary is an hour-long hike to some caves. We decide to skip it and carry on to Lalungla Pass at 5,050 meters. Everyone in our group is feeling ill from the high altitude and from bouncing over these rough roads. I have developed a headache.

We arrive in Lhatse at 9:30 PM and I go straight to bed. I sleep for a short time, until my headache becomes too much to bear and I have to take some painkillers. We are at 4,050 meters (13,287 feet).

The roads are atrocious! The surface is dirt, gravel, rock, and many large potholes. As we drive higher into the mountains the road seems to get narrower and the side of the road drops steeply into the valley. I feel thankful that I'm not riding my motorbike through here. In the high passes wind blows steadily and whips our scarves around our necks when we step off the bus. We see a lone Tibetan woman trudging across the barren land, far from any dwellings, carrying a large basket on her back. Sometime later we see a man on a horse. I have no idea where they came from or where they are going—nothing but bare mountaintops are in sight. At the high mountain passes we are met by nomads, posing with decorated yaks, waiting for tourists to take their pictures. Of course there is a slight charge—just one of the many innovative ways to make a bit of money. But my heart goes out to them, standing in this cold wind.

We stop at little villages high in the mountains. Our guide speaks to a woman on the street and asks if we may tour her home. She agrees and motions for us to follow her. The living quarters are up a narrow, steep set of steps that lead to a small room immediately off the kitchen. The kitchen is long and narrow, and at one end is a large wood stove for cooking and heating the home. A long table stands at one end and benches run the length of both walls, extending from the stove to the end of the room. At night the benches are used as beds. A bedroom is just off the kitchen, but our guide asks us not to go in there. On the ground floor, under the main living area, reside a couple of donkeys, maybe even a yak.

We stop and tour several Buddhist monasteries built many centuries ago. Our guide tells us that many of the monasteries were destroyed during the Chinese invasions beginning in 1950. Precious artifacts were stolen or destroyed, and thousands of monks were killed. The Drepung Monastery, the largest in Tibet, once housed up to ten thousand monks. Now only six hundred study and worship here.

Every stop we make brings the children running with their hands outstretched. They crowd in the front door and bang on the side of the bus. Those who are tall enough reach up and tap on the windows. I get the feeling that parents prostitute their children as beggars, scamming the tourists. Unfortunately, well-meaning tourists, who continue to offer handouts, feed this whole nasty business.

Finally, on the fifth day of bouncing and banging around on the bus, we arrive in Lhasa, the *Land of the Gods*. Disappointment sweeps over me as we drive through wide paved streets lined with streetlights and stores with Chinese signs and decorations. This is not at all what I expected. I imagined seeing the Potala Palace high on a hill overlooking gardens and the ancient city of Lhasa. I cannot even see the palace. We spend the next day touring two other working monasteries and attending a *monk's debate*. The *debate* is more like a classroom study group where students are paired off and quiz each other. The added movements and expressions of the monks create an interesting and often entertaining scene.

I have been nursing my leg morning and night, and taking my antibiotic pills. The gash on my shin is looking better every day, the pain is subsiding, and I no longer walk with a limp. I am relieved that it is healing nicely, especially since I did not see a doctor. What else could a doctor do? Most likely he would have instructed me to care for it in this same manner.

Day seven, our last day in Tibet, our guide takes us to the Potala Palace. This is what I have been waiting for and why I made the treacherous journey across these mountains. I have read some history of the Dalai Lama, including how he is chosen to succeed the previous leader, and how the current Dalai Lama (Tenzin Gyatso) made his escape from Tibet during the Chinese invasion.

The Potala Palace has been the home of the Dalai Lamas for centuries. The complex comprises the White and Red Palaces and their ancillary buildings. It sits at the top of Marpo Ri (Red Hill) Mountain at an altitude of thirty-seven hundred meters, rising one hundred and seventeen meters into the air and three hundred meters above the Lhasa valley floor. It measures four hundred meters east to west and three hundred and fifty meters north to south. Today not one picture of the fourteenth Dalai Lama, now exiled to India, remains on the palace walls. The Chinese have removed all memory of him.

My feelings of anger surprise me as I wander through the palace and absorb the ramifications of the Chinese invasion. This enormous structure was once home to the Dalai Lama and his staff; it was the seat of Tibetan government where ceremonies of state were held; it was a school for religious training of monks and administrators; and it was one of Tibet's major pilgrimage destinations. That has all been taken from the Tibetan people. My heart aches for their loss.

From here we visit the Summer Palace of the Dalai Lama, surrounded by gardens and trees. It is here where the young Dalai Lamas studied and learned their roles as leaders, and it is here where their leader lived during the cold winter months. The rooms in this building portray a more "homey" feel than those at the Potala Palace. One picture of the fourteenth Dalai Lama at age thirteen hangs above the throne in the main meeting room.

April 11 is our last night in Lhasa. Tomorrow morning we leave at 6:30 for a two-hour bus ride to the airport where we'll fly back to Kathmandu. Visiting Lhasa is one of my dreams come true. I sigh and wonder what it would have been like to visit this city before the Chinese invasion …

— *Back in Nepal*

On April 12 I fly back to Kathmandu. I am relieved that we don't have to cross those horrible mountain roads by bus again. My plan is to get my visa for India and Pakistan, then pack up and start my journey through India.

April 13 is New Year's Eve in Nepal, so I am delayed getting to the Embassy. I wait until the 15th before I walk to the Indian Embassy only to find it is still closed. The next morning I return at 9:30 and join the already long queue at the gate. We line up just to sign in and go through the security cameras. Two hours pass while standing in lines. Finally I reach the wicket for a third time and am told to come back April 22 with my application and three thousand and fifty rupees.

The morning of April 20 I walk out into the street and sense that something is not right. The shops are closed and only a few people are out. I notice a crowd at a distant intersection and ask a bystander what is going on.

"There is a general strike to protest the government's lack of action in bringing to justice the police officer that shot and killed a university student in Butwal two weeks ago," he explains. The shooting occurred when students held a protest to voice their concerns over the forty per cent price hikes on gas and diesel. The streets remain quiet all day.

I have developed a cough again since returning to Kathmandu. I suspect it is caused from the pollution in this city. My throat and nose burn continually and no amount of cough candies seems to ease my discomfort.

The next day I walk for three hours looking for the Pakistan Embassy. According to the guidebook it should be on Presidents Road. Mansions, surrounded by two or three-meter high brick fences, line this street. The homes are very majestic, reminding me of the vast differences between rich and poor in Nepal. My feet ache by the time I finally find the Embassy. After an hour in line I am told that it is too soon to apply if I plan to spend a month in India. I will have to try again once I reach Delhi.

At 8:30, the morning of April 22, I return to the Indian Embassy and wait for the gates to open at 9:30. There are only twelve people in front of me, and I feel hopeful this will go fast. I watch as several Israelis ahead of me hand over a stack of passports each. Several times an agent comes in through the back and places another stack of passports on the desk of the lone man handling the processing. I suspect these are from tour groups. Finally, two hours later, I present my passport at the wicket and the officer tells me to come back at 4:30. This is so frustrating and seems completely ridiculous, but there is no point in arguing. I leave and return at 4:30 along with sixty other people. This time the line moves quickly. An officer directs the Israelis into one line and the rest of us into another. There are about fifty in their line, compared to fifteen in ours. When it is my turn at the wicket I pay 3,050 Nepal rupees and receive a ninety-day visa for India in my passport. That is the most expensive visa so far.

My cough is not getting any better, my throat hurts, and my nasal passage burns. My leg is healing nicely and I no longer have to wrap my wound. I make contact with my family via e-mail to let them know I will be leaving Nepal and crossing into India in a couple of days. I pack up the rest of my things, ready to leave Kathmandu on April 24.

The manager of Kathmandu Garden House drapes a silk scarf, symbolizing good luck, around my neck before I leave. I like this tradition—it feels good.

I make my way out of the hectic Kathmandu traffic and ride twenty-nine kilometers to Naubise before turning south onto the Tribhuvan Highway, which will take me to the Indian border. In only four kilometers I reach a line of traffic going nowhere. Carefully I ride alongside the vehicles until I come to an accident. A very small child is lying in the center of the road covered with a large square blanket. Someone indicates that the child is dead, having been struck by a vehicle. The road is barricaded with benches and poles at both ends. Someone moves a bench and the crowd separates, creating a path for me to ride through. I am not sure what to do but they wave me on, so I ride past the body and out through the other end of bystanders. It is an eerie feeling going past the tiny body.

It has taken me six hours to cover 136 kilometers. I stop in a town close to the Nepal/India border, but do not want to cross late in the afternoon. I expect proceeding through the border will take time, so I will get a good sleep tonight, and cross tomorrow.

Chapter 3
India

I have no problem exiting Nepal. It is smooth sailing through Customs and Immigration. My passport and carnet are stamped and I ride into Raxaul, Bihar—the poorest state in India. I reach customs at 9:00 AM and hand over my passport and carnet. The officers take some time investigating my papers, and then tell me I must wait until 10:00 for another office to open. One of the officers tells me to wait in a building nearby that looks like a garage. Inside, the room is drab and smells strongly of some kind of disinfectant. Maybe this is the quarantine shed. The only furniture is two old filing cabinets resting against one wall, and a long old table with a couple of chairs in the center of the room. I decide to wait on the sidewalk. Immediately the officer comes back and says, "You wait in here."

"No," I reply. "It stinks in there." Besides, I am not entirely sure they won't close the door and lock me in.

When the officer realizes I am staying outside, he leaves and returns shortly with a chair for me to sit on.

I get out my camera to take some pictures of the fancy trucks, bicycle rickshaws, ponies, steers, and longhorn Brahmas pulling hand made wooden carts. Instantly the guard looks at me and barks "No pictures!"

"I just want a picture of the ponies. Not even the ponies?" I ask.

"No. No pictures here!"

"I don't understand your country. What are you trying to hide?" I mumble.

The officer makes no reply, so I suspect he did not understand me. That is probably a good thing. I sit and patiently wait, watching the hustle and bustle of border activity. The landscape has become flat since leaving Nepal.

At 10:05 I yell across the street to the customs officer sitting in his tower, "Ten o'clock" and point at my watch. A guard standing on my side of the street says; "Ten minutes."

Sure enough, at 10:15 another officer arrives dressed in a stark white shirt, loose tan pants, and shiny black shoes. This man must be the head customs officer. I wonder how he keeps his shoes so shiny walking on these dust-filled streets and sidewalks.

I am ushered into the strong-smelling building and asked to sit. Two officers sit opposite me and look through my carnet and passport. They chatter back and forth, seeming to decide on what to do with this paperwork. Finally the first officer gets up and retrieves a huge ledger and "Head Officer" begins to record all my information. While this is going on, another officer comes in and offers me a Coke. I am very appreciative. It is hot here and my throat is parched.

When all is recorded, I am released and told to stop at the immigration office under the bridge to get my passport stamped. I ride over the bridge past small shacks and rundown buildings on both sides of the street. I cannot see a building that looks anything like a government office. I turn and ride back to a row of shacks under the bridge. I had not seen them going in the other direction. I stop at an open front stall to ask directions. To my surprise, this little *hole in the wall* is the immigration office! The officer is an elderly man dressed in a muscle shirt and loose cotton pants. He takes my passport and records the information in another humungous ledger before stamping my passport and handing it back. Finally, I am free to start my journey into India. The date is April 25, 2003.

It is stifling hot, and I look for a shop in the next village to buy water. No one understands me, and they appear to be unwilling to sell me water or food. I return to the bike, having now attracted a huge crowd of men and children. Nervous and uncomfortable with all those eyes on me, I dig out my cookies and warm water so I can have a snack. I offer the children some cookies but they are shy and do not take any, until an older man tells them it is okay. When I start my bike, the crowd parts and forms a path for me to ride out.

Later in the day I stop again at a petrol station. The heat has zapped my energy and I need to rest. I park near the entrance, remove my jacket, and dig out an orange and some water—both are hot. I walk across the driveway and sit on my haunches under the shade of a tree. Immediately there is a circle of men and boys around my bike. I watch tentatively, ready to run, because I have left my tank bag, coat, and helmet on the bike. At the same time, a man brings a chair from the petrol station and places it under the tree for me. Very soon the crowd surrounding my bike moves toward me and stands staring. Occasionally these bystanders say something to each other, but no one speaks to me. They make no motion to leave.

This is too much! Now what do I do? I finish my orange, drink some water, and head back to the bike. All this attention is just too unnerving.

I decide to leave the main highway at Saqauli and cut across country, riding through flat countryside and small farming villages. Farmers have placed sheaves of grain on the road so passing traffic can grind out the kernels. I slowly and carefully make my way through these patches. I meet men hauling grain in wooden hay wagons pulled by steers or water buffalo. I cannot help but wonder what farmers do if these animals eliminate on the grain spread across the road.

I really need some cold water and something to eat. I stop in a small village and find a little roadside shop that has bottled water. When I ask for water the young man does not understand. I go back to my bike and bring out my empty bottle. A man working in the booth brings out a stool and says, "Sit!" I graciously accept and he hands me a cold bottle of water. Once again a crowd of men surround my bike, then come and form a circle around me and stare. Will I ever get used to this?

I continue on and when I reach the main highway again, it is mid-afternoon. All I have had to eat are a few cookies, water, and a Coke. I stop at a larger center hoping to get some food, but again people don't understand me and will not sell me anything. I return to the bike and drink the warm water I purchased just twenty kilometers back, attracting another crowd of curious men and boys. Just as I am about to leave, a well-dressed English-speaking gentleman comes over and asks if I need anything.

"Do you have cold pop?" I ask. If I can't get any food, at least I will get some energy from the sugar in pop.

This gentleman says, "Come with me."

He takes me to a small vendor and I get a cold Fanta. When I pull out my money to pay the man says, "No, I pay for this—a welcome to my country." He introduces himself as Amar.

By this time a crowd is forming again and my new friend explains, "They do not see many foreigners so they gather out of curiosity." Then he asks me to say something to them and he will translate.

I say, "I am from Canada. I'm enjoying your country; people are very kind to me." Smiles light up the many faces. I finish my pop and leave.

Amar had told me there are hotels in the town about thirty kilometers down the road. After riding more than that distance, I do not find a town. I stop a couple of times to ask, but no one understands. The last time I stop I ask the crowd that has gathered, "Does anyone speak English?"

After asking two or three times I hear a voice behind me. "What do you want, Madam?"

I ask about a hotel and the stranger directs me farther down the road to Gopalganj. When I reach the town I stop once to get my bearings, then ride on. Soon a fellow on a small motorbike is beside me and asks where I am going. I tell him I need to find a hotel and he points me in the direction of the Shabnam Hotel. It looks clean and well cared for so I go in and ask for a single room. The clerk questions me, "You want single, no double?"

"Yes, single is fine. It is just for me." He finds it hard to believe a woman would be traveling alone. For one hundred and fifty rupees I get a small room with a single bed, toilet, sink, shower, and balcony. The room is not great, but it could be, with a little effort. This whole establishment could be a five-star hotel, with a little tender-loving care and business sense.

Gopalganj is a fairly good-sized city with a population of over fifty thousand. I figure I should be able to find a bank to exchange some money here, or use my bankcard. Today is Saturday so I can only hope there will be a bank open.

I ride into the heart of the city and find the State Bank of India open. I walk in and wait in front of the tall, barred gate attended to by a guard. The steel pipe gate is about three meters wide and extends four meters to the ceiling, strongly resembling what I imagine you'd find in a prison. It appears that only a certain number of people are allowed in at one time. When it's my turn the guard unlocks the gate and I enter a large, grey room with a dozen or more wickets running down the whole length of one wall. I present my Nepal rupees and a twenty dollar US bill but the clerk will not accept either. I then give him my bankcard and credit card but he shakes his head no. Now what am I going to do? I leave feeling dejected and wondering what my next move will be.

Back at my bike, I find a bazaar crowded with people and decide to stop and look around. After strapping my helmet to the handlebar, I sling my jacket over my arm, and make my way through hundreds of people packing the sidewalk. I try to buy a pop with my Nepal rupees, but no one will accept them. I hear a familiar voice behind me and turn to see Amar standing there. He asks what I want and again buys me a pop. I tell him about my money dilemma and he says, "Come with me. I will take you to the bank."

I ask Amar if my bike is safe where it is—because my tank bag, helmet, and back seat rolls could all be removed. He assures me it will be fine. We walk up the street to the Central Bank but still have no luck. Then we try Amar's bank and he introduces me to the manager. We sit at a desk while the manager makes a couple of phone calls, but again I am refused money on my cards or exchange for my cash. *I'm screwed!* I will need fuel today. I go back to my hotel and check out, handing the desk clerk my credit card. He shakes his head and says, "Cannot take that …"

"That is all I have, I do not have any Indian rupees yet. I have Nepal rupees and twenty US dollars," I explain, losing my patience. I stand my ground and finally he accepts my credit card.

Wow, that is one problem solved. Now I must get out of this state and into Uttar Pradesh. Amar has assured me I will have no problem using my credit card or bankcard once I reach Gorakhpur; in the much richer state of Uttar Pradesh.

I am still faced with one more problem: *Fuel.* I most definitely don't have enough to get me out of Bihar. As I ride west to Kushinagar I keep my eyes open for a gas station. I stop to ask directions and a fine gentleman points me to Kasia, a few kilometers back. When I find the station I pull up to the pump and instruct the attendant to fill it up. The tank is close to empty. Once it's full they will have to accept my money. I'm sure they won't drain the fuel out.

I enter the small building and present my credit card. "No, that is not acceptable," exclaims the attendant. I offer Nepal rupees or my US twenty. Again, he shakes his head and refuses to take it. I explain that this is all I have, not entirely sure how much he understands. He motions with his hands for me to wait, and leaves to get the owner. In a few minutes he returns with a short, sturdily built man, dressed in a light tan salwar kameez (loose cotton pants with a tunic to the knees). Without introducing himself this man asks, "Why you not want to pay?"

"I do want to pay. I only have Nepal rupees or US dollars. My one thousand Nepal rupees are worth six hundred Indian rupees." I reply.

He whips out his calculator and says, "Six hundred and twenty-four."

I quickly say "I will accept six hundred."

"We are not a bank—why you not get money changed at bank?" he asks in a sharp tone.

"I have not been able to get to a bank yet. I was told I need to go to Gorakhpur, but I don't have enough gas to get there."

"You should get your money changed in a bigger center," he snaps.

"*Yes, yes, yes, I know.* I have not been to a big center yet and I am out of fuel."

Suddenly a chair is placed behind me and I am told to sit. My interrogator sits in an armchair facing me and begins asking dozens of questions: "Where are you from? Why are you here? Where is your husband? Do you have children? Aren't you afraid to travel alone?" On and on he quizzes, while his right hand rubs his inner thigh. I am very conscious of his actions, and keep my gaze directed at his eyes. I'm also aware that the custom here is for the woman to lower her eyes when she speaks to a man, but this situation calls for courage and self-confidence. When my interrogator is finished asking questions, he lectures me for a few more minutes, then takes my twenty dollars. He does not want the Nepal rupees. He hands the American money to one of the other men and speaks to him in Hindi or Urdu. Then he turns to me and explains that his man will find a moneychanger.

As we wait my captor continues to lecture me on the safety of traveling alone in India, but his tone and manner have become friendlier. He sounds like he may even be genuinely concerned.

Twenty minutes later the man returns with the money, keeps four hundred rupees for gas, and returns five hundred and ten to me. I know I am being ripped off. One US dollar is equal to forty-seven Indian rupees—but at this point I don't care. I need money to get through today and tomorrow. Tomorrow is Sunday and I will not be able to get to a bank until Monday. I thank the men at the gas station politely and return to my bike, feeling relieved and jubilant about winning my battle.

I ride the few kilometers back to Kushinagar and decide to stay for one night. It is here where Buddha *expired*. I like this word; I will adopt it into my vocabulary. When I am asked if I have a husband, I will reply, "No, he has expired." Not entirely a lie—just a new term for divorce. Divorce is scorned upon here and as foreign as a woman traveling alone. *Expired* will come in handy.

Kushinagar has a population of approximately thirteen thousand and is a celebrated pilgrimage center for Buddhists. Lord Buddha's last words were, "Impermanence is inherent in all things. Work out your own salvation with diligence!" This event is known as the "Final Blowing-Out" or "Parinirvana", in Buddhist parlance.

I find the Nirvana Stupa, housing a colossal sandstone statue of Buddha in the reclining position. It was built in the fifth century. I also find the Muktabandhana Stupa, erected just after Buddha's death, and believed to be sitting on the spot where Buddha was cremated. Many of the stupas and viharas date as far back as 230 BC to AD 413.

As I ride through the streets I find the Thai, Chinese, and Japanese Temples and the Royal Residency Hotel. A guard stands outside the locked gates to the hotel grounds. I stop and ask him if I can go inside and take a picture of my bike in front of this beautiful building. He graciously swings open the gate and I ride in. I wonder if I could get a room here, and if so, for how much. Oh well, not today. I only have a few rupees on me.

I find a room at the Buddhist Temple and Guest House; recommended in the Lonely Planet guidebook, for one hundred and fifty rupees. I spend thirty-nine on food, thirty-two on water, and have not even spent half the rupees remaining from my twenty US dollar exchange.

My room is a rectangular cell in an old monastery. It has no windows except for a small opening above the heavy door and a small square hole near the top of the bathroom wall. The bathroom has a squat toilet and sink, but no shower. A fan hanging from the ceiling works as long as the power does not fail. I sleep peacefully tonight.

I am up early and packing my bike before 6:00 AM. Upon exiting my cell I discover cots on the driveway where people have slept. If I had known that, I would have done the same. I wonder if women are permitted to sleep outside under the stars.

At Gorakhpur I try to find a restaurant, to no avail, so I buy two oranges. Later I stop for a Pepsi—this will have to do for breakfast today. I continue on to Varanasi, arriving at 2:00 in the afternoon. It has taken me more than half a day to ride less than two hundred kilometers. The congestion in the cities and villages slows me down, but there is no way around it. All I can do is pick my way carefully through. Taxi drivers barrel through the streets, laying on their horns. I have learned that the horn is a most vital part of a vehicle. Had I been using my horn in Nepal I might have avoided that accident with the woman in the red sari.

Varanasi is situated on the banks of the River Ganga (Ganges) in the state of Uttar Pradesh. It is known for its many temples that line the banks of the river, and is one of the oldest continually inhabited cities in the world, dating back thousands of years. It is a holy city in Hinduism and one of the most sacred pilgrimage places for Hindus. More than one million pilgrims visit the city each year. Their belief is that bathing in the River Ganga will cleanse their sins and that dying in the holy city aids in rebirth. I stay two nights here and spend one whole day exploring.

My money problem is solved now that I can use my bankcard in the bank machines. I take a boat ride up the river to see the ancient architecture from the water. The captain calls out the names of many of the buildings, and points out the water line high on the cement structures, left behind from floods of years gone by. Water has reached such levels that it flows through the buildings, flooding the streets of the city. We glide past steps, leading from buildings into the river, packed with people waiting to swim. I cringe at the thought of going into this filthy water. We pass people doing their laundry in the river and laying sheets and towels out on the large rock steps to dry. Some have even strung up a clothesline. We also go by the *ghats* where cremations take place.

Back on land, I visit the Mother India Temple. A huge map of India made of one hundred and seventy-six pieces of marble, covers the main floor area. A wide walkway surrounds the map so visitors can view it from all angles. It is truly an impressive piece of art.

As I walk the last few blocks back to my hotel, I constantly fight off the rickshaw drivers trying to entice me to accept a ride. They seem not to understand the word *No*. Today has been a long and tiring day. I pack up my bags for tomorrow and retire early.

At 6:30 next morning I leave for Allahabad, one hundred and forty kilometers away. In the first few kilometers I come upon an overturned truck. I see no evidence of another vehicle involved. A few kilometers farther and I see another overturned truck. This one looks like he dropped off the edge of the road. Some time later I see another one. I wonder what the problem is, and make a conscious note of paying close attention to my own driving and the traffic around me.

After four hours of riding I finally arrive in Allahabad only to ride around another hour looking for a hotel. The first area of town I arrive in looks pretty shabby, so I try another area. One hotel wants eighteen hundred rupees for a single room. I decline and keep looking until I find the Hotel Tepso for three hundred and fifty rupees. That's a much better price, and it is a perfectly good room.

After lunch I go in search of Anand Bhavan—the Museum of the Nehru-Gandhi family and the birth home of Jawaharial Nehru and Indira Gandhi. I walk along the path where Indira Ghandi was shot when she was prime minister.

A group of college boys stop and talk to me. They have all sorts of questions about Canada, and then invite me to go to the Jawahar Planetarium with them. I accept. They ask about my bike and where I am going. As we talk, I find out they are here to apply for the army.

I am too tired to leave early the next morning so I decide to spend another day here. After breakfast I ride out to the fort built by Emperor Akbar in 1583 A.D. This is the largest of the Akbar forts and is now used by the army. It is an amazing structure.

I return to my hotel and go for a walk. I am enjoying myself, taking in all the sights, when I step in a pile of soft runny cow shit! Now what do I do? My feet, sandals, and pant legs are a mess. I look around for something to clean myself with and notice a pump a short distance away. I scurry over and start pumping. I try to be quick but cannot finish before a small audience gathers. I pump faster and clean up as best I can, then hurry off. I remind myself that cows are sacred here in India, and that I must be more careful to watch out for cow pies.

The next morning I leave at five to beat the heat. Days become unbearably hot wearing all this riding gear. I do not have far to go, but it takes me four and a half hours to reach Chitrakut, only 122 kilometers away. I ride comfortably for a few kilometers until the road starts to decay. Part of it is under construction and the base is thick, fine sand. In one stretch of construction the detour directs traffic down the ditch for a few meters, and then back up on the road. I pick a track and head down the bank into the ditch. I am doing fine, and when the track leads back up to the road I accelerate easily near the top and hit a thick patch of sand. The back wheel slides out and I go down, sand cushioning my fall. As I pick myself up, two men jump out of their jeep and help lift the bike back up on its wheels. One fellow asks in a surprised voice, "Who told you to take this road?"

"No one did, I am just following my map." I reply.

The kind gentleman shakes his head and asks if I am okay. "Yes sir, I will be fine once I get out of this construction."

A bit farther down the road I come to a bridge, floating on huge pontoons, crossing the Yamuna River. The deck is made from wide planks, producing an uneven surface, and wide enough for a bike and one vehicle. The railing on either side is, three strands of steel rope supported by steel posts.

I stop for a picture, then pick my way through the traffic to the other side, right into another mess of sand and construction. After a few more kilometers I finally ride back onto hard surface, arriving in Chitrakut at 9:30. It is only mid morning and I should keep going, but the guidebook suggests this is a place worth stopping at.

I find the tourist bungalows and secure a room before checking out the sights. Then I ride down to the river, park the bike, and go walking. It is said that Brahma, Vishnu, and Shiva were incarnated here; thus it is a holy place and pilgrims flood the area to have their sacred bath in the murky water. I look down from a bridge and witness people brushing their teeth, washing their hair, and bathing. There are some impressive temples standing tall on the shoreline. I spot the cremation ghats towards one end. My guidebook tells me that one can see parts of bodies floating down the river from time to time. The remains of bodies are sometimes pushed into the water before they are completely cremated.

I stroll along the fronts of the building facing the river, then wander through the streets behind. The smell of urine is strong. People stand or squat wherever they are. Men pee up against brick walls or fences. In this heat the stench is foul. Needless to say I do not linger here, but return to my bike and ride back into town.

Early the next morning I make my way to Khajuraho, using secondary roads, having to stop several times to make sure I am still heading in the right direction. I ride through farming villages and see people working early in the morning. Women and children are picking berries off the road that have fallen from the *mahua* tree. Later I am told they are used to make liquor.

I arrive in Khajuraho before noon and check into the Hotel Yogi Lodge. My room is wonderful. I park my bike inside the fenced yard where I can see it from the hallway window. After I pack my gear up the stairs and into my room, I take a short nap. Getting up at 4:30 and 5:00 every morning requires a nap by noon.

Half an hour later I feel refreshed and am ready to tour the sights. I take a look out the window before going downstairs, and notice four or five young men surrounding my bike, while one is sitting on it. I race down the stairs and talk to the hotel attendant. He wastes no time sending the fellows packing, and assures me they will not touch it again.

I walk to the square of the Khajuraho Temples, also referred to as the *Temples of Love*. It is known for the erotic sculptures carved into the walls and steeples. They were built in a one-hundred-year span from 950 to 1050 and are now listed as a UNESCO World Heritage Site. Today there are twenty-two temples remaining.

I admire the intricate architecture as I wander from one temple to the next. While in the western group of temples I meet a woman from Brazil and she asks if I would like to join her in hiring a guide.

Our guide gives us the history of each temple and tells us to which God each is dedicated—Lord Shiva, Lord Brahma, Lord Vishnu, the Sun God, and the Goddess Kali ... He explains the erotic sculptures on Kandariya Mahadeo Temple, the tallest structure at thirty-one meters. "They knew how to make love and transfer their physical energy into spiritual energy," he says. Each panel of sculptures tells a story of what transpired in that era. Scenes show figures of humans and animals copulating, followed by an army of men in pursuit to punish them for their offensive deeds. Orgy scenes depict people of royalty engaging with their subjects. Our guide relays these stories and many more as he leads us through and around each temple.

On my way back to the lodge I stop at some outdoor vendor stalls selling jewelry, trinkets, statues, and other paraphernalia. A slight wind has picked up, stirring up the dust and catching the tablecloths and canopies that cover the vendor stalls. I return to the lodge and ask the desk clerk about other things I should see while in Khajuraho. He suggests touring the town by bicycle, and visiting Yogi Ramprakash Sharma who is a very wise and mystic man. That sounds like a great idea.

Early the next morning I rent a bicycle for the day for a mere twenty rupees (less than a dollar), and ride to the Yogi Sharma Ashram. I listen to the yogi for an hour. His views on life, God and self, are interesting. He says, "Your Soul is God. We must take time to sit in front of the Master (Our Soul) to question and find out about *I*." He talks for an hour, his words filling me with inspiration, and closes with; "We must always retain our right to question." I leave satisfied, with a well-spent hour of inspirational messages.

I cycle back into town for breakfast reflecting on the yogi's words and am proud to say that much of what he speaks is what I believe. We have the ability to accomplish whatever we set out to do if we can believe and trust that all things will come to us at the right time and in the right place.

After breakfast I visit the Jain Temples then cycle into the old part of the village. Very quickly a young boy about twelve years of age rides beside me on his bicycle. His name is Jahr. He speaks pretty good English and asks where I am going, at the same time chasing away other boys as they gather on their bikes. I guess I have myself a guide. Jahr chatters incessantly as we visit the volunteer school, shops, and some homes. He points out the home of some newlyweds with brightly painted designs on the outer walls, and explains that the tradition is to make the home lively for the new couple. We go into an antique shop that just happens to belong to his older brother. Jahr invites me in to see his home. I am not sure that I should enter but he pulls me along. Some family members are sitting cross-legged on the floor having lunch and they invite me to eat. I thank them and politely decline, then follow my young friend on a tour of his room. It is a typical boy's room with his things scattered around. I notice there are no windows or door, just an archway with a curtain covering the entrance. The walls are cement or some kind of plaster over brick. He is proud of his room and shows me everything. Soon his older brother arrives and takes me through the antique store. I really do not want to buy anything, but manage to find a couple of small brass ornaments that I can fit in my bike.

I pay my little guide a few rupees before making my escape from the store and cycling back to find a restaurant. India has some wonderful vegetarian restaurants and today I enjoy an excellent meal of rice and veggies prepared in a spicy curry sauce.

I have this bicycle for the whole day so I explore for another hour before returning it. The air is so hot the slight breeze burns my eyes, forcing me to return to the lodge early.

At 5:10 next morning I am on the road. It is cooler this morning but the air is filled with dust and smoke. It is hard to breathe and I find myself taking short, shallow breathes. My cough seems to have come back. I put on 316 kilometers today and make it as far as Agra. By the time I find the Tourist Rest House it is after 2:30. I unpack, shower, and go down to eat.

Since entering India it has been difficult to find restaurants open in the morning, so my breakfasts have consisted of fruit, water, and pop. Today all I have eaten by 2:30 is fresh fruit, four cookies, and water. No wonder the pounds are falling off me.

On the morning of May 5 I visit the Taj Mahal and the Agra Fort. I am up early so as to get to the Taj Mahal by 6:30 to watch the sunrise. As I walk along, following my map of Agra, rickshaw wallahs (men) and touts who solicit for hotels and retail shops constantly bother me. I find it difficult not to be rude.

Emperor Shah Jahan built the Taj Mahal as a mausoleum for his second (and favorite) wife, Mumtaz Mahal. She died giving birth to their fourteenth child in 1631.

The building is constructed of marble, with intricate carvings and inlaid semiprecious stones forming floral and motif designs. In the inner part of the mausoleum the patterns are so detailed that over sixty pieces of stone makes up one small flower. The cenotaphs of Mumtaz and Shah Jahan are housed inside, but the actual tombs are in a locked room of the main chamber, which is underground and roped off to the public. The grounds surrounding the Taj Mahal consist of three acres of immaculately kept lawns, flower gardens, trees, and walkways. I watch two men mowing the lawn—one riding a mower pulled by two long horn Brahma steers, and the other walking alongside. Both men carry a white staff in one hand.

A tall red sandstone wall, with guard towers at each of the four corners, surrounds the Taj. There is a mosque on the west side of the Taj and an identical building on the east side for symmetry. The main gate is to the south of the Taj, separated by a very long, narrow reflecting pool with fountains and lights. Beyond the main gate is an outer courtyard with entrance gates to the east, west, and south. The Yamuna River runs past the lawns facing north.

From here I walk about two kilometers to the Red Fort of Agra, the most important fort in India, constructed between 1565 and 1571. The powerful walls of red sandstone rise up twenty-three meters and form a two-and-a-half-kilometer enclosure surrounding the imperial city of Mughal rulers. The fort is crescent shaped, flattened on the east, with a long, nearly straight wall facing the Yamuna River, and is encircled by a moat. Inside the walls are spectacular buildings of sandstone and marble. The Diwan-I-Am (Hall of Public Audience) has sixty-four pillars with sculptured arches designed in an isometric fashion so that whatever direction you approach from, the pillars are in perfect line. The Shah met officials and commoners and listened to the petitioners in Diwan-I-Am. The famous Peacock Throne made with gold, silver and precious jewels and ordered by Shah Jahan, was kept here until 1739 when it was removed by the Persians and later destroyed. This is only one of the many impressive buildings inside the fort walls. I am in awe as I stroll through rooms, down hallways, up flights of stone and cement stairways, and sit on wide cement windowsills to enjoy the best views. It is hard to pull myself away.

The past two days I have enjoyed tasty meals at highly recommended restaurants that serve excellent vegetarian dishes. But, yesterday I felt stomach cramps coming on and wonder if the spices were too much for me. In the evening the cramps become severe, turning into full-blown diarrhea. I hope this clears itself up quickly.

My bike needs washing and the chain needs lubing. I have run out of silicone spray so will have to get my bike greased at a shop and try to buy some spray. The young men who handle car and motorbike washes are wide-eyed with excitement when they see my bike. I am sure there is a team of five or six working on it. When the job is done I let them each take a turn sitting on it.

I am up early and leave Agra at 5:30. Dust hangs in the air and the temperature is cool, but I know it will be around forty degrees Celsius by noon. The road between Agra and Delhi is a nicely paved four-lane, divided highway. Riding is pleasant until I reach Delhi at 8:30 and am faced with total chaos. I seem to ride in circles for an hour before finding a shopping center where I stop for breakfast and look for a better Delhi map than the one in my guidebook.

Unable to find a map, I ask directions to Connaught Place where I hope to find a Guesthouse or Hostel. People do not know how to give directions. One man says, "Go out here, turn right, then left, and go straight." As soon as I am on the road I realize this will never work. I have to stop twice more before I find Main Bazaar Road near Connaught Place. The first two Guesthouses I check look fine but parking is in the alley. With all the activity in this area, that will never do. I continue to ride through the busy streets, weaving my way past crowded markets until I find the Hotel Relax. It looks great compared to most places I have seen and I expect it will be expensive. I go in and ask anyway. They want eight hundred rupees—way too much. I bargain with the man until we settle on five hundred rupees.

A female clerk shows me to my room. I am very impressed. This is a grand old hotel with marble floors and wide staircases leading to a large central foyer on each of the three floors. My room is on the second floor. The foyer is long and spacious, decorated with chairs, sofa, settee, coffee table, antique vases, and statues. It has seven doors leading off to guest rooms and garden doors at the end leading to a patio overlooking the busy bazaar below. The manager tells me to park my bike in front of the lobby window. He assures me it will be safe there as the desk clerk will be able to see it clearly.

I unpack my gear and cart it up to my room before showering and striking out into the busy market streets. This is an old part of Delhi where vendors open their doors and place their products out into the street. A narrow part of the street down the center is left for vehicles, bicycles, rickshaws, motorbikes, cows, and people. I spend the afternoon strolling through the Super Bazaar, popping in and out of shops and enjoying the activity around me. I find a fabric shop where they make clothes and pick out some material to have a sari made. Maybe if I wear the traditional dress I will be less conspicuous.

On May 8 I take a taxi to the Pakistan High Commission to apply for my visa. All I get is the application form, and I'm told to return with a permission letter from the Canadian Consulate and a bank draft for 3,250 rupees—the cost for a ten-day transit visa.

I walk to the Canadian High Commission, located in an impressive building. Upon entering the main doors I feel like I have stepped into a room from Star Wars. The smoked glass doors open automatically with a sensor. I walk into an ultra modern waiting room decorated with oversized abstract pictures and furnished with comfortable armchairs organized in two groups around coffee tables. The receptionist cage is a circular enclosure made of polished steel and bulletproof glass. The clerk speaks to me through a microphone then asks me to take a seat. If I want to speak to her I have to dial a phone in the waiting area. I don't think we have anything this elaborate at home.

When my turn comes a voice over the speaker asks me to please enter the cubicle. I go through another polished steel door, closing myself off from the rest of the world. Shortly afterwards an official comes to the window, after punching in a pass code, and asks how she can help me. I explain that I need a letter of permission from the Canadian Consulate to get my visa for Pakistan. She replies that they are not issuing a permission letter but will give me a standard form letter stating "The Canadian Consulate is not advising Canadian citizens to travel in Pakistan as it would be inconsistent with their travel advisory at this time." The borders between Pakistan and India have been closed for a few weeks due to a battle of ownership over the state of Kashmir, in northwest India. I wonder what to do, and then quickly decide to get the letter anyway. Maybe the people at the Pakistan High Commission won't read it thoroughly. I ask her about Iran. "No problem," she says. "Travel advisory has been lifted there." I wait for a few minutes and am issued both letters.

I must get a passport picture taken, with a scarf covering my head, for Iran. I go back to Main Bazaar Road to find a shop that does photos, and then venture out farther walking towards the city center. Delhi is designed with three inner circles with main arteries leading out from the center circle to the third circle (Connaught) like spokes on a wheel. At Connaught more main roads continue out to other parts of the city.

The next morning I ride back to the Pakistan High Commission. I give my letter to the man and explain that it is the standard form letter from the Canadian High Commission. "Is this letter okay?" I ask.

He does not really say yes, but pushes my forms back to me and says; "Three thousand, two hundred and fifty rupee bank draft." So off I go to find a bank. The hawkers cannot handle a draft this large so I proceed to the Ashok Hotel and the Central Bank.

When I reach the Ashok I enquire about a bank and am told that they do not open until 10:00 AM. Wow, someone was misleading me. The hawkers told me they open at 9:00. The Pakistan High Commission is only open until 10:30 to receive applications so I have to make it quick once the bank opens in order to get back in time.

I am the first person in the bank door when it opens and ten minutes later exit with my bank draft. Now I must find a taxi to get back to the High Commission. I make it with only minutes to spare. The clerk takes my papers and bank draft and tells me to come back at 4:00 PM.

When I return at 4:00, my passport has a ten-day transit visa pasted on one page. I would have liked at least a month but I will have to accept this and ride through Pakistan quickly. Now that I know I can get into Pakistan, I can apply for the Iran visa. Today is Friday and unfortunately the Iran Embassy will not be open until Monday.

With the weekend coming up I book a bus tour of Delhi for Sunday. On Saturday I pick up my sari and get the girls at the hotel to help me wrap it so it stays on. There is a special technique to this so it won't come loose halfway through the day.

On Monday morning I sleep in until after 9:00. During the night I was freezing and had to put on extra clothes. Then I was burning up and sweating so much my sheets and pillows were soaked when I awoke. I sure hope this is the end of the little bug that has been giving me stomach cramps and zapping my energy for the past few days.

Today I go to the Iran Embassy. After waiting an hour I am told they require a letter from me detailing my life history. They want to know where I was born, where I lived while in primary school, who my teachers were, where I went to college, every place I worked, et cetera. That letter gets sent to the Embassy in Iran and in about two weeks they will have an answer regarding an entry visa.

This is terrible news. By the time they get an answer my Pakistan visa will have expired. Do I fly from Delhi to Turkey and bypass Pakistan and Iran? Do I take a chance that I will be able to obtain my Iran visa when I get to Pakistan? My mind is working overtime trying to sort it all out.

As I walk back to my hotel I find myself on a street with a high cement wall on my right. The smell is horrid; it is plain to see that the wall is used as a urinal. With temperatures around forty degrees, the stench is wicked. That, combined with the Indian habit of spitting everywhere, grosses me out. Men chew on something called beetle nut and spit the unsightly red goop on the ground and sidewalks.

Back at Main Bazaar Road I wander through the markets. The streets are especially littered with garbage today and a slight breeze whirls it around. I pass a cow or two and remember to watch where I step so as not to repeat my horrible incident in Allahabad.

I return to the shop that made my sari and stop to thank them for the excellent job they did. Then I find an Internet café and post a message on Horizons Unlimited Web site asking for input from anyone who has obtained a visa for Iran and what the best procedure might be. Many world travelers frequent that site and post some very good information and advice. I must make a decision before entering Pakistan.

On May 14 I leave my hotel at 6:30 AM, and am quickly lost in the maze of streets that follow the circular plan. I stop several times to ask directions but by the time I realize people do not really know where they are directing me, I have traveled twenty kilometers south of Delhi. I want to find Highway 1 going north. It is now 9:10 and the sun is shining through the haze, so I use that as my guide. Finally I see a sign for Chandigarh and make my way out the north side of the city.

At 10:30 I stop for breakfast at a nice roadside hotel restaurant. Before I park the bike another motorcycle, loaded down with milk cans, pulls in. He must be making a delivery to the restaurant. I quickly get my camera and ask if I may take a picture of him and his bike. He obliges but does not speak enough English to answer my questions about what he is hauling.

I arrive in Chandigarh at 2:30 in the afternoon, riding only 254 kilometers. Back home I would have done that distance before breakfast.

Accommodations in Chandigarh are more expensive than I have been accustomed to paying. The city is known for its clean wide streets and nicely manicured boulevards. No cows or rickshaws are allowed here. After trying a couple of hotels I take a room at the Hotel Regency for eight hundred rupees. The first price the clerk quoted was thirteen hundred and I bartered with him until we agreed on eight hundred. Unfortunately, I can only get the room for one night, as they are booked up for tomorrow and the weekend.

In the morning I move to the Kwality Regency and have to pay a thousand rupees. It is the beginning of the weekend and I cannot barter them down any lower. I check out the room and find it is beautiful, so decide to pamper myself. After all, one thousand rupees equal about thirty dollars Canadian.

After checking in I spend the rest of the morning searching out airlines. I find Air India and Indian Airlines and neither one flies out of Pakistan (passenger or cargo). There goes my idea of flying my bike from Pakistan to Turkey. I still don't know what I should do.

Later that afternoon I happen upon a large outdoor shopping area with a wide pedestrian-only street that runs for three blocks and is lined with upscale shops on both sides. I enjoy the afternoon poking around window shopping and relaxing in an outdoor café. I check my e-mail and am disappointed that there are still no messages from anyone who has traveled to Iran.

The next morning I leave for Shimla, heading north into the mountains. Shimla is situated high in the hills at over twenty-one hundred meters above sea level and is surrounded by hilly green pastures and snow-capped peaks. It was discovered by the British in 1819 and was declared the summer capital of India in 1864. In 1903 it was named the capital of the state of Himachal Pradesh and is a major Indian Hill Station. The architecture of the restored buildings resembles that of a small English town. Temperatures, although hot in summer, are cooler at this altitude, making it a popular tourist destination.

I stroll around town and take the lift up to a large outdoor mall built along the top of a mountain ridge. When I return to the bike it is 4:30 PM. Accommodation is hard to find here so I decide to ride farther north. After twenty-five kilometers I find myself on a narrow, bumpy, twisty road with curves so tight rounding the mountains that I use my horn continually. The first hotel I find is full so I have no choice but to continue riding. It is getting late and I begin to worry about being caught out here after dark. At Tattopani I find the Rainbow Guesthouse built on the banks of the river. There is no water in the taps but I can have a hot bath in the sulfur tubs, so I stop for the night. At four hundred rupees it is very much overpriced since it is so isolated and has no running water. However, the view is spectacular and makes up for what is lacking.

I have breakfast at the Guesthouse and do not leave until 8:00. The road becomes rougher and narrower and when I meet oncoming trucks or buses I pull off to the edge and stop. I am riding on the cliff side and am very close to the edge with no official vehicle pullouts. To make matters worse my horn has quit working. The scenery is breathtaking, but I can only sneak the occasional quick glance.

At one little roadside home I see some interesting paintings on huge rock boulders and stop to take pictures. A man dressed in a salwar kameez with a long orange shawl draped around his shoulders comes out to meet me. He invites me to stop for a smoke or a drink. I am not sure what kind of a smoke or drink—it sounds and looks suspicious— so I continue riding. It is 1:30 in the afternoon when I reach Mandi and I have only traveled 170 kilometers. I stop early knowing that it is over a hundred kilometers to Dharamsala and it could take four or five hours. I do not want to be on these mountain roads after dark.

Great news! I have a response from my message on the Horizons Unlimited Web site. A fellow biker suggests that I e-mail Ramin from Sireh Travel in Iran and request my visa through their agency. He had similar problems when he applied and was advised to go this route. Processing, he explains, will take about two weeks, but it is almost certain that I will get my visa. When I reach Dharamsala tomorrow I will fax my passport and other information to the travel agency.

I leave Mandi shortly after 6:00 AM. The road improves for some short stretches and several times I come to a Y in the road with no direction sign to be seen. I stop several times to ask directions, which is a good thing because twice I was heading off on the wrong arm. Before I reach Dharamsala I spot a little shop alongside the road where two men are working on motorcycles. I stop and ask if they have time to fix my horn. One man speaks very little English so I have to show him the problem. He motions me into the shop, pulls out a stool, and waves with his arm for me to sit. In no time at all he has fixed the horn. My chain needs adjusting, so I show him that it is loose and rub my finger across indicating it needs grease. He says, "No problem." and sets about doing the job.

When the work is done I ask, "How much?" and pull out my money to pay him. He shakes his head no, waves his hands and says; "Your thank-you is enough."

"No, I expect to pay for the work." I reply.

He repeats; "Your thank-you is enough."

Wow! I thank him again and again before leaving. There are some terrific people in the world. My thoughts drift to my belief that the Universe provides our every need. Somehow we are all connected and play a part in the lives of those we come in contact with.

I reach Dharamsala around noon and ask a storeowner which street takes me up to Upper Dharamsala. He tells me the road is very steep, and then looks at my bike and exclaims, "You have no problem with that bike, it has lots of power!"

I begin to wonder if it is safe to ride up. The guidebook recommends staying at the top for majestic views of the Dhaulandhar ranges above and the Kangra Valley below. Dhaulandhar, which means "white ridge", rises out of the Kangra Valley to a height of five thousand, two hundred meters (seventeen thousand feet) forming part of the outer Himalayas. Upper Dharmasala, also referred to as McLeod Ganj, sits at one thousand, eight hundred meters and is home to the Dalai Lama. The monastery was an abandoned hill station once used by the government, and offered to the Dalai Lama at the time of his exile from Tibet. The mountainsides are covered in pine, Himalayan oak, and rhododendron and deodar forests. The local Indians farming the Kangra Valley below grow rice, wheat, and tea.

Streams of Tibetan refugees from all over the world flock to McLeod Ganj to receive blessings from His Holiness the Dalai Lama. The village has a definite Tibetan character with shops strung out along narrow streets selling traditional Tibetan arts and handicrafts, and restaurants serving Tibetan food.

The narrow road I take to reach Upper Dharamsala ascends about six hundred meters in four kilometers. It is very steep in places but

I reach the top safely and locate a hotel on the main road with a spectacular view of the mountains and valley. I manage to negotiate the price down to five hundred rupees.

I park my bike and begin to carry my things up the wide staircase to the third floor. The young man who checked me in stops me and asks how old I am. I don't think that is necessary for his hotel records so I do not tell him.

He continues to tell me that he likes older women, that he has powerful sexual desires, and that he had sex with another older foreign guest five times.

I stand there stunned, not sure if I should continue to carry my things in or find another place to stay.

He continues, informing me that he uses condoms and that he has eight inches and is only twenty-six years old.

I wonder if he thinks it will continue to grow as he gets older? Is he in for a surprise!

Then he adds, "If you need any let me know."

I chuckle and tell him, "No thanks, I won't be needing any."

By this time I am thinking he is perfectly harmless, and continue to bring my bags up to my room. I shower and eat then go walking through the narrow streets packed with shops. I find a shop where I fax my passport information to Sireh Travel in Iran and send an e-mail to the agent, Ramin. Today is Sunday, May 18; if all goes as expected, I should have my visa in ten days.

I send an e-mail to three Pakistan Servas members in hopes of meeting someone when I reach Lahore.

I continue to stroll through the streets and stop at clothing shops looking for a pair of lightweight cotton pants. These blue jeans are just too hot. At one point a Tibetan lady comes running after me with my camera in her hand. I had left my camera in a shop a few doors down. Wow, that is two good deeds I have received today! Here I am in a country where people could easily rip me off and, instead, I receive exceptional treatment.

I stay four nights here, packing in as much sightseeing as possible. The Monastery is first on my list. Maybe I will be fortunate enough to see the Dalai Lama. One can make an appointment to have an audience with Him, but it must be booked months in advance. Many monks study here and can be seen sitting cross-legged on padded mats laid in long rows on the cement floor, practicing their debating techniques.

The temple complex is always busy with services held daily and attended by lamas, monks, nuns, and lay people. Visitors are welcome to observe and must follow the tradition of removing their shoes and walking clockwise around the temple past the chorten (prayer wheels) before sitting down.

There are no automatic bank machines in Upper Dharamsala so I have to go down the hill four kilometers to the Baroda Bank to get money on my credit card. I should have withdrawn money when I came through Shimla, but how was I to know? At the bank I present my visa and have to fill out a "request for money" form, then come back tomorrow to get it. That means tackling this hill twice. The walk down was quite easy, but going up is a little more difficult. A little beggar boy latches on to me halfway up the hill and will not leave me alone. He keeps walking in front of me, pushing me over to the cliff edge of the road. I finally have to get very angry with him before he leaves. I notice that the zipper on my purse is half open. I wait until I get up to the hotel to check. Nothing is gone but I wonder if the little guy was trying his hand at pick pocketing. I am told that the children here are very adept at this.

The next morning I head back down the hill to the bank. My leg muscles are sore this morning and I scold myself for not being more consistent with my yoga exercises.

On May 21 I am sitting in an open-front coffee shop having breakfast when I notice a crowd of people gathering at the end of the street towards the monastery. After finishing my coffee I walk down to see what is going on. I cannot get anyone to tell me so I find a place in the crowd and wait. There are officers amongst the crowd so I ask one and he mentions something about the Dalai Lama leaving on tour today. A monk tells me the people have been waiting since 8:00 this morning—it is now 9:15. I gradually make my way to the front of the crowd, keeping my elbows out so as not to lose my position. At 10 o'clock the procession comes around the corner and down the hill. A man at the edge of the crowd steps out with a bucket of water and sprinkles the road to settle the dust. The first vehicle is a jeep with five armed security guards; the next car carries the Dalai Lama and more security guards. For a change I chose the right spot—as the vehicle passes I see the Dalai Lama, smiling widely with his hands at his face in a half *namaste* position. Of course I do not have my camera with me, but this is a special moment, so I remember every detail about him as though I've captured it all in a photograph. Four more vehicles with security guards follow behind the car carrying His Holiness.

There is a lot to see and do here and I should stay a week, but I'm anxious to get moving and into Pakistan and Iran. I have received an e-mail from Servas host, Mohammed Naseem, in Pakistan and he has invited me to stay with his family when I reach Lahore. He also states that he will meet me at the border.

May 22 I leave Dharamsala/McLeod Ganj shortly after 6:00, early enough to miss the busy tourists and local traffic through town. I ride far enough to get away from this madness before stopping at a little roadside restaurant for breakfast. I visit with the owner over toast and coffee. He proudly tells me about his business, but is concerned that tourism has slowed down in the past year. I continue on to Amristar where I stay one night. Tomorrow I will cross the border into Pakistan.

I try to make a phone call to Mr. Naseem, but am not allowed. Because of the unsettled issues between Pakistan and India at the moment, the government of India will not allow phone calls between the two countries. The border is still closed to local traffic. I hope I don't have problems getting in. The best I can do is send an e-mail telling Mr. Naseem I will be at the border at 8:00 AM.

Chapter 4

Pakistan

On May 23, 2003, at 8:00 AM I arrive at the gates dividing India and Pakistan only to find they do not open until 10:00. I'm concerned that my Pakistan Servas host will have been waiting for two hours. In my e-mail I told him I would be crossing early. Now I have no way of contacting him to relay this setback.

I cross the border to Pakistan against the advice of the Canadian High Commission in Delhi. The border has been closed to local travelers for several months now, so there are very few people crossing between India and Pakistan. The two countries are quarrelling over the boundaries of the most northern state in India, "Jammu and Kashmir" (more commonly referred to as *Kashmir*). India considers the entire state as its sovereign territory, but has control of only half the area. Pakistan controls one third of the state and the remaining portion is administered by China. This territorial dispute has been ongoing for years and at this point in time Pakistan and India have closed their borders to one another. I am crossing much farther south of the disputed territory so am not overly concerned about aggressive activity in the areas where I will be traveling. Kashmir lies mostly in the Himalayan Mountains.

It is 11:00 AM by the time I reach the Immigration and Customs office for Pakistan. It takes about half an hour to get my passport stamped before being sent on to another customs office to get my motorbike checked in. Another *sit down and wait* exercise while the officials figure out what to do with my carnet. After another half an hour a man walks in and introduces himself to me as Mohammad Naseem. Wow, is this ever great! This is my Servas host—the head of the family I will be staying with for a couple of days in Lahore. I was sure he would have grown tired of waiting and gone home.

Once Mohammad appears the officers seem to know exactly what to do, and they complete my carnet immediately. It feels good to have a friend in my corner. As a Servas member I know he is just that— another friend I have yet to meet.

We stop to have a pop and get acquainted before going on to Lahore. Mohammad is a jolly man, not much taller than myself, weighing around two hundred pounds. He is the National Secretary for Servas Pakistan, and a gracious host. During our "get acquainted" visit I soon realize that he does not have a vehicle. He came to the border by bus and is expecting to ride back with me. My thoughts are spinning. It would be rude to tell him he has to take the bus back, after coming all this way to meet me. The back seat of my bike, which is not really a seat at all, is loaded down with gear. How will I fit him on too? It is very obvious that he plans to ride back to Lahore with me—but where?

As we continue our visit my mind is rearranging the gear on my bike to accommodate my gracious host. I truly do not know if this is possible, but I must try. We finish our drinks and walk towards my bike. Mohammad is saying he will catch a ride back, but by now I have a plan. I tell him to give me a moment and I will see what I can do. I un-strap the two rolls from the back seat and attach the bigger one to the top of my trunk. I strap it down carefully, check that it is tight, and am satisfied it will not fall off. Now we just have to worry about the small roll. Mohammad quickly offers to hold it on his knee. Okay, that might work. I get on the bike and instruct him to get on behind, then hand him the blue roll which he props upright on his knee. Great, this will work just fine. I give my passenger a few instructions on co-riding and we are off and running.

It is nice to have someone give me directions so I can pay attention to the roads and enjoy a bit of the scenery. I am thankful that the traffic is light and the roads are good. The bike is loaded down to maximum capacity and I realize how odd we must look—me with my full riding gear of heavy jacket, pants, boots, gloves, and helmet and my co-rider in shirtsleeves, with no helmet, and wearing sandals on his feet. I chuckle as the picture flashes across my mind.

When we reach Lahore, a city with a population of over one million, the traffic becomes like that of many cities I have been to in the past few months. The major streets are wide, but, as for the rest, they are very narrow, dusty, and congested with a wide assortment of vehicles, motorbikes, cycles, donkeys pulling carts, pedestrians, and anything else that rolls or walks, going in all directions. I stay one hundred percent focused as Mohammad directs me through the busy streets to his office. I am all too aware of the responsibility I have undertaken by having him as a passenger and I am relieved when he instructs me to pull up in front of his office.

As soon as we enter the building my host asks if I would like something to drink (Pepsi, water, chai). I accept a bottle of water, which is brought in by a young boy about ten who turns out to be Mohammad's nephew. Shortly afterwards I am introduced to Shaista and her three young sons who are Mohammad's younger brother's family. Shaista is a petite lady with long black hair pulled back off her face and bound at the back of her neck. She is very pretty with a welcoming and genuine smile. Her youngest son is about six and tugs at my heartstrings with his huge brown eyes and permanent smile that reminds me of my second grandson. I am thinking—*how can you look like my grandson when your hair is black and his is blond, and your skin is dark and his is light?* In spite of the differences, every time this beautiful little boy smiles, I see my grandson, Liam. For a moment I feel homesick and find myself blinking back the tears.

In a few minutes Shaista brings in three cups. I thought she would be joining us, but not so. The third cup is for another friend, Mohammad Khan. I quickly learn that *Mohammad* is a popular name in Pakistan. Mohammad Khan owns a garment and costume factory nearby. My host, also a business owner, runs a mattress factory that produces top-quality mattresses.

It is interesting visiting with these two men. They are curious about my life and ask many questions about my family, whether I am married, the kind of work I do back in Canada, where I have traveled, and where I am going.

The women of Pakistan work and also run businesses, but the

thought of them traveling alone is totally foreign. My being there without a man is shocking to these good people.

After a lunch, prepared by Shaista, we ride to Mohammad Khan's garment factory. Mohammad K is riding a little 100cc Honda, and my host, once again, rides behind me. Our first stop is a costume factory where I meet the employees, who are all women. They seem to be enjoying what they do and smile broadly when I come near. Each woman leaves her post and comes forward to shake my hand, giggling as we are introduced. I must be a curiosity to them—an independent woman traveling by motorbike, *and without a man*. Mohammed then says something in their language, which produces great laughter. I am curious about what was said but never do find out. Maybe they were laughing about the strange custom of women shaking hands. Soon, to my delight, they have me trying on some of their beautiful costumes while Mohammad takes pictures. I feel like a teenager being accepted into a group of new friends.

Our next stop is the big factory. Here is where the men work—cutting fabric and sewing uniforms, suits, et cetera. The atmosphere in here is much more serious. Mohammad K talks to me about his business and asks if I have any contacts for him. He exports his costumes to several countries including the USA.

After the tour I am offered more chai, pop, and water. I have had so much to drink I think I will burst. We make a few more stops that afternoon, to meet more Servas members and friends, and by the time we head to Mohammad's home it is dark. Driving in Lahore in daylight is bad enough, but at night it is horrendous! I pick my way carefully through the traffic and narrow streets lined with night markets, and finally, about forty-five minutes later, we arrive at the Naseem home.

The Naseem family lives in an apartment-style, two-bedroom home situated above a grocery store. The buildings on the whole block are of dull grey cement and seem to be all connected. I go up a long flight of narrow stairs leading to an open-air hallway. There is a sink and washing machine in the hallway on my right and at the end is a door leading to the kitchen. Three doors on my left lead to bedrooms and a living room. The bathroom is behind me at the other end of the hall. It is about three by four feet and consists of a squat toilet, sink, and shower. At the moment the shower is not working so there is a large tub of water in the corner, which is used to sponge bath. At this end of the hall there's also a stairwell leading up to the rooftop where Mrs. Naseem hangs the laundry.

Once I haul my gear up the stairs I meet the rest of the family—Mrs. Naseem, their sixteen-year-old son Naumand, and twenty-year-old daughter Monessa. The children both speak pretty good English and Monessa takes extra classes in the evening to improve for university. They are wonderful young people and have a host of questions for me. They especially want to know about Canada, then they ask about some of the other countries I have been to. The whole family is very curious about why I am traveling alone. "Don't I get lonely? Isn't it frightening or dangerous?" They just cannot imagine being that far from home *and* alone.

By this time I am exhausted and would like to sleep but I cannot be rude. It is 9:00 PM and Mrs. Naseem has dinner ready. She spreads a colorful cloth on the floor in the first bedroom, which doubles as a dining area, and sets out the plates and food. We all sit cross-legged on the floor and eat a wonderful meal of rice, vegetables, meat with sauce, and some sort of flat bread. Since I have become vegetarian I pass on the meat but try everything else. The food is prepared in a lot of oil and is much spicier than what I am accustomed to, so I keep plenty of water handy. The flat bread is used to scoop up the food and using one's fingers is quite acceptable. I find my legs becoming cramped and must change my position often during the meal. Members of the Naseem family have no problem sitting cross-legged for the entire time. We finish off dinner with another cup of chai and I find I am having trouble swallowing this thick, sweet liquid. I must admit, I would have been happier with a bottle of water.

Finally it is time for bed. I have been wondering where I will sleep with only two bedrooms in the apartment for four of them plus one of me. They set up two wide cots, end to end, in the hallway, and then make up the beds. The air is still hot so there is no need for heavy covers. A sheet, light blanket, and pillow is all that is required. I am given the choice of taking one of the bedrooms or using one of the cots. I opt for the cot. I cannot pass up the experience of sleeping under the stars in Pakistan. Mrs. Naseem and her son sleep on the other cot.

I have a wonderful sleep out in the open air. By 5:00 I am awake and open my eyes to the sky above. What a beautiful way to start the day. Muslim people rise very early in the morning to perform their religious rituals before going about their duties for the day. In this family the parents head off to their separate jobs and the children to school. Today Mohammad and I will go sightseeing. He enjoys riding on the back of my bike and since he does not have a vehicle, it is either that or take a taxi. It is quite apparent he prefers the bike.

Our first stop for the day is the Lahore Museum. The admission for a foreigner is one hundred rupees, and for a local person ten. Later I notice my ticket stub reads *Foreigner adult, fifty rupees*. I am not sure why I was charged one hundred. This sort of thing seems to happen all too often. The museum is in a beautiful old building with several domes on the roof and an ornate entrance with arched doorways. They have done an excellent job of displaying artifacts from Pakistan—stones, wood, jewels, carvings, statues, antiques, and more.

Our next stop is to visit Haseck Ahmed, one of Mohammad's friends. Mr. Ahmed is a tall, attractive man who operates a money exchange shop. His doors are locked to the public today because another moneychanger was murdered a couple of days earlier and the businesses are protesting his death by closing their doors for a day or two. After introductions, Mr. Ahmed offers chai, Coke or juice, and asks if I want something to eat.

I am feeling a bit hungry so I accept. Mr. Ahmed sends his employee out to buy a pizza. I am expecting that it will be a pizza for all of us, but the young man comes back with a small pizza just for me. I protest, but they will not listen to anything I say. This pizza is for me and only me. So I concede and eat my pizza in silence while they converse, mostly in Urdu, leaving me in the dark.

By the time I finish my pizza there are a couple more visitors present and we converse in English, with Mohammad interpreting for the gentlemen who do not understand or speak my language. Mostly they are interested in hearing about Canada. I field the typical questions about our health care and education systems, some politics, and a lot of personal questions about myself.

Before leaving Mr. Ahmed asks if I would like a hotel room for one night. He suggests that I might like some privacy after spending a few days in the cramped quarters of a Pakistan home. He has a complimentary room at the Ramada Hotel and would like to give it to me. Immediately the red flags go up in my mind. I express my concerns to Mohammad, but he assures me it is an honorable gesture.

I wish I could have understood what they were talking about earlier while I ate. I accept the offer and Mr. Ahmed books a room for me at the Ramada Hotel for Monday night. In all honesty, I look forward to some time alone.

It is early afternoon when we leave Mr. Ahmed's office and go to meet more of Mohammad's friends. We walk past a huge bicycle bazaar and many fashion shops before turning into a narrow alley of clothing and fabric shops jam-packed with merchandise. The shops are not individual enclosed storefronts as we are accustomed to, but rather open front market stalls in a very large area under one low roof. There are long racks of vibrant salwar kameez outfits and tables full of beautiful, brightly colored cotton fabric. I am itching to stop and try on some outfits, but do not want to appear rude so I follow Mohammad into a back room where his friends are having lunch.

There are four men and one woman in this group. She owns and operates one of the fashion shops and speaks only a few words of English. One of the men is a doctor who has traveled extensively so he has many questions for me about some of the places I have been. Aside from this, most of the conversation is in Urdu and, I am sure, about me. I try hard to ignore that fact and just enjoy the atmosphere.

Once again I am offered more to eat and chai. Finally, after about an hour, we make our intention to leave. Uroog, the only lady in the group, gets up and tells us to wait a moment. When she returns she has a gift for me—a set of six gold-colored bangles with multi-colored carvings around them. I am thrilled to be presented with such a beautiful gift.

From here we walk to the post office before returning to Mr. Ahmed's office to retrieve my bike. We go into the office and are served more chai by Mr. Ahmed's assistant. I really do not know if I can stomach another cup of this sweet stuff. I sip as much of it as I can before going out to start my bike. By now I am tired and hope we will be heading home, but Mohammad has other plans. He says we will stop by his older brother's home first, to meet his mother, sisters and sister-in-law. I am tired but do not argue. I really do want to meet all these people, just not all in one day!

It is about four o'clock when we arrive at the home of Mohammad's brother. We enter through a low door (I have to duck to get in) cut into the side of a high cement wall, and go up three flights of stairs. The bathroom is on the landing at the top of the stairs. It is modest, has a squat toilet, sink and shower head that, when used, would spray water over the complete room. This is a typical bathroom in a modest home in Pakistan. We turn to go into the next room, a large rectangular space with no roof and one side open to a view of the city. There is a cement wall about a meter high running the length of the opening and a bed against the opposite wall. There are four other doors going off from this outer room; one is a kitchen, I assume two are bedrooms, and one is a large living room. In this room there is a mantel at one end, a colorful area rug on the floor, and cushions lining the outer walls. Along one wall there is a built-in bench covered with cushions on the seat and upright against the wall.

In the Muslim culture the eldest son is responsible for aging parents and other siblings, especially women and their children. Consequently there are several people living in this household—the grandmother, three sisters, and a couple of nephews. Upon our arrival all the women are in the big room reading the Koran (the Muslim scriptures).

While we wait for the women to emerge, I sit and visit with Mohammad's eighty-year-old mother. She looks more like ninety-five and moves very slowly. Women in Pakistan are very weathered and look much older than Westerners. I anticipate that this is from being in the sun 365 days of the year. This grand old lady does not speak English but she makes me feel very welcome just by her actions. I show her pictures of my children and grandchildren that I carry in my wallet. At that moment the other women come out from their worship. They are all excited to see me and gather close to see the pictures. A couple of the younger women speak a little English but are too shy to try. Most of our conversation is with the help of Mohammad's interpretation.

The next day Mohammad arranges for his sister-in-law, Shaista, to make me a salwar kameez. After a short visit and more chai, she takes me to a shop to buy material for the project. I pick out two different patterns, one in multi-colors of bright blue and the other in a bold orange, black, and yellow. I am excited about getting the finished product so I can wear the traditional dress and blend in a little. I chuckle at that thought, given my white skin I would not blend in regardless of my clothing.

When we get back from shopping I am sure we will be heading home for the day, but Mohammad informs me we will be going to

Mohammad Khan's home for dinner. So off we go on my motorcycle. I am very tired and should have insisted on going home but do not want to disappoint my host. I continue carefully on to Mr. Khan's residence, following Mohammad's directions. Many of the roads he directs me on are narrow, full of potholes, crowded, and require all my skill and concentration. I am very glad to reach our destination.

The entrance to Mr. Khan's home is off a narrow street, wide enough for only one vehicle to pass. I know I cannot leave my bike out there so I inquire about where I can park it safely. Mr. Khan opens up a large gate-like door to his home and tells me to ride it in. This is the foyer to his home—a large square room nicely decorated with shiny tile flooring. I hesitate, but he insists. Wow, what hospitality! I cannot imagine one of my friends or family members at home opening up their front door and inviting me to ride in.

Mr. Khan escorts us down the hallway into a large living and dining room. The floor is covered with brightly patterned, heavy area rugs. A long chesterfield is placed along one wall with another one positioned across the room in front of an antique-look cabinet. An end table sits at each side of the chesterfields with lamps, flowers or ornaments decorating their tops. Heavy drapes line the end wall, but I do not remember seeing a window from the outside. At the other end of this huge, long room are a large dining room suite, china cabinet, and other smaller furniture. I can tell this is a home of a more prosperous family.

I sit on the chesterfield but soon move to sitting cross-legged on the floor to join my two hosts. I expect to meet Mr. Khan's wife but as we visit I realize that is not to be … yet. I meet his six-year-old son, who captures the spotlight, and his teenage nephew who works at the garment factory.

Several people also live in this home. Along with his wife, son, and infant daughter, three of his sisters live here. One sister is widowed with a teenage daughter and son. Mr. Khan relays to me that it is his responsibility to look after his family. If any of his sisters were to be widowed or divorced, they would be welcome to live in his home.

I ask what his wife thinks of this. He replies; "Sometimes she complains and would like to have a home of our own with some privacy. But she understands that, as the eldest, it is my duty to take care of my family."

As we continue to sit cross-legged on the floor, I wonder if we will eat at the dining room table. I do not have to wait long for an answer to my thoughts. The nephew brings a large square tablecloth and spreads it on the floor between the two chesterfields. Then, with the help of Mr. Khan, they bring out the dishes, utensils, and food, and we eat right where we are. I think I like this tradition, but it would take a few weeks to build up my muscles to sit comfortably for any length of time. It disappoints me that the women do not join us, but this is the custom in many of these cultures.

After dinner Mr. Khan takes me into the kitchen to meet his wife, sisters, and niece. The women make me feel completely comfortable. Mr. Khan interprets, "My wife and sister would like to know if you would spend a couple of nights in our home?" I thank him for the generous offer and explain that I only have a ten-day transit visa for Pakistan, which does not allow a lot of time to make it across the country to Iran.

By the time Mohammad N and I leave for home it has grown dark outside, making riding more dangerous. The streets are still as busy as they had been during the day and I exercise extra caution for what seems to be a great distance back to the Naseem home.

May 25 marks my third day in Pakistan, and I have yet to leave Lahore. Mohammad wants to introduce me to so many people that he asks me to stay longer. I explain that I can't; I must coordinate my Iran visa before my Pakistan one runs out. If the visa for Iran does not come through I will have to return to India. I only have eight days to get this all organized. Today is Sunday so Mohammad tells me, "Tomorrow I will take you to the Iran Embassy and apply with you. If they think you are accompanied by a man, the visa may be easier to obtain." That sounds reasonable—let's hope it works. This will be my backup plan just in case I do not get an e-mail from Ramin, the travel agent in Iran through whom I ordered my visa.

This morning we are off to visit a couple of teachers, including Mr. Musleh who is also a scout leader. His wife makes up some beautiful drinks and serves them to her husband, Mohammad, and me. She then retreats from the room, leaving us to get acquainted. I am saddened by this custom and feel cheated that I cannot spend more time with the women. Mr. Musleh wants me to stop by his school tomorrow.

While I have been spending time with the men, the women have been gathering gifts for me. Later, when we go to another room to talk with the women, Mrs. Musleh gives me a Pakistan pin and Mr. Musleh's sister, who is also a teacher, gives me a huge card she made and a box of twenty-five wrist bangles. I thank them and take several pictures. They are excited to meet me, and love having their pictures taken.

From here we go to visit a popular drummer group in Pakistan called *Safis Soul*. En route we notice an extremely tall bicycle parked on the street and Mohammad tells me to stop. He explains that this bicycle holds the *Guinness World Record* for the tallest bicycle in the world. I am honored to meet Mr. Hussain, who is the owner and engineer of the bicycle. He agrees to give me a demonstration and climbs up to the top seat, about three meters off the ground. All I can say is *"Wow*, this man has balance!"

Mr. Naseem seems to know everyone so there are a few more introductions and short visits before we continue on to the home of *Safis Soul*. We turn down several narrow, rough streets lined with grey cement buildings before stopping in front of the home of Gonya Sain, the lead drummer for the group. We enter through a low door, which goes directly from the street into a small room lined with cushions around the exterior and a built-in bench along one wall. Family photos line the walls along with photos of the musical group in various performances. Mr. Sain and his brother are sitting cross-legged on the floor talking and laughing. He is well known in the music industry in Pakistan, and I soon realize he is blind. Most of the conversation is in Urdu and Mohammad interprets some for me. I learn that drums are called "dhols" and that Mr. Sain has been playing for many, many years. He has been blind since birth and is married to a wonderful woman who is his constant companion.

The younger brother has a Pakistani wife and is proud to show us the pictures of his recent marriage to a Japanese woman. I simply cannot understand this custom, but it is quite normal in the Muslim culture for a man to have more than one wife. A man is allowed to have four wives, presuming he can support them and their families.

By now it is late afternoon and after three days of meeting people and fighting traffic in this hectic city, I have had enough. I tell Mohammad I cannot visit anymore this afternoon, and that I need to go home and rest.

In the evening Naumand, Mr. Naseem's sixteen-year-old son, wants to take me to the big shopping plaza. It is still light out when we leave on my bike and I am happy that we do not have to ride far before reaching our destination. Naumand does not want to wear a helmet but I insist. Nobody wears a helmet here and he is worried that one of his friends may see him. Once we reach the shopping area the traffic seems to multiply. I have a difficult time finding a parking spot and have to ride down several narrow streets with tightly parked cars, trucks, and bikes. It takes awhile but finally I manage to squeeze into a space in a partially dried up mud-hole. Traffic is horrendous and I am ready to take any spot I can find.

I am completely amazed at the size of this shopping plaza. First we walk through the open market of vendors with stalls displaying products from Pakistan of everything imaginable—furniture, mattresses, clothing, trinkets, tools, et cetera. Naumand is a good guide and talks continually, throwing in questions about my life, my family, and Canada. When we leave the market we stroll past stores with nicely displayed merchandise in the windows. This is the newer shopping mall with several fashion stores for men and women, fabric shops, pharmacies, and many others.

It is very late by the time we return home and Naumand's parents have been worried about us. They did not expect us to be gone this long. Parents everywhere in the world are the same when it comes to protecting their children.

Today is Monday, May 26—my Pakistan visa is quickly expiring, and I still have not heard from the travel agent about my visa for Iran. This morning Mohammad and I go down to the Iran Embassy to fill out another application. We are sent home with the forms and told to return at 8:00 tomorrow morning with photocopies of my Pakistan visa and the identification page of my passport. Mr. Naseem also has an application. Wow, this is making things really tight! After today I have only six days left on my visa. Nothing happens quickly in these countries.

After visiting more Servas members and having lunch, we ride to the hotel Mr. Ahmed booked for me. I am looking forward to a peaceful afternoon and time alone.

Mohammad accompanies me into the hotel to secure the booking. I am handed the key and am expecting Mohammad to leave but he insists on coming up to check out the room and make sure everything is okay. He makes a thorough check of the room and then, to my surprise, decides to take a shower! I am a bit miffed, to say the least, but then I recall that his shower at home has been out of commission for a few weeks, so I figure no harm is done by him using the shower before he leaves.

I relax on a nice easy chair, but am feeling just enough on edge that I do not get too comfortable. My intuition is telling me something because shortly there is a knock on the door and I open it to find Mr. Ahmed standing there. He comes in and makes himself comfortable before asking about Mohammad. I tell him Mr. Naseem is in the shower and should be out soon. I am not happy with this turn of events.

Mr. Ahmed starts asking me questions. They are pretty general at first, but gradually take a personal turn. He asks if I have a friend. I say; "Yes, I have many friends, in the biking community and elsewhere." I am fully aware that is not what he is asking, but I decide to play dumb.

Now the questions get more direct. "Are you in a relationship? Aren't you lonely? Don't you want a relationship?" Moments later he asks, "Are you afraid to stay here alone tonight? One of us can stay with you if you are afraid."

Oh-my-gosh! I have traveled halfway around the world alone and this man thinks I am going to fall for that?

Mr. Ahmed suggests I make myself comfortable, take off my boots and socks, and stretch out on the bed if I like. "Don't be shy," he says.

I am still sitting with my riding boots on and ready to bolt for the door if I have to. I am becoming annoyed that Mohammad is taking so long in the shower. He has been in there about half an hour already.

Finally Mohammad makes an appearance. *It is about time!* The men speak to each other in Urdu, and of course I have no idea what they are saying. My mind is racing and I know that I am not spending the night here. I formulate a plan in my mind, and then tell Mohammad that we have to go out to get our passports and visa application forms photocopied. I remind him that we have to be at the embassy at 8:00 in the morning so we cannot delay on this. He agrees and we leave with our documents in hand, Mohammad telling Mr. Ahmed that we will be back shortly. I am thinking, *you might be, sir, but not me.*

On our way out of the hotel I turn to Mohammad and ask,

"What on earth was that all about? What kind of a deal goes with this room?"

Mohammad looks shocked and asks me what I mean. I cannot mince words here just to be polite so I tell him straight, "I am not interested in exchanging sexual favors for a nice room!"

Mohammad is clearly confused and asks what Mr. Ahmed said to me. I give him a short version of Ahmed's inquisition and say again that I am not interested in this little game. Mohammad apologizes profusely for his friend and says he had no idea about all this and that I will return to his family home. I am quite relieved.

After getting our photocopying done, Mohammad directs me to a warehouse where liquor, beer, and wine are sold. The large storage room is at the back of a very nice hotel. I am confused at first but then he explains that it is illegal for Pakistan natives to buy alcohol. This is a bootleg outlet. He explains that, as a foreigner, I can get a permission slip to purchase two hundred dollars worth of booze. What many foreigners do is buy the alcohol and then bootleg it to the locals.

"Sorry Mohammad, I really don't want to buy any." I say.

As we are returning to the bike Mohammad tells me that Mr. Ahmed had told him I wanted some beer. I realize now just how accurate my intuition was back at the Ramada Hotel, and am glad to be returning to the Naseem home.

Later that evening I accompany Monessa to her English class. She is excited to bring a guest, and to ride on the back of my bike. Her instructor is a Pakistani man who speaks very good English. He instructs for the first half hour of the class and then asks me to come up to the front and tell everyone about myself. I talk for about ten minutes, telling the students a little about Canada and my family, and then I ask if they have any questions. These are university students who love the opportunity to practice their English, so each of them asks one question.

On Tuesday, May 27, Mohammed and I are at the Iran Embassy before eight o'clock. We take a spot under the trees with the rest of those in line. There seems to be a lot of Pakistani people wanting visas for Iran. Finally it is our turn and we are sent down a narrow hallway to the officials. I find out that I cannot get a visa on the spot; they have to send my application to Iran, and then I must wait ten days for it to come back ... or not. This is not good for me. My Pakistan visa will have run out by then. Oh dear, I have to take time to think about this. As my host would say, "What to do, what to do?"

I decide to stop at the Pakistan Embassy and try to extend that visa. I am hoping that I can stay for another ten days. After an hour of waiting in line and being sent from one window to another, I am told that I have to apply for an extension in Islamabad. Wow, the problem keeps mounting. Now that means an added two or three days. I was not planning on going there, but I guess I have no choice. Tomorrow I will ride to the capital city of Pakistan.

Before returning to the Naseem home we ride to Mohammad Khan's house for lunch. I get behind a bus belching blue smoke out of its pipes and try to sneak around it. Unfortunately this is a bad decision. When I see that I will not make it I hit the brakes and we take a tumble. With these high temperatures the pavement can become greasy. Fortunately it is a minor spill—I only suffer a small scrape to my elbow and Mohammad remains unhurt. We pick up the bike and continue on.

When we arrive at Mr. Khan's home I am all too glad to park the bike, sit down and rest. I just close my eyes and relax while the two men visit.

The two Mohammads occasionally speak to each other in Urdu and before I know it Mohammad K is asking me if I want to see a doctor about the scrape on my elbow. Mohammad N has told his friend about our little incident earlier today and they both seem terribly concerned. I insist that I am okay and the scrape is nothing. I am sure it will be fine once I put some medicated ointment on it. Mohammad K insists that I see his doctor. He says they must take the baby in for her check-up, so I should come with them.

It is obvious that I am not going to win this argument. We all pile into Mohammad K's old pick-up truck with a wooden box on the back, and head off to the doctor's office. Mr. and Mrs. Khan, their baby, and son ride in the cab while Mohammad N, the Khan's nephew and myself ride in the box. There is a wooden bench and a metal chair in the box and I am given the chair to sit on. I would have been quite happy on the bench, but I don't argue. We bounce along on these pitiful roads for what seems like forever until we arrive at the doctor's office. Mr. and Mrs. Khan and their children are ushered into one room while I am sent off to another. It appears that they have sent the doctor to me first since I don't have to wait long. I feel like I am wasting the doctor's time, because it really is a minor scrape. The doctor cleans my wound and puts some ointment on it, then asks if I would like a tetanus shot. I refuse since all my shots are current, and again, I feel like I am wasting his time.

The doctor goes in to see the Khans and invites me along. We all wait while the baby is checked over, given her medication, and the okay to go home. Then, to my surprise, one of the clinic staff brings in pop and cookies. Now, when was the last time you were served a snack at your doctor's office?

A few moments later, another surprise—the doctor invites us up to his home, which is above the office and clinic, for chai. He has two sons and three daughters; one of his daughters is sixteen and studying in university to become a doctor. She speaks good English and has several questions for me. I enjoy chatting with her and admire her ambition. It is great to see women of her generation getting such a good education in Pakistan.

On the way home we stop at a few bike shops to see if we can get my windshield fixed. The cracks from my accident in Nepal have now become definite breaks and I will either have to remove the windshield or repair it. We're in an area of the city filled with mechanical shops of all kinds, as well as retail shops selling products for vehicles and other machinery. Mohammad inquires at several little shops until he finds a mechanic whom he is satisfied will do a good job at a fair price.

It has been another long day. We arrive home after 8:30 and have dinner at 9:00. I am wondering if they always have such busy days here and such late meals. I'm not used to this, especially after getting up at 5:00 every morning.

May 28 is day six in Pakistan and I still do not have a reply on my Iran visa. I work on my Web site in the morning, then Mohammad takes me shopping for groceries. I will make the family a Western dinner tonight. They are used to very spicy food so I hope they won't be disappointed. All of a sudden I question my ability to cook. I have not made a complete meal for almost two years. These people have been so hospitable that I do not want to let them down.

Shopping for meat in Pakistan is not that straightforward. I want to buy beef, but today is Wednesday and beef is not sold on Wednesday. We find a vendor with chicken and I receive the surprise of my life. The chickens are kept alive in large, wire cages stacked several layers high. The vendor reaches in and grabs a chicken by the legs and before I know it, he has grabbed the chicken's head, given it a flip, and snapped its neck—all in about two seconds! In about thirty more seconds, he has it skinned, gutted, and cut up for us to take home.

I pull out one thousand rupees to pay the man. Mohammad takes the bill from me and says, "That is no good." I am thinking he means it is too large a bill, but he continues with, "This bill is counterfeit."

"What? What do you mean it's counterfeit?" I exclaim. "I got this money from the money changers at the India border gates. How can it be counterfeit?" Mohammad shows me the difference between a good bill and a counterfeit one. When you know what to look for it is easy to spot the fake. I am very upset and embarrassed because now Mohammad has to pay for the chicken. I am wondering how many other bills in my wallet are counterfeit. After returning home we check my other bills and find two thousand rupees of counterfeit money. Mohammad cautions me not to try and use them. If I am caught it could create very serious consequences. I take them out of my wallet and tuck them away. The last thing I need is to be sent to jail for using counterfeit money.

Every evening at 6:00 PM there is an opening/closing of the gate ceremony at the border between Pakistan and India. This evening Mohammad and I ride to the gates to watch the ceremony. I am amazed at the number of people from both sides of the border who attend this very professionally performed ritual. The officers from both countries are in full uniform and do a series of marches before raising the flags and opening the gates. There is a cheer from the crowds and then the closing ceremony begins with the flags being lowered and the gates being closed. Another roar from the crowd and it is all over. The complete ceremony takes about forty-five minutes.

When we first arrive for the ceremony, Mohammad and I stand on the right with the rest of the crowd, but soon an officer comes over to tell me to move. At first I do not understand, but then I realize I am the only woman standing amongst all these men. The officer wants me to go sit with the women on the other side. Mohammad tries to convince him to let me stay because I am a guest, but I can see that he is not going to budge. I quickly assure Mohammad that it is okay, that I do not mind moving to the other side. Besides, there are very few women over there and I can get a good place to sit. On the male side we are standing because all the bleachers are full. From the female side I enjoy a great view of the ceremonies and later get my picture taken with one of the Pakistani officers in full uniform.

When we return home I still have to make dinner. It turns into a complete disaster! First of all it is late when we arrive, then it takes me forever to prepare a meal of chicken, potatoes, and vegetables. When we finally sit down to eat I can see they are not impressed. Everyone is very polite and claims to like the meal, except for Naumand. At sixteen, he is still being honest about his feelings and admits that he does not like it. My hosts are used to very spicy food and everything fried in lots of oil. I guess I should have made pasta; at least I could have added a few more chili peppers to the sauce.

On day seven of my visa I am up at 5:00 to finish packing for my trip to Islamabad. Munjee makes a mango shake for me (to die for) before I leave. She is concerned about me traveling alone and suggests that Mohammad should go with me. I assure them both that I will be just fine. I have been touring the world alone for two years now. I am also thinking that I need to escape this hectic schedule.

There are two highways from Lahore to Islamabad. Both are good roads, but one is a freeway where motorcycles are not allowed. I get out of Lahore and am soon at the entrance to the freeway. There are a couple of officers stationed here, so I stop and ask if I can ride through. The officer says, "No, go that way," pointing away from the freeway.

"But my bike is big, it can travel as fast as cars," I reply.

This produces a laugh from the officer, but he points and says, "No, that way... " Then he adds, "Have you taken chai this morning?"

I decline his offer and head towards the slower route. I seem to be tired this morning and have to stop a couple of times for a rest. My bike is making a clicking noise that I've not heard before—this worries me. Shortly after noon I arrive in Islamabad and begin searching for the Pakistan Embassy only to find out they just take applications in the morning. I do manage to find someone to give me an application form so I can have it completed for the next day.

From here I go to the Canadian High Commission. I have one page left in my passport so I must apply for a new one. No problem finding it, but by now it is two o'clock in the afternoon and the guard tells me they are closed. He can see my frustration and decides to pick up the phone and call. I am relieved and very grateful to him, telling him how much I appreciate his help. Once in the office I state my case about my passport and am delighted to find out that they can add pages, and that I do not have to apply for a new one. They take my passport, add ten pages arranged in accordion fashion, and tell me this can only be done once. When these pages are full I must apply for a new passport. At least the problem is taken care of for now.

It is three o'clock when I leave the Embassy. The only thing I have consumed all day is the mango shake Mrs. Naseem made for me this morning. I stop for a sub and a pop before checking into the Hotel Marina and crashing for two hours. I am completely exhausted from my last five days in Lahore.

The next morning I am at the passport office by 8:30. I wait in line with all the rest just to be told to go to the Ministry of Interior in the Parliament area. I ask directions before I leave and make my way easily across the city to find that the office is closed on Fridays. The guard tells me to come back tomorrow between eleven and twelve noon. Now why couldn't they have told me that at the passport office?

Today is Friday, May 30, the eighth day of my ten-day visa. That means it expires on Sunday and I can only hope that I will be issued an extension tomorrow. I have no choice but to play this out and hope it all falls into place.

Islamabad is a very nice city, much cleaner than any I have seen in Asia so far. The streets are wide and traffic is normal. There are no donkey carts, cows, or exhaust belching rickshaws and buses allowed here.

After lunch I search out a motorcycle repair shop to get my bike looked at, and hopefully find out what is causing the clicking noise. I find a shop where the mechanic is willing to take a look. They only work on small bikes but he seems competent and I agree to let him pull it apart.

The first thing they do is place a chair on the sidewalk outside the shop window, and tell me to sit. The mechanic is working on my bike at the edge of the sidewalk. I feel all eyes are on me as people pass by. I have become somewhat used to the *stares* since riding through Southeast Asia, Nepal, and India, but it still feels awkward.

The owner of the shop next door comes over and asks if I would like something to drink. I noticed earlier that they make mango shakes, so I order one. When the young attendant brings it to me I give him twenty rupees and thank him very much. Seconds later the owner returns with my money and exclaims, "Please take this, you are our guest!" I am overwhelmed by their hospitality.

I watch the mechanic while enjoying my mango shake. He has the cover off the front sprocket and cleans out the grease before showing me that the sprocket is wearing badly. I ask if he can get a new one. He does not think so. I ask him to put it back together and I will see what I can find tomorrow. He refuses to take any money for his time.

I return to the hotel and ask the desk clerks if they can refer me to a good bike shop that works on bigger bikes. One of the men offers to make some phone calls and will let me know.

I retire to my room and watch TV. I cannot understand the words coming out of the tube but the actions tell a pretty good story. The scenes with a man and woman kissing are blacked out unless the couple is married. The legs or knees of a woman are also blacked out. The actress wears a shalwar kameez, which covers most of her body, leaving no chance to expose the arms, legs, knees or shoulders.

On Saturday morning I return to the Ministry of Interior with my visa extension application. When I finally get in to see the officer he tells me they do not extend transit visas. I plead with him that I need more time because I have not received confirmation for my Iran visa and besides, it will take at least five days to cross the country to Iran. He agrees to give me seven days starting from today. I ask him for ten days. He throws the application down and tells me to come back on Monday and he will give me a letter. Heaven only knows what that means.

Sunday is a holiday for most people and many of the shops are closed today except for the market. I am lucky that the repair shop the hotel clerk recommended is open and works on big bikes. Although I do not see anything bigger than a 125cc here, the mechanic assures me he can find a sprocket and fix my problem. I have to leave the bike there all day and pick it up in the evening. He estimates the job will cost fifteen hundred rupees.

I return to the hotel and spend a relaxing day catching up on my journal writing. I find an Internet café and am elated to read an e-mail from the Iran travel agency telling me my visa is approved. They have included a reference number and instructions for me to pick it up at the Iran Embassy in Quetta before Friday. Now I just have to pray that

I am given an extension for my Pakistan visa tomorrow. How do I get myself into these binds?

On Monday morning I ride to the tourist office to pick up a map of Pakistan before heading off to the Ministry of Interior. My visa expired yesterday and I am in a vulnerable position. I join the lineup and keep my thoughts positive. When it's my turn I am sent out to wait for another officer. After another twenty minutes I ask, "Why haven't I been called yet?" They direct me in to see a Mr. Islam. He gives me a letter of extension for seven days starting from May 31st. Today is June 2nd. That gives me four days to return to Lahore and cross the country, about two thousand kilometers, to Iran.

I am not finished yet. I must now go back to the passport office across town to get my visa stamped. Hopefully I can make it before they close at noon. I get to the wicket and am told to fill out the original form again and get a photocopy of my passport and visa. I am really losing patience. I have to go to another building across the street for photocopies. Back and forth I go to comply with these requests. I return to the wicket and the clerk asks for the receipt for the money I deposited.

"What do you mean? No one told me to deposit money!"

"You must go to the National Bank of Pakistan in Karachi area, deposit sixty-five dollars US, and bring the receipt back here," the officer explains.

I ask where the bank is and the officer gives me some vague directions. I am running out of time so I quickly go outside and find someone who can give me accurate directions. I get to the bank, make my deposit, and return with about five minutes to spare. I have decided I will not leave until someone issues my visa. I am told to wait fifteen minutes because the officer who signs the visa extension is out. The clock shows 1:00 PM so I predict that he is out for lunch. Thirty-five minutes later I go into the head honcho's office and ask whom it is I am waiting for. This fellow instructs another officer to take me to the next building to wait in another office.

There is a male clerk in the office but he has no authority to issue my visa. I must wait for another officer. Finally a man comes in with some papers, rummages through piles of ledgers and papers on the desk, and leaves without so much as a look in my direction. I begin to think that maybe this is the day I should offer a bribe, but I just don't want to take the chance. Who knows, maybe they would lock me up for bribing an officer.

Ten minutes later the officer returns and starts searching through more files. The young clerk is speaking to him and finally he looks in my direction. I think the clerk told him what I had said earlier. In my frustration I told the young clerk that I think they have a problem dealing with women and push us aside like we are nothing. The next thing I hear, the older officer is telling me he needs a confirmation letter from the Ministry of Interior.

I jump out of my chair and point to the letter he holds. Speaking more loudly than normal, I state; "That is the letter I gave you, signed by the officer who authorized an extension for seven days!"

"We need a confirmation letter," he replies.

I repeat, pointing to the letter, my voice getting louder. "That is it, right there—that is what he gave me!"

The officer tells me to sit down. I do as he asks and shake my head in disbelief. He then gets on the phone and smirks as he speaks to a person on the other end whom I can only assume is the officer at the Ministry of Interior. When he finishes on the phone he sends me back, with all my papers and passport, to the head honcho in the first building. This man sends me back to the wicket clerk who was the first man I spoke to when I arrived at this building. *I have come full circle.* Finally the clerk puts all the official stamps in my passport and returns it to me. It is now 2:30. I am starved and angry, but when I look in my passport I see an expiry date of ten days from today. *Halleluiah!*

On my way back to the hotel two young men on a little 100cc bike ride up beside me at the lights and stare at my bike and me. This is a common occurrence but today I stare back and smile. Then, completely out of the blue I say with a laugh, "Nice toy!" The rider quickly puts his bike in gear and pulls up between the traffic. I can't stop laughing—it makes my whole day better.

I stop at Subway to appease my hunger. Before leaving I buy a pizza sub for two little children who hang around outside the door every day. They are a boy and girl about seven to nine years of age. I have seen them every day since I arrived, and today I need to do something good to ease my feelings of anger over earlier events of the day. I am rewarded with big, beautiful smiles that light up their faces, and lift my spirits tremendously.

This evening one of the hotel staff invites me to attend a wedding in their banquet room. I am thankful for the salwar kameez outfits Shaista made for me in Lahore. At least I won't walk in looking like a biker. I do not attend the ceremony because I feel like it would be an intrusion, but I go to the reception for about an hour. The bride is gorgeous, in a beautiful, light green, satin/crepe gown and shawl with gold trim, but I never see her smile. Most marriages here are still arranged by the parents, and the bride's face indicates to me that she does not like this arrangement.

I am ushered up to the front of the room to visit with the bride and groom, a sister, and one of the mothers. The bride never speaks, only the groom and his sister. Another woman, dressed in a lovely salwar kameez gown, her head and face covered, and a veil over her eyes, comes and sits beside the bride. She speaks very good English and directs a few questions to me. She appears to be well educated and sounds like a happy woman. The costume makes me think that she does not want to be recognized. Yet, I am sure this is not the case, since she is probably a family member.

The groom insists I stay for the buffet and eat with them. There is an abundance of food and I eat well. I cannot begin to tell you what all the dishes are, for the variety is endless, but I enjoy the feast immensely.

On June 3 I am up early and leave Islamabad at six o'clock. Already it is hot but I will be back in Lahore before the worst of the heat hits. I arrive shortly after noon and am somewhat annoyed that Mohammad has filled up the rest of my day with more visits to friends. He and Mr. Khan try to talk me into staying another two days so they can take me to visit a village in the country. I would love to but have to decline, because after today three days will have already elapsed on my ten-day visa. I have to allow at least one extra day, in case of emergency, to get across the country.

The next morning I start my journey across Pakistan to Iran. Mrs. Naseem serves me two large mango shakes while I am packing the last of my gear. She is very concerned about me traveling across the country by myself and tells me to be careful. I leave my newfound friends with mixed feelings—anxious to get out of these crowded quarters, but at the same time sorry to be leaving these wonderful people.

I realize that I know so very little about Muslim people. From this trip I have learned that they are very dedicated to their religion and their families. Mr. Naseem has told me that whether his neighbors are Christian, Buddhist, white or black, it makes no difference; it is his responsibility to look out for them and help them any way he can. I feel like we, in the Western world, have become so individualized and accustomed to having our own space that we do not even know our neighbours.

Once I get out of the hectic traffic of Lahore the road is good and the ride is nice. I have ridden about one hundred and thirty kilometers when two highway patrol officers on motorcycles stop me. One officer pulls in front of my bike and the other alongside. The questioning goes something like this:

Officer: "What is your country?"

Me: "Canada."

Officer: "Where you going?"

Me: "To Multan."

Officer, looking over his shoulder: "Another bike?"

Me: "No sir, only me."

Officer: "Only one?"

Me: "Yes sir, only one," as I hold up one finger and point to myself.

Officer, after a moment's hesitation: "Excuse me, are you a man or woman?"

"I'm a woman," I reply with a smile.

Officer, with a shocked look on his face: "Aren't you afraid to travel alone in Pakistan?"

Me: "No sir, people have been very helpful and kind to me."

Officer: "You take chai, or cold drink?"

I look at my watch and see that it is about 8:30. I have been on the road for over two hours and it is time for a break. "Okay, is there a place nearby for a cold drink?" I ask. The day is hot and I cannot bear the thought of warm chai.

Officer: "The next station, follow me."

Off we go, the two police bikes with their blue lights flashing and me following close behind. We stop about three kilometers down the road at a service station where I am ushered into a comfortable lounge. Shortly, one of the attendants brings in three bottles of Pepsi and in the next half hour I am peppered with all kinds of personal questions.

Officer: "What about your family, any children?"

Me: "I have two sons and one daughter. They are all adults," and I hold my hand up to indicate *tall*.

Officer: "Are you married?"

Me: "I was, many years ago."

Officer: "And?"

Me: "He expired a long time ago."

Second Officer, in a concerned voice: "Was he ill?"

I brush it off as though I do not want to discuss it and say, "It was a long time ago."

Officer: "What is your job?"

I explain and the conversation continues in this manner until the younger officer, who had been doing most of the talking, asks, "How old are you?"

"Well sir, tomorrow is my birthday and I will be fifty-five."

Officer, looking very surprised: "You look very good and are in good shape. Women in Pakistan look old at fifty. They are sick and have medical problems, and are overweight because they stay in the home and do not do any exercise."

"Is that because they have not been allowed to develop their own lives?" I ask.

The look on his face is something between embarrassment and shock. I quickly continue by saying, "But things are changing, aren't they?"

The conversation continues for awhile until the young officer asks if I would like to have lunch with them.

"Well, I have not had breakfast yet and I must stop soon. Okay, is there a place nearby to eat?"

Officer: "There is a hotel a little farther up the road—I will arrange for lunch."

I start out ahead of the two officers while they are on their radios arranging lunch. I come to what is one of Pakistan's many Y's in the road and take the wrong arm. In seconds the police bike is beside me, motioning me to turn around and follow him. I don't know where he came from. I had been watching in my rear-view mirror and am sure he was not behind me. He escorts me the rest of the way, showing off doing some zigzags with his bike. I'm thinking he is crazy, especially after just telling me the pavement is hot and greasy, and very dangerous.

We pass a police jeep on the way to the hotel. I see the heads of the officer's turn as their eyes follow me. I am sure by now the whole police jurisdiction has been informed about this big foreign bike being ridden by a woman.

We arrive at the hotel restaurant, get seated, and are shown the menu. The officer apologizes that we cannot get lunch because it is too early. I assure him that is just fine, and order coffee and toast. The officers order chai. Our conversation rallies around how I came to traveling around the world (alone), my country/his country, my family/his family, and that I should be afraid to travel alone. I tell him I have four grandsons and a granddaughter. He shares that he is just recently married and wants to start a family. Then he says, "If I guessed your age by how you look, I would guess 40."

Wow, that makes my day!

After breakfast they escort me out to the bikes and when we say our goodbyes the young officer says, "God Bless You."

I am touched, and as I ride on to Multan I thank the Divine Spirit of the Universe for the wonderful people I have met and the many blessings in my life.

I reach Multan shortly after noon, stop at KFC for fries and pop and to ask directions for the road to Dera Ghazi Khan (D.G. Khan). The manager is very helpful, and before I finish my fries he brings me a mixed fruit sundae. "Complimentary, because you are our guest," he says.

The hospitality continues.

It takes almost three hours to ride ninety-eight kilometers to D.G. Khan. It is now 4:00 PM, so I start looking for a hotel immediately. After trying three and being told, "We're full, no room left," I become suspicious. I search out a fourth hotel and get the same response. This time I dare to ask the clerk, "Are you really full or you just don't want to rent to me because I'm a foreigner? Or maybe because I am a woman?" I add. He makes no reply so I continue, "If I were Pakistani would you have a room for me?"

The clerk looks around the room and behind him, as though confirming that no one is within hearing range. Then he leans over the counter and says in a quiet voice; "We cannot rent to a foreigner unless you have an approval letter from the Chief Commissioner."

Now what do I do? I am extremely tired and weak from the heat and all I want is to get out of these heavy biking clothes and lie down. I ask him where I can find the police commissioner. He looks at his watch and says, "Office is possibly closed." At this point I am at a loss. It is too late to ride back to Multan so I ask him for directions to the police station. Maybe I can enlist their help.

I find my way easily, park my bike outside the gate, and walk in. As I go through the gate an officer meets me and tells me to bring my bike inside. He escorts me to the office where there are about ten officers sitting around a long table talking and laughing. It only takes a moment before all eyes turn in my direction. One of the officers asks what I want and I quickly explain my predicament. The officer who appears to be the chief says, "You can stay in the police rest house. There is security and it will be safe there."

A few murmurs spout from the other officers as they discuss the situation in their language. I get the feeling that offering this to a man would be okay, but not entirely so for a woman.

I am only there a few minutes before two reporters come in. They saw me ride through town and followed me here. One reporter asks if they can be of help, and then requests an interview. I would prefer a shower and bed, but it does not appear that I will be going anywhere soon; so I sit and talk to the reporters. They finish with their questions then promise to help find a room. Before they leave they tell me they will celebrate my birthday with me later.

About an hour passes before another officer (possibly the Chief Commissioner?) arrives and promptly asks one of his men to escort me to another precinct. I am surprised to see the same two reporters there when I arrive. True to their word, they have been trying to get some action from the police to find me accommodation.

I sit and wait, for what seems another hour, while the head officer makes several phone calls. Finally he tells me I have a room at the DG Hotel. I feel a rush of relief and thank him very much. He continues speaking and tells me that one of his officers will escort me out of town tomorrow morning.

His statement takes me by surprise and I say, "That's fine, but I will be leaving at six in the morning."

He assures me that his officers will be there at 6:00 AM.

When I get up to leave he tells me to sit down. "My officers will escort you to the hotel," he says. So I wait. Eventually three officers appear, driving a nice white jeep, and escort me through town. The local people stop whatever they are doing and look. It is obvious they recognize the jeep and wonder about this big, shiny, black bike.

We arrive at the hotel and I am glad to see there is covered parking. The officers make sure I am checked into my room then show me where the restaurant is. Before leaving they ensure that I understand that I am not to leave in the morning until an officer comes by to escort me out of town.

I am exhausted by now and flop down on the bed to sleep for half an hour before showering and going down for dinner. I walk across the parking garage to the restaurant and enter through the door on the right. The room is large and there are several tables occupied. I look for a place to sit but am intercepted by a host who takes me into the next room. It is an equally large room with several tables set for dinner, but the place is empty.

The waiter brings a menu and I ask him about sitting in the other room where everyone else is. He explains that I must stay here because the other room is only for men. I had not noticed that it was occupied entirely by men.

I have a nice dinner of rice and veggies, then go back to my room and lie down while I wait for the two reporters to come by. They said they would call in about half an hour—that was two hours ago. By 10:00 I am too tired to wait any longer so I turn in for the night.

Five o'clock on the morning of June 5, my 55th birthday, I hear a soft knock on my door. It is a police officer letting me know they are here to escort me out of town. I pack up and go down to the lobby to pay my bill. With that complete, the clerk hands me a nicely decorated cake and tells me that two reporters brought it by late last night.

Wow, *they didn't forget.* But what do I do with this cake now? I ask the desk clerk if he can bring some plates and forks, then I share my birthday cake with three police officers and the hotel staff. Fantastic! What a great way to begin the day.

Shortly after 6:00 we are ready to leave. Now, picture this: here is little old me on my 750cc Honda Magna loaded down with gear, following a 125cc Honda loaded down with two very large (about 250 pounds each) police officers. The officer riding passenger is holding a rifle upright on his knee with the nozzle pointing up to the sky. They lead me through their town to show me some of the sights, and then out onto the highway. After about thirty kilometers they stop to tell me they are leaving me now, and I am to go to the next police checkpoint a short distance up the road. There will be another officer to escort me from there.

I do not travel far before I see a police truck coming towards me. It makes a u-turn off the road and pulls right back out in front of me. I easily maneuver around them and pick up my speed to eighty. I want to see if they are here for me or if I should be concerned about their presence. Sure enough, they catch up to me, pass, and slow down to seventy. I follow them to the next police checkpoint.

About twenty minutes later we arrive at the check post where I am ordered to wait for a patrol truck. I believe this is the border into the province of Balochistan. I have heard rumors that this province is not safe to travel in. The officers invite me to sit and take chai with them. We exchange a few words—no one speaks English, so it is more like a game of charades—and I wait. Twenty minutes go by. I have taken chai and watermelon with them and am becoming impatient. I ask, "Can I go now?"

One officer replies "Yes", looking proud that he can answer in English.

I get up to leave and two officers *shoot* out of their chairs like they have been hit with a jolt of electricity. They wave their arms excitedly and motion for me to sit. One of them says, "No! No! No! Patrol truck, police, police, patrol truck!"

I cannot help but laugh as I sit back down and wait.

Another ten minutes roll by and finally the truck arrives. A few pleasantries are exchanged amongst the officers with curious glances in my direction. Several forms are filled out and I am asked to show my passport and bike papers. When all my data is recorded I take out my camera and ask, in motions of charades, if I can take their pictures. They are all smiles and eagerly pose beside my bike and in front of the police truck. With the technology of a digital camera I show them the picture immediately, which produces laughter and chatting amongst the officers.

It is now time to leave. I shake the hands of the officers at the check post and follow an old police truck carrying three officers in its cab. For about an hour we take roads that alternate between pavement and sand until we reach the next jurisdiction. The sand is thick in places and I am thankful for the truck ahead of me—just in case I should wipe out.

At each new jurisdiction I am asked to write down my name, passport number, the date I entered Pakistan, and my bike information, then wait until they decide who is going to escort me further. From the second check post I am escorted by five officers—three in the cab of the truck and two armed officers in the box. I suppose I should be frightened but the situation seems quite humorous.

At the next jurisdiction I am offered lunch and chai. I have to wait for an important man to arrive, so I relax and enjoy my lunch. This man is the head educator and speaks English. He suggests that they load my bike on the back of the truck and I ride in the cab with the officers. "It would be much more comfortable for you," he says.

"But why would I not ride my bike?" I reply. "That is why I'm here, to ride my bike across your country." With no argument he concedes and then proceeds to choose which officers will escort me. This time I am blessed with two officers in the cab of the truck and three armed officers in the box. I feel like a visitor to the Queen!

The road has not improved all day. It boasts pavement for some stretches, and then drops off sharply into sand, then back onto pavement. At one such area I bottom out and fight desperately to stay upright. The truck is far enough ahead that they may not see me if I go down. I must be more careful in these sections. We stop in a couple of small villages and I grab the opportunity to take some pictures. There is nothing much out here except grey hills and sand.

A couple of hours later I am delivered to the Mekhtar jurisdiction. The officer in charge has to issue a receipt for proof of delivery to the delivering officers. Again, I find this quite amusing. I want to say, "Really guys, I am not that important."

I take pictures of my delivering officers after they have been discharged and thank them for looking after me. Then, to my surprise, the Mekhtar officer tells me that I will stay here tonight.

"But I want to go to Loralai today!" I exclaim.

He looks troubled, and then tells me that his truck is in Quetta and will not be back until tomorrow night. His father, who is Chief of Police for this jurisdiction, is on an errand in Quetta and would be angry if he were to allow me to continue alone.

"I cannot stay an extra day here, my visa will run out. I must leave early tomorrow morning."

He agrees that I can leave in the morning and tells me that I will stay with his family in the village. I resign myself to that, although I am not confident that he will let me leave tomorrow morning without an escort.

I wheel my bike into one of the rooms surrounding the courtyard of the police compound. It looks like this could be a large holding cell.

I take what I need off the bike and the officer slides a huge bolt into place and secures the lock. *No one will be stealing this bike!*

He walks with me to his home and introduces me to his sisters, sons, daughter, and other relatives before returning to work. The first thing I am offered is more chai. I politely refuse and ask for water. I try to explain that I want bottled water but do not make much progress. I am so thirsty that I settle for drinking well water. I know this could be risky but the air is so hot and dry here that I have some anyway. My thoughts drift back to my years growing up on the farm. We drank well water then and it never hurt me. How bad could this be?

Everyone is excited to have a foreign guest and they try hard to communicate with me. Some of the younger children know a few words of English. They are very proud of this and like to practice what they know. Soon other people from the village are dropping in to see the foreigner. This has probably never happened in their village before. One young man is a teacher and takes me on a walking tour. As we walk the entourage of children becomes larger, and it soon seems like most of the children in the village are following us.

My guide wants to take me to the only "green area" in the village. We are in the middle of the desert, and every direction I look there is sand and dirt, so I am curious to see this area. We have to climb a bank and a fence to get to it, but it seems to be important, so I scramble over and under and soon am standing in the middle of a green patch measuring about fifty meters square. It looks like weeds to me. I think it is grown to feed the few animals in the village.

I am intrigued with the structure of the homes here. The one I am staying in is built in a large square. The outside wall is about three to four meters high and half a meter thick, and surrounds a big open courtyard. Rooms are built along three sides of the wall, with doorways facing the courtyard. There are no windows, and doors remain open— some with a curtain pulled across. A flat roof covers the rooms, which consist of two or three bedrooms, a kitchen, prayer room and family room. The animal yard is the last door on one end of the courtyard and goes out behind one wall of rooms. The courtyard and animal yard are open to the sky. At night cots are pulled out into the courtyard and the younger members of the family sleep under the stars. I am given a choice of sleeping in one of the bedrooms or in the courtyard. I cannot pass up the opportunity to sleep under the stars in the middle of the desert in Pakistan.

It is great to wake up in the fresh air. It actually got cool overnight and I had to pull the bottom blanket around me. The family rises early and spends time in prayer before starting their day. The temperature is nice at five in the morning and I enjoy the reprieve from the heat that is sure to envelop us shortly.

After a cup of chai and biscuits the officer takes me back to the compound for my bike. I must get fuel before I leave, but the power went out overnight so the pumps are not working. They assure me it will be available in the next village. I hope they are right. I buy an orange pop and leave.

Fuel in these parts of Pakistan is often sold out of barrels or jerry cans at the side of the road. I am never too sure how good or clean it is, but when that is the only thing available I have no choice but to use it. So far it has been okay.

Today I am not feeling well. The farther I ride the weaker and more tired I feel. I reach Loralai, get fuel and water, and then continue on to Ziarat. I stop several times to ask if I am on the right road and how much farther to Ziarat. Three times I am told "six kilometers", but six kilometers goes by and still no town. The highway is taking me into the foothills of the mountains bordering Pakistan and Afghanistan and this worries me.

As I ride I can feel the nausea begin to build. It is becoming almost unbearable and I know that once I stop I will be sick. I must stop before reaching Ziarat, because I do not want to throw up on a street in town. At the same time, I know I can't stop too far out in these mountains either, so I push myself to keep riding. Finally I see a building that looks like a restaurant. As I pull into the yard I can see that the building is boarded up and there is no one around. Good thing too because I only have time to pull off my helmet before I expel everything left in my body. Once that is over I have to find a spot behind the building to empty out from the other end. I have never felt so drained and exhausted in all my life!

I make my way back to my bike, take out a bottle of water, and sit down with my back against the building. I find myself fighting to stay awake. It takes all my willpower not to lean my head back and close my eyes. I know that if I allowed myself, I would be asleep in seconds—but

I cannot let this happen out here in the middle of nowhere. I drink a few swallows of water and mentally force myself to gather some energy to get back on my bike and ride. I am sure it is not far to Ziarat—I must make it that far. Maybe I can get some toast and summon up enough energy to ride on to Quetta.

Finally, a few minutes later, I reach Ziarat and stop at the first hotel along the main street running through town. I am extremely tired and weak. I park my bike in front of the restaurant and go in. The place is empty except for one table near the entrance occupied by two men. The hotel clerk is standing behind his counter and a waiter is walking across the room. All eyes turn toward me as I enter. If I were not so weak and tired I would probably feel intimidated, but all I can think of right now is, *let me sit down and rest.*

I take a chair at the next table and fight the urge to lay my head down. The waiter comes over and I order toast and tea. Lucky for me he speaks a little English and understands that I want black tea (not chai) and dry toast. I ask him how far it is to Quetta, wondering if I have the energy to make it today.

"About four hours," he replies.

It seems like people do not measure in distances in most parts of Asia—they measure everything in hours.

While I wait for my toast and tea I rest my head in my hands and struggle to stay awake. When my order comes I am horrified to see a stack of six slices of toast on the plate. I know I will never eat that much, but how can I complain? It takes me twenty minutes to force down all but one bite of the first slice of toast. I am trying hard because I know I need the energy, but that is as much as I can manage. I sit for about an hour trying to gather up the energy to leave. Finally I give in and admit to myself that I cannot do it.

I beckon the waiter over and apologize for not eating my toast. Then I explain to him that I am sick. I ask him if they have a room available, and he goes to speak to the desk clerk. A horrible thought crosses my mind—what if it's the same here as it was in D.G. Khan? "Oh, please don't let it be. I am so tired I just need a place to sleep."

The waiter returns with good news—they have a room. I am *so* relieved I do not even ask how much. I ask him about parking my motorbike, and he kindly helps me bring it through the locked gates and into the courtyard. I un-strap my gear and struggle to carry the lighter bags up a long flight of stairs while the waiter carries the heavier ones. I thank him and give him a generous tip, then lock the door and push a small dresser in front. I take off my riding gear and flop down on the bed, fully clothed. I am out in a flash.

Two or three hours later I am awakened to a knock at my door. It is the waiter; he wants to know if I want something to eat. I tell him no, but he will not accept that. "You must eat," he says.

Finally I agree to let him bring me some toast and tea. A few minutes later he returns carrying a tray with scones and tea. This time I do a little better—I am able to eat one of the scones.

The energy it takes to get up, move around, and eat seems to exhaust me. I go right back to bed and sleep the rest of the afternoon away.

At about 7:00 PM I awake to another knock on my door. The waiter says they are concerned that I have not eaten all day. He insists on bringing me a plate for dinner, but I refuse. I ask him to bring me toast and tea, which he does, but not without showing his disapproval. I am touched by his compassion and assure him that I will be fine. I just need to sleep.

I sleep soundly all through the night and early the next morning pack up my gear. I still feel weak but do not have time to spend another day here. It is not far to Quetta where I will pick up my visa from the Iran Embassy. I am on the road by 6:00 AM.

I arrive in Quetta before 9:00 and head directly to the Iran Embassy. First I must complete another form, and then I have to go to the bank and make a deposit of 2,610 Pakistan rupees, and finally, return to the embassy at 3:00 in the afternoon.

I immediately find a bank and make my deposit. I can feel my energy draining fast so I look for a hotel. The first one I see seems very nice, but it is much too expensive. The clerk there directs me to the Muslim Hotel, but their directions are all but clear and I end up in the middle of a busy section of town fighting traffic, heat, and major energy depletion.

My first (near) disaster is in an intersection controlled by a traffic cop. I drop my bike in an effort to avoid a collision with a jeep that comes barreling into the intersection. In spite of the officer's "stop arm" pointed in his direction, the driver of the jeep does not stop. Consequently I slam on the brakes and go down, simply too weak to hold the bike up. The officer and a couple of other men are there immediately to help me pick it up and get moving again. As I continue, feeling more and more tired, I begin wishing I had taken the expensive hotel room.

Quetta is a dusty frontier town with lots of activity and traffic. Once more I drop my bike while turning a corner and going over a huge speed bump. My strength is gone. I simply lose my balance on the bump and fall over. A man appears immediately and helps me pick it up. Finally I make my way out of this hectic area of town and find a street of hotels. I check the Muslim Hotel and find it is a dive. The next one I stop at is the Maryton. It is clean and comfortable, so I check in here. I need to rest before going back to the embassy to pick up my visa.

I park my bike in the underground garage and haul my gear up to my room. Today this is too much for me. I drop everything on the floor, crash on the bed and sleep for a couple of hours. When I awaken I order toast and tea before riding back to the Embassy to pick up my visa. By the time I return to my room, Iran visa in hand, my energy is completely zapped once again. I decide to stay another day to sleep and regain some strength.

I spend most of Saturday in my room sleeping. On Sunday, June 8, still tired and weak and with three days left on my Pakistan visa, I decide to stay one more day. I am sure it will only take me one day to reach the border, so I rest most of the day. In the afternoon I take my bike to the service station to get fuel, check the oil, and have it washed. In these countries you do not wash your own bike—it is washed for you. I quite enjoy sitting back and watching as the young fellows wash and polish. For a small fee it is well worth the wait.

While I wait a young man approaches and speaks to me in English. He is a teacher here in Quetta and his wife is a nurse. He invites me to his home for dinner and to meet his family. He offers to pick me up on his little 75cc Honda. Under normal circumstances I would have refused and taken my own bike, but today I am tired so I accept his offer for a ride.

Asjed arrives at 8:00. By this time I am ready to sleep and almost regret having accepted his invitation. However, I cannot be rude. The ride to his home takes about twenty minutes, and as we travel he tells me a little about his family. His aging parents are sick and that is why he chose a wife from the nursing profession. That sounds so cold and uncaring—more like a business deal, I think, as he tells me the story. But then, how can I judge when we have a divorce rate of over fifty percent in our country.

We finally reach the home after maneuvering down dusty, narrow, bumpy streets. I am glad I do not have my bike. Asjed leads me up a flight of stairs into a nice, large apartment-style home. It is much bigger than I expected. His family occupies the upper level and other members of the family share the lower level. I ask him about his home and he tells me they rent it and that it is one of the nicer places in town, but quite expensive.

I am escorted into a large rectangular room, which I take to be the living room. Long, thin cushions line two outer walls with thicker cushions scattered here and there. The only other furniture in the room is a television and stereo. Everyone, even the aging parents, sit on the long thin cushions in a cross-legged fashion.

The family is wonderful. Asjed's mother was once a teacher and his father was in the army. They seem delighted to meet me. They do not speak English but do understand a few words, and their son translates for them.

Dinner consists of rice, meat, vegetables, and creamy and hot sauces, and is served in the traditional style on a tablecloth laid out on the floor. We sit cross-legged with our plates on our laps. One of Asjed's sisters comes in and joins us for dinner but not his wife.

After dinner my host proudly shows me their wedding album and insists on giving me one of their pictures. I don't want to take it but he seems offended, so I accept. As he talks I realize that he has an ulterior motive for inviting me here. He asks if I know someone who will sponsor him to come to Canada. Being the eldest son, he is responsible for the family but cannot make enough money here as a teacher to support them. He would like to go to America to work and send money home to help his family.

I admire the family unit and dedication the male members have. They take their responsibility very seriously. Asjed tells me that his wife would like them to have their own home, away from his family, but he will not think of it. That seems to be a common feeling amongst the wives, but they adjust and accept their husband's responsibility.

After dinner I meet his wife and another sister. The sister asks where I am staying. When I tell her I'm staying in a hotel, she states; "Next time you come to us first and you stay here." I feel honored.

The next morning I am up early to pack my bike. I am feeling a bit stronger after resting a day and eating a good meal last evening. At 6:20 I am on the road. It is cool and a bit breezy but I know the temperature will rise quickly. As I leave Quetta I can see a windstorm ahead, and within a couple of minutes I am riding right into it. The wind is very strong and sand is blowing heavily across the road. I consider turning back but wonder if this is an everyday occurrence. I am worried about not making it out of the country before my visa expires, so decide to keep going. Fortunately I ride through the storm quickly and the rest of the day is calm. I am thankful for that.

I have to buy fuel out of a roadside barrel, and shortly thereafter my bike starts to sputter. I think it could be the fuel. I have been traveling through a lot of construction areas and my bike is full of sand. Several kilometers back I hit a big rock going through one of the detour stretches. Maybe I damaged something. The sputtering concerns me and I hope it is nothing too serious. I will get it checked out at the border town of Taftan.

I arrive in Dalbandin at about 1:00 PM in temperature above 40 degrees Celsius. I have only ridden about four hundred kilometers across the desert. It is simply too hot to continue so I get a room at the only hotel in town. There is no air conditioning but there is a fan hanging from the ceiling, which does not seem to make much difference. I lie down for awhile before going into the restaurant next to the hotel. Several men occupy the chairs inside and everyone is watching television. The waiter shows no sign of waiting on me, so I go out to the little shop down the street and buy a juice and biscuits. This will have to do until later.

Before returning to my room I check my bike over and find an oil leak. With all the sand I have come through I can easily see that oil has been spraying out onto the pipes and the saddlebag. This does not look good. I check the oil level and it appears to be fine. I cannot find where the leak is coming from but it is definitely there somewhere. I walk about a block and find a small mechanic shop but am unable to make myself understood. In the end I believe they work on large vehicles, so probably would not know what to do with my bike. I silently hope that I will make it to Taftan.

At about 6:00 PM I am feeling hungry, so I try the restaurant again. This time I find a man who speaks a little English, who helps me order rice and vegetables for dinner. I am only able to eat a small portion of it and the cook looks offended. I apologize and feel bad, but my stomach is still not one hundred percent, and I cannot force down another bite.

The next morning before leaving, I check the oil in my bike once again. It is still not showing low so I cannot be losing too much. It sure looks like a lot with all that sand stuck to the bike. It is 6:10 when I leave Dalbandin and I know I must make it to the border today or I will be paying a penalty for an expired visa. I wonder if they arrest people for expired visas?

The highway is pretty good. After about 165 kilometers it becomes a good paved road with a centerline. The wind has picked up and I fight the force against my bike, plus the blowing sand that stings my neck and wrist where my skin is exposed. Even with my face shield pulled down, sand stings my eyes. The wind is so strong in places it continually whips my face shield up and forces my helmet so hard against the right side of my face that my jaw hurts. I get fuel in a little place called Nokkundi. I think about stopping at a mechanic stall, but am not sure they would be able to do anything for me here. The village consists of small wooden stalls and shops lining the main road. The few people I see seek reprieve from the sun inside buildings or in the shade of working stalls. The temperature is already creeping up to unbearable heights.

Twenty minutes down the road my bike starts sputtering and running very rough again. Is it the fuel or the oil leak? I stop and check the oil—still not low. I think about the sand that has been blowing and wonder if sand is somehow getting into the crankcase. The bike runs good for a few kilometers then goes through another series of spurts and sputters. I keep a mental countdown of the distance left to the border. Finally, to my relief, I reach Taftan. I flag down a police officer and ask him where to find a bike mechanic. He leads me to a shop where the mechanic looks at my bike and says he cannot fix it here. I should go to Zahedan, Iran, eighty kilometers across the border. *I hope we make it.*

I get to the border crossing and patiently present my passport and bike papers at several check stops. In less than an hour all documents are stamped, and I exit the gate out of Pakistan, riding a short distance to the Iran Customs building.

Chapter 5

Iran

Today is June 10, 2003. It is my mother's 86th birthday and I wonder what she would think if she realized I have traveled through Pakistan and am about to enter Iran. My heart and thoughts go out to her.

I ride through the gates leaving Pakistan behind, and am bombarded by moneychangers wanting to exchange my Pakistan rupees for Iran rials. I have checked the exchange rate so I can negotiate an acceptable deal. Now that I know what to look for in counterfeit money, I take the time to check each bill carefully. This will give me a bit of money until I find a bank machine.

The earth is hard packed, dry, and dusty. Not much rain falls in this area. I park my motorcycle outside the Iran Customs and Immigration office, gather all my papers, sling my helmet and jacket over my arm, and walk inside. It feels great to have my jacket off in this heat. The room is full and I join the long line of people waiting patiently for their turn. Finally I get to the wicket where they take my passport and tell me to wait. I choose a spot on the floor against a wall and sit. It seems like an hour has passed before my name is called. I quickly gather my things and make my way to the wicket. A little man on the other side of the bars barks, "Cover your head."

"I'm sorry," I reply. "I left my scarf on the bike."

"Cover your head!" he barks back loudly.

Stunned and not sure what to do, I quickly take my helmet from my arm and place it on my head. At this point the customs officer slaps my passport on the counter and shoves it under the bars at me. I pick it up, ask about my *carnet de passage*, and am sent to the next wicket. In a short time I receive my carnet and make my exit. As I leave the building I resolve to myself that I must never forget to cover my head once I remove my helmet.

My first stop in Iran is a little town called Mirjaveh, just minutes from the border. As I ride through the main street I see a man carrying a tray of doughnuts into a shop. I make an abrupt stop, park, and follow him in. It is almost noon and I have not eaten yet today. I order two muffins and a Pepsi and relax at one of the tables. Soon, two young men join me. One speaks a bit of English and offers me some of his cake. Of course these two fellows are very curious about what I am doing here. They are amazed when I tell them I'm traveling around the world, and even more shocked when they realize I am traveling alone. I ask directions to a fuel station and take my leave.

At the gas pumps I find a long line of cars and motorcycles waiting for fuel. I pull around to the back of the line of bikes and wait a few minutes before a man comes out and motions for me to ride around to the side of the building. When I round the corner I see an army truck being fuelled. A mixture of thoughts run through my head—am I heading for trouble here? Will it provoke anger if I'm served ahead of the people who have been waiting in line much longer? I really don't know what to do, except follow instructions. The man directs me to go behind the army jeep where he begins filling my tank. It all happens so quickly and smoothly. I feel privileged to receive special treatment and I thank the attendants profusely before paying and riding away.

My bike runs much better on the ride to Zahedan—no more sputtering. Now I am sure the earlier sputtering was due to dirty fuel I bought back in Nokkundi. When I reach Zahedan I search out the Hotel Saleh, shower, and lie down for a short rest. The extreme heat on top of my recent illness zaps my energy quickly.

It surprises me that no one speaks English here. Usually someone appears who wants to practice English on me. Even the clerk at the hotel reception is unable to understand or speak to me. I go in search of a restaurant, but eventually give up. Instead I buy some fruit and two tomatoes and walk back to the hotel. The hotel kitchen staff is very kind and allow me to wash my fruit and tomatoes in their sink. They even offer lettuce, cucumber, and dressing so I can make a wonderful salad.

I must find a repair shop and determine where my oil leak is coming from. I ask the hotel clerk for directions, but she simply cannot understand me. I will have to wait until tomorrow. Maybe the morning clerk will speak English. It has been a long day so I retire early.

First thing next morning I speak to the desk clerk, to no avail. As I am leaving I notice some police cars across the road performing a check stop. Maybe they can help. I ride down the street to a traffic circle, come back, and pull up behind one of the police cars. I lift my face shield and ask, "Does anyone speak English ... a little bit?"

After a moment's hesitation one of the officers replies, "No."

I motion for him to follow me, and show him the oil mixed with sand sprayed over the pipes and saddlebag on the right side of my bike. He immediately calls two other officers over and they discuss my situation. Now it is his turn to motion *follow me*. Three officers get into a police car and lead me to a motorcycle repair shop. The street is lined with many small, open-front shops or stalls with men working on all sorts of things. We stop in front of one such stall and the officers speak with the two fellows working there. One man, whom I presume is the mechanic, takes a look at my bike and immediately goes to work while the other man brings me a stool to sit on. My instincts tell me my bike is in good hands. In a short time they have the oil drained and the crankcase pulled off. With the oil wiped clear the mechanic shows me a small crack fracturing the bottom. That probably happened from one of those rocks or broken pavement I hit in the construction area, or maybe it's from one of the speed bumps I took too fast and bottomed out on.

The mechanic now has a new helper—a little boy no more than six years old. I watch as this little guy hands tools and cleaning rags to the mechanic, cleans the oil catch basin, and brings water and tea. He knows every tool required and at times supplies it before the mechanic has a chance to ask. I watch in amazement; this little fellow is brilliant.

While I sit and wait, another little boy, about four or five years old, rides in on his bicycle. His bike seat needs fixing. He talks to the men in the shop then finds the wrench he needs and does the job.

About two hours have passed. The crack in the crankcase has been welded and my bike is back together and running great. The mechanic takes it for a ride and is beaming from ear to ear when he returns. I pay my bill, thank the man for his wonderful work, and go in search of a tourist information center.

I am trying to find a map of Iran. The small maps in the *Lonely Planet* guidebook are not quite adequate. I need a map that shows the roads throughout the whole country. I end up at a travel agent's office and am befriended by a woman dressed in the traditional black outfit from head to toe. The headdress she wears is called a "hijab", which is usually a one-piece item fashioned to slip over the head and extend down to cover the neck and chest. I am wearing a very large, light blue patterned scarf that ties under my chin. Here women wear long skirts topped with a knee-length tunic that covers their arms, legs, and body. Even their feet are covered. Most of the women I see are wearing black or tan-colored outfits.

My friend walks with me to three or four shops but we have no luck finding a map in English. Not all is lost, though. At least I have an interesting chat with this woman, who is shocked and excited when I tell her I am traveling by motorcycle, alone.

The next morning I leave the hotel early to find a gas station before leaving Zahedan. The first two stations I find will not serve me because I do not have a local gas card. As I ride down the street I spot a soldier and stop to ask for assistance. He does not understand a word I say but another vehicle has stopped and the young man driving speaks a little English. He takes me back to the gas station and attempts to get fuel for me. No luck, they simply are not going to serve me.

This young man does not give up. He leads me to a black-market gas stall and I get six liters of fuel from a barrel for twenty-two thousand rials. That is about four dollars Canadian. Not bad, you say. Well, I would agree except that fuel at the pumps is ten cents per liter. Nonetheless, I am grateful. I could not start out for Bam with a partial tank of fuel.

The highway to Bam crosses the Kavir-e Lut desert. The road is paved but rough from cracks and heaves, no doubt caused by the extreme heat. Temperatures can soar to sixty degrees Celsius or more. I ride about a hundred and fifty kilometers before stopping for fuel at another roadside stall boasting old barrels with hand pumps. I remember those hand pumps from my farm days as a kid.

Back on the road I start having trouble almost immediately. I curse the man for selling me dirty fuel and nurse my bike a bit farther. The sputtering grows worse and then it just dies. *Now what?*

I search my mind trying to remember the last time I saw a vehicle. Maybe a truck will come along and we can load it up and take it to the next town or village. Walking in this heat is not an option. Anyway, I cannot leave my bike out here with everything on it. After discounting those options, my mind flashes back to an article I read on the Horizons Unlimited Web site about a biker who had a similar problem that turned out to be a loose battery connection. Oh, to be so lucky. What do I have to lose? I am not a mechanic but I do have some natural instincts about my machine.

With that thought I proceed to unload my packs and take the seat off the bike. When I check the battery connections, sure enough, one is loose. "Please let this be the problem," I plead. I dig out my tools and tighten the cable, then turn the key in the ignition. Bingo! I am up and running. I breathe a sigh of relief as I replace the seat and strap my gear back on.

I reach Bam, a little town bordering the south edge of the desert, at 12:30 PM. The temperature is too hot to continue riding. Besides, I need to explore this historic city. I find Ali Amiri's Legal Guesthouse (not sure of the significance of *Legal*) and check in. It seems I am the only person in here. I ask the attendant how secure it is and where I might park my motorcycle. He tells me to park at the "big house" a few blocks away. The owners of the guesthouse live there, and their yard is fenced and secure. This sounds just great to me so I get directions before I leave to go in search of a bank.

My first stop is a variety store where I ask directions to a bank. A male clerk tells me that banks are closed already today and not open on Friday—tomorrow is Friday. The good news is they do open Saturday. I will just have to spend an extra day here.

Back at the guesthouse I unload my things before riding over to the big house. Two women meet me in the yard, show me where to park my bike, and then invite me in for tea. I gratefully accept as I have some questions to ask. I must find a moneychanger, and an optometrist to get my glasses fixed. I hope these women can direct me. It would be wonderful if I could take care of both today.

I enjoy my visit, and then ask my most pressing question. "Do you know where I can exchange some US dollars for Iran rials?"

They think about this and discuss it between themselves, then send me off to see a friend with a shop who might change some money for me. I hurry away before it gets too late and find Amar, who agrees to change forty US dollars at seventy-eight hundred rials per dollar. I know the rate is about eighty-one hundred per dollar, but this man is not negotiating. He probably suspects I am in a jam, with the banks closed tomorrow.

By the time I return to the big house it is 8:00 PM. I inquire about a place to get my glasses fixed, and this time, the women refer me to a relative who owns an optical shop. That will be my first task tomorrow morning.

Dinner is prepared Iran style and we sit cross-legged on the floor to eat. Rice is the main dish fancied up with spices I cannot identify, and served with vegetables, nuts, and Nan bread. My appetite has diminished over the past year so it does not take much to fill me up. I leave feeling quite satisfied.

It is 9:30 and dark by the time I leave. It is four blocks back to the guesthouse and I express my concern about walking alone after dark. The women assure me it is quite safe. The guesthouse entrance faces an alley instead of a main street so I take a quick look around before making my way to the door and letting myself in. There is still no one else in the building and that makes me a little nervous. I will sleep lightly tonight.

I make it through the night without incident and after breakfast find the optical shop. As I wait and watch, my glasses are welded together at the break. Not a pretty job, but it will have to do until I work out a better solution. On my agenda today is a tour of the ancient city of Arg-e Bam, which was started in the period before Christ. This walled city is constructed entirely of mud bricks, clay, straw, and the trunks of palm trees. It occupies six square kilometers, contains thirty-eight towers, four hundred houses, and at its peak had nine thousand to thirteen thousand inhabitants living within its walls. It was once a major trading center on the famous Silk Road.

I pay a nominal fee to enter and spend a big part of the day wandering through narrow hallways and corridors, imagining what life was like here during the city's heyday. Many of these small rooms would have housed a complete family; others would be businesses, maybe even a school and hospital. I climb the stairs to towers along the outer edge where the ruler's elaborate quarters were, and finally reach the highest point overlooking the entire walled city. From here I can get a picture of the complete maze below.

I meet an Iranian family with two small boys and a girl. The children are having a great time scrambling through the narrow passageways. We exchange greetings then take each other's picture before continuing on our way.

Note: I am extremely blessed to have visited this site. On December 26, just six months after my visit, the city of Bam, including Arg-e Bam, was destroyed in a devastating earthquake that claimed over thirty thousand lives and left thousands more injured. Many reports claim that over 60 percent of the city proper was destroyed. My heart aches for the people who lost their lives, those who were injured, and for the ones who are left to rebuild.

I leave the hostel early next morning and walk to the big house to collect my bike. The women have charged me an exorbitant price for breakfast and the one dinner I ate there. I am shocked and concerned at how quickly my Iran rials are disappearing. I ride back to the guesthouse, pack my things, and continue on to Kerman. My route still borders the desert and I ride in extreme heat the first part of the morning until a cloud cover forms and offers a slight reprieve.

Not many people in this part of Iran speak English. I struggle to find the Omid Guesthouse in Kerman, and finally meet a young man who understands enough to direct me. I have learned that businesses shut down between 1:00 and 5:00 PM to avoid the hottest part of the day, so I check in and sleep for a couple of hours before going out to buy some very fresh rolls, tomato, cheese, and a banana. It is too hot to be out so I take my food back to the guesthouse and retreat to my air-conditioned room.

The next morning I continue on to Yazd and stop early in the afternoon. The first hotel I check wants sixty dollars US. I keep looking and find a nice one for seventy thousand rials—less than ten dollars. I continue to search for a bank or business that will give me money on my visa, mastercard, or bankcard. Still no luck! I am running short on US money to exchange. For this reason I cannot spend too much time in these places.

From Yazd to Esfahan is 335 kilometers on very good roads with plenty of rest stops along the way. When I reach Esfahan, the craft market capital of Iran; I ride toward the center of the city and find the Amir Kabir Hotel. This is a larger and busier city so I am hopeful about getting money on my card here. I stop at Bank Melli, but once again, they refuse my request.

The time is mid morning and too early to check into a room so I go to the restaurant for breakfast while I wait for my room to be cleaned. I am standing at the counter asking for hot water to add to my cup of very strong coffee, when a voice behind me says, "Can I help you?"

Hearing English sends a feeling of relief and excitement through me. The gentleman introduces himself as Magid, and I invite him to sit and chat. He tells me he is with Iran Tourism. This could be very helpful.

"We do not see many foreign tourists here," he says. "So when one comes in I like to talk to them."

I explain my predicament about running low on money and my problem at the banks, and ask him if he knows where I can get money on my credit card. He says he may be able to help but first would like me to come to dinner and meet his family.

Later that afternoon Magid picks me up and we go to his home, a large cement building similar to an apartment with a few large suites. Their flat is spacious and comfortable. The living and dining room is one very long room with beautiful Persian carpets covering the floor. The furniture and décor is not much different than what you'd find in North America. There is a large dining room table at one end, and I wonder if we will eat at the table or sit cross-legged on the floor. Magid has four children ranging from seven years to twenty-five. The oldest daughter is in university and the eighteen-year-old son will soon follow. Both speak very good English and have many questions about Canada.

Magid's wife has made a wonderful meal of rice and veggies, potato salad, tomatoes, and cucumbers. The traditional Nan bread (chapita) accompanies the meal. Lunch is served at the dining room table.

The women shed their hijabs and required dress when in their home, and wear clothing more suitable to the climate. The daughter no longer has her arms and legs covered, and explains that women are required to be completely covered only when out in public.

After lunch my host takes me to an art shop in Emam Square. He knows an art dealer who buys and sells with Dubai and just may be able to sell me some US dollars on my credit card. It may mean buying a piece of art from him but if that is what I have to do, so be it. Magid tells me that many credit card transactions from North America are never paid; that is why businesses refuse to accept them. Political relations between Iran and the United States are not good.

The owner of the art shop has one hundred and fifty dollars US available and will put that amount on my credit card as though it is a purchase. I browse around the shop and find a miniature painting of

Romeo and Juliet on camel bone for thirty-five dollars. Much overpriced, I feel, but at least now I have money to exchange. Hopefully this will be enough to get me out of Iran. If I head straight to the Turkey border from here I will be fine, but I want to see more of this country before leaving. This will most likely be my only opportunity.

Magid spends time walking me through some shops in the outer walls of the square, introducing me to people, and explaining the many crafts sold here. We walk past intricately patterned Persian carpets hanging from the walls; metal smiths hammering out designs on large silver plates, vases and bowls; ceramic and glass wear, jewelry, and other trinkets; hand-crafted furniture, art stores, food stalls, and much more. It is obvious I will not see it all today, so we call it quits and Magid drops me off at my hotel. I decide to stay another day to explore more of Emam Square.

Early the next morning, as I walk towards the square, I pass by a shop selling fresh bread shaped long and slender like French loaves. The front wall of the bakery is open from the counter to the ceiling and several people crowd to the front to make their purchases. I watch one man pay for his bread, tuck the loaf under his armpit, and stroll on down the street. No, the bread is not in a bag. I chuckle at the scene and watch until the crowd thins out. When I have a chance I ask the bakers if I may take their picture standing in front of the huge brick oven and holding their long wooden paddles (used to place and retrieve the loaves).

I continue on to the Si-O-Se pedestrian bridge that crosses the Rud-e Zayandeh (Zayandeh River). This is the famous *Bridge of 33 Arches*. It actually consists of two layers of 33 arches—a beautiful work of architecture.

From here I walk to the Emam Square and spend the morning browsing through the shops and markets, taking pictures. The mosques that border the square are covered with blue, white, yellow, and green tiles placed in precise patterns from the ground to the highest peak. I chat with the owner of a carpet shop and he asks if I have been to the Tea House. "It is the oldest tea house in Iran. You must visit our famous Tea House," he says. "And you must try a water pipe."

The Tea House is just a short walk away and this kind gentleman escorts me. There are two rooms divided by an arch. In the farthest room from the door, only men are allowed. The walls are covered in carpets, ornaments, pictures, and ornate lamps. The rooms seem very dark and busy with all the paraphernalia. I take a seat on the side for women and families, and order tea. My friend encourages me to try the "water pipe"—a vessel that looks like a tall, skinny, glass lantern with water in the bottom, coals in a metal dish at the top (with your choice of flavour) and a tube that protrudes from the lantern near water level. To smoke the pipe you suck on the tube and if you suck hard enough the water bubbles and you inhale the aroma, which is usually some kind of fruit or herb. As I try to master this skill I cannot help but wonder if there are drugs in here. All I taste is an apple flavour.

I follow the covered alleys that go on for blocks and blocks leading out from the square. One could get lost in this huge bazaar. Esfahan is famous for its handcrafted merchandise. This is the first place I have been where I've had the desire to buy souvenirs to send home. The crafts are the most beautiful I have seen in all my travels. If I had unlimited money to spend I would buy one of these intricately woven Persian carpets and send it home.

As I walk back to my hotel I start thinking about the noise my bike is making again. It sounds the same as it did before I had it worked on in Islamabad. Now I wonder if they replaced the front sprocket with an old one, or did they replace it at all? I will have to keep a very close eye on the chain tension.

On June 17 I leave Esfahan at 6:00 AM. It is actually cool riding for the first two hours. What a treat! All too soon the heat hits and I remove my fleecy sweatshirt from under my riding jacket.

The noise from my bike is getting louder. I worry that something may become seriously damaged. I try a bike shop in Quom, but no one understands me. A gentleman passing by the shop suggests I should try a mechanic in Tehran and directs me to the main road out of town. The noise is not bad when I keep a constant speed; it is just when I accelerate.

I make good time today. The highway is wonderful and I am able to ride at a steady speed. The first hotel I check does not have parking and I would have to leave my bike several blocks away at a public parking lot. This is not acceptable so I look for the Hotel Naderi. It looks nice and well kept and has a fenced garden area out back where I can park my bike. My room is big compared to most places where I have stayed and it has a large, clean bathroom—all this for ten dollars US.

After lunch I check out a bike shop a couple of blocks away. They sell new bikes here and I look around briefly before going to the counter. I stand there for several minutes feeling like I am invisible, before anyone pays attention to me. I explain the problem with my bike, but the men behind the counter are not at all helpful. They only sell Kawasaki's and a local brand of bike. I ask, "Do you have a mechanic here?"

"No, we do not work on Hondas," the clerk replies.

"Where can I find a motorbike mechanic who works on Hondas?" I ask.

A man, who appears to be the manager, gives me the street name where many bike repair shops are located, then says in an abrupt tone, "But you cannot go there alone. Women do not go there."

By now I am feeling a bit agitated and want to say "Too bad!" But I bite my tongue and leave the shop.

Back at my hotel I talk to the young man behind the reception desk and try to get directions to these bike repair shops. "Women do not go there," he says.

Well, I have a bike problem and it needs to be looked after, so I go to my room and retrieve my riding gear. When I come down the stairs carrying my jacket, helmet and gloves, the clerk stops me and tells me I should not go there alone. He then makes some quick phone calls and when he hangs up he says; "I have found a mechanic who will come to the hotel at 6:00 PM." Then he adds, "It is better for you if he comes here." It's after 7:00 when two men arrive to look at my bike. I explain about the noise and what is happening. They start the engine, and of course it sounds just fine. I explain that the noise is not there when it's idling, only when I accelerate. Soon they agree that I should bring the bike to their shop and they give me the address and directions. I am pleased that they will at least try to resolve the problem.

The hotel restaurant does not open until 10:00, so early the next morning I walk down the street to a corner stand that makes fresh cantaloupe shakes. I brush the shoulder of a man walking in the opposite direction and he turns and says something to me. It takes a moment to register. I cannot be certain, but it sounded like, "Watch your back." At the corner stand I order my cantaloupe shake and the owner invites me to come in and sit. This is not a café and no one else is invited in, so why do I receive special treatment? I begin to feel like I should not be out on the street. I am wearing my scarf and a long t-shirt over my jeans but my arms are not covered. Maybe that is the problem, or maybe it's because my scarf is of a light blue pattern, and not solid black or brown.

In spite of all this inner turmoil I enjoy my shake before returning to the hotel for my bike. I follow the directions Aghar gave me to what I think is going to be a big Honda shop. I pass by many stores, shops, and offices, feeling like I have ridden a lot farther than I should have. Several times I stop and ask for directions. On one such stop a business owner offers to come with me. He hops on the back seat and we continue for another eight or ten blocks. This is great! When we finally find the repair shop I offer to give him a ride back, but he insists that he will walk.

By now it is 9:30 AM. Aghar meets me in front of the shop and I am surprised to find a small stall with room for one or two motorbikes. The space is very tidy and clean but certainly not a large Honda shop. I hope they can fix the problem.

Aghar picks up the phone, and in minutes, two other men arrive to help him. I am given a stool to sit on while I wait. Throughout the morning several men drop by. Most of them pay me a quick glance, but they are here to see this huge foreign motorcycle, not me. Besides that, men here do not look a woman in the eye.

After an hour Aghar offers to take me to his mother's house for tea. I believe they feel uncomfortable having a woman in the shop so I accept and get on the back of his little 125cc bike. Away we go, weaving in and out of traffic, turning left then right, down narrow streets, making more turns until I am completely lost. Finally we stop and enter a cement building where a little old lady sits cross-legged on the floor. The room is sparsely furnished with rugs on the floor and cushions propped up against the walls.

I sit cross-legged on the floor and sip tea brought in by a younger woman, whom Aghar introduces as his sister. The mother does not speak English so Aghar interprets our conversation—or rather, the interview. The questions go something like this: Where is your husband? Do you have children? Why do you travel alone? Are you not afraid to travel alone? I do manage to get some chuckles out of her before I leave, but she clearly thinks I am odd.

Finally we return to the shop and my bike is ready to go. They were not able to replace the sprocket but made some adjustments, lubed the chain, and it sounds much better now. I hope it will get me to Turkey where I stand a better chance of getting the chain and sprockets replaced.

After lunch I go to the Central Bank of Iran in hopes of getting some money on my mastercard or visa. They refuse, so I exchange one hundred dollars that I got in Esfahan for 813,500 rials. The bank clerk is sensitive to my problem and suggests I go to my embassy for assistance. He even phones to inquire about their hours of operation. I am in luck—if I go now I should make it before they close.

While waiting in line at the bank I am befriended by a young couple with two children. They kindly offer to give me a ride to the Canadian Embassy. The father says, "When we studied in Italy people were very kind and helpful to us. Now we must repay this kindness by being helpful to visitors in our country."

Wouldn't it be wonderful if everyone in the world thought that way?

At the Canadian Embassy I explain my problem about not being able to get money on my bankcard. The woman behind the wicket gives me a lecture on not finding this out before entering Iran, then passes me a form to fill out, and returns to her work. When all is complete, I receive 1,350,500 rials. The clerk informs me that a bill for two hundred and fifty dollars Canadian will be sent to my address in Canada, and must be paid immediately upon receipt. I feel so relieved. Now I can continue my travels in Iran.

I walk back to the main street to catch a bus back to the hotel. When the bus stops I make my way to the front door, but am told to go to the back door. I quickly realize that women sit in the back half of the bus and men in the front. There is a door halfway down the side of the bus where women may enter. My initial reaction is to protest but I remind myself I am a guest in this country, and not here to judge or change their system.

I leave Tehran next morning with my bike running and sounding much better. At 6:00 AM the traffic exiting the city is moving smoothly, and I soon find myself on a beautiful four-lane highway. Next thing I know there is a tollgate ahead and a road sign for Tehran. Just as I realize I am going in the wrong direction, a police truck pulls in behind me with his lights flashing.

Now what! I stop and immediately pull out my map. When the

officer comes to my bike I quickly hold up the map and ask if this is the road to Chalus.

"No, Tehran," he says, pointing to the tollgates. Turning around he points in the opposite direction for Chalus.

Then the officer says, "Follow me."

He leads me to the tollgate, makes a u-turn, and then points me in the right direction telling me to watch for the sign exiting right. I thank him and continue on my way, relieved that he does not interrogate me.

The scenery north through the mountains is beautiful, but as I climb higher in elevation the clouds and fog roll in. The temperature drops fast and water and mist form on my windshield and visor. The road is wet and traffic is moving slowly. My body shivers and my hands begin to feel the cold. About fifty kilometers click by before the fog lifts and I ride down the other side of the mountain range. In minutes I begin to warm up and quickly forget about how cold I felt.

At Chalus I make my way to the Caspian Sea. The shoreline here is rocky and I ride slowly on hard-packed sand until I find a safe place to park. I quickly substitute my helmet for a scarf, shed my jacket and riding pants, and walk out on the rocks. I rest awhile, enjoying the sound of the waves crashing against the shoreline. There is something very calming about the sea. Only a handful of people are out here, and even though the sun is shining and the temperature is warm, they are dressed from head to toe in the required costume. No bikinis and bathing suits here.

As I relax and enjoy the tranquility of the moment, I look out across the Caspian Sea and realize that just across these waters, to the northwest, is Stavropol, Russia—where my father was born. I wonder if I will be successful in reaching it. Reluctantly, I pull myself from my thoughts and return to the bike.

Before I have my riding gear back on, a gentleman about 45 years old approaches me and introduces himself as Jim. He tells me he owns a hotel nearby and will give me a good rate. He speaks very good English and I immediately know that he is a foreigner to this country. I follow him to his small resort, consisting of a large central hotel with smaller cabins, situated along the ocean. I book a little round cabin close to the water where I can hear the sound of the waves.

Everyone is interested in my bike and Jim asks me to bring it to the front of the hotel so he can take pictures of it with the staff, himself, and me.

I ask about an Internet café and Jim instructs his young attendant, Jahar, to go with me. Jahar is about 30 years old, six feet tall, slim, and very good-looking. He rides behind me on my bike and directs me to an Internet café and small market. When we return and I thank him, he has a big smile on his face and places his hand over his heart. I guess this must mean, "You're welcome," or "It is my pleasure."

Later, as I stand on the flat cement rooftop watching the waves crash against the rocks ten feet below, Jahar appears again. He stands quietly awhile, and then begins to tell me in Persian how the waves crashed so hard the spray rose up this high and completely soaked him. I do not understand a word he is saying, but his actions tell the story well. What an inspiring and spiritual experience.

At about 9:00 PM I go to pay for my room so I can leave early in the morning. I visit a short while with Jim and find out he is from the United States. He and his wife moved here several years ago. The tourist business is slow and they are thinking of returning home if things do not pick up. They have a great location along the ocean and once had a thriving business. But because of the government in place for the past ten years, things have changed drastically.

I pay my bill and Jim says, "Jahar wants me to tell you he likes you."

I chuckle and say, "He is a very nice young man—about the age of my son."

Jim translates this to Jahar, and then laughs. I ask him what they said and he replies, putting his hand over his heart, "What does it matter when it's of the heart?"

The two of them exchange a few more words and I hear Jahar say, "Zst, Zst." I'm not sure what all that was about, but I think I hurt his feelings. Once again I find myself wishing I were twenty years younger. Then again, maybe it is a good thing I'm not …

The next morning I head west on the highway bordering the Caspian Sea. Riding is slow as I pass through one small seaside town after another. These are vacation spots for tourists—mostly Iranians. It is a very pretty area so I take my time and enjoy the scenery, stopping a couple of times to walk by the sea. The shoreline varies from hard-packed sandy beaches, to pebbles, to large rocks and boulders. My destination is Bandar-e Anzali, the most important seaport in Northern Iran and known as "the world capital of precious caviar." When I reach Rasht, a fairly large city, I find myself going in circles again and decide to stay here one night. I will ride through Bandar-e Anzali tomorrow and then on to Astara.

With a little help I find my way out of Rasht in the morning and back to the ocean road, riding west, then north. Bandar-e Anzali is only forty kilometers out and wish I had continued yesterday. It is a much prettier town than Rasht.

I reach Astara around noon. My plan is to stay here a day or two. Astara is a border town between Iran and the Azerbaijan Republic, lying in both countries. On one side it borders the Caspian Sea, and on the other, the mountains. With the help from a couple of young men on a small motorcycle, I find the Astara Tourist Inn. It is very nice but they want thirty dollars US. I negotiate the price down to twenty-five. This is still more than I want to pay, but I take it and enjoy.

I unload my bike, get a small map from the desk clerk, and go in search of lunch. People are friendly and talk to me as I walk past their shops. As I turn on to Bazaar Street a tall, good-looking man joins me, walking with me through the bazaar. He introduces himself as Nasaar, and then explains that it is siesta time and most of the shops and stalls are closed until about 5:00. We continue strolling to the sea and along the beach. Nasaar picks up a cardboard for me to sit on and we stop and talk awhile. He owns a restaurant in Astara but often goes across the border into Russia to work. He asks me all the usual questions, which, by now, I am quite prepared for. "My husband has expired, my daughter is married and no, I am not afraid to travel alone."

There are a few men on the beach and in the water, but I do not see any women. I ask Nasaar where the women swim and he says, "Come, I show you."

We walk over a rock berm to another bay where the rocks form a crescent, offering privacy from the main beach and people passing by. There is no one in the water right now but this is where the women swim.

Up to this point Nasaar has not touched me, but now that we are far from sight of anyone, he takes my wrist as we continue to walk out on the huge black rocks towards the water. We find a secluded spot beside the water and stop to talk. Nasaar tells me I can take my scarf off here. "It is private and no one can see us," he says. He tries to convince me to go swimming, but there is no way I am taking my clothes off and jumping in. If I were caught they would probably throw me in jail. I tell him I'm happy just to sit here and enjoy the peacefulness.

Waves slap lightly against the rocks, the sun is shining, the scenery is spectacular, and here I sit with a gorgeous, extremely fit, forty-five year old man. We talk and laugh at each other's stories, and he reaches over and kisses me on the cheek. In another time and place I might relax and enjoy this, but here in a strange country where the culture differs so greatly from mine, my guard goes up. I think it's time I made my escape. Either I am getting old *or* I have acquired some wisdom in my old age. All I know is that I am not prepared to risk my freedom, no matter how attractive he is.

Nasaar is a gentleman. We climb back over the rocks and make our way back through the bazaar and to his little café. He makes tea and introduces me to some friends who come in for pizza. Two men from the shop next door come in for a visit. During our conversation one gentleman reveals his age as fifty-seven and the other as fifty-three. They both look much older.

Before returning to my hotel I stop at an Internet café. It turns out they are also a service provider for the area. The attendant speaks good English. He wants to hear about my travels and is amazed that I am traveling alone. When I prepare to pay he tells me, "The Internet is free for visitors."

The next morning I go for a walk to watch the sunrise over the ocean. I walk a few blocks before climbing a high hill that overlooks the city to my right and the ocean to my left. The sun has not risen yet. Making my way along the ridge I see a group of women sitting amongst the rocks, and say good morning. They smile and reply in their language. One woman asks, "Are you alone?" Women do not go out alone. They are either with a man, another woman, or a group of women.

In a few minutes the sun is rising and creating a brilliant beam of light across the sea. The view from my spot on the hill is perfect as I watch the city come to life with the first rays of dawn.

At noon I ride to Nasaar's café for pizza. He is not in today but his partner, Amin, serves me and visits between serving other customers. I just start eating when a police officer comes in and asks whose bike is parked out there. Amin interprets for me.

"It's mine," I reply.

The officer asks in a gruff voice to see my passport. He does not sound very friendly and I do not understand what he is saying.

My friend interprets again. I give the officer a copy of my passport and tell him that my official passport is at the hotel (it is a law in Iran that, upon check-in, you turn over your passport to the hotel clerk where it is locked in a safe until you leave). The officer says something in Persian, then turns and leaves. My friend tells me I am to go with him. I had just started eating before this interruption and figure I can at least finish my lunch first.

A few minutes later a man comes into the café who speaks English. He tells me that the officers want to speak to me, pronto! I retrieve my jacket and helmet and go outside. When I get to my bike the officer puts out his hand for the keys, and the interpreter tells me to ride in the police car.

I address the man interpreting as I point to the short, chubby officer, "He wants to ride my bike?" "No way, he is not riding my bike. No one rides my bike!"

I hold fast to my keys as the interpreter talks to the officer, then turns back to me with, "You should ride in the car."

I repeat myself, this time with much more emphasis, and pull my helmet on over my scarf. Now the officer backs down and gets into his car. The interpreter tells me to follow them to the police station a few blocks straight down this street.

As I follow the police car I am thinking I cannot go to the station without my passport. My hotel is a block or two off this road, just two blocks from the police station. I have to make a major decision and my gut instinct tells me to get my passport. When we reach the traffic circle the police car goes straight through and I turn off on the first quarter exit. Immediately their lights and siren comes on so I pull over and stop where I am. I watch as the police car turns and comes to me. The officer is yelling something at me and I am pointing to my hotel and saying, "Passport, hotel, passport, hotel." I continue riding and when I stop at the hotel the officer is still raging on about something.

The officer requests my passport from the hotel clerk and I go to my room to get my carnet de passage. Now I will follow them to the police station.

Once inside I am led to a waiting area near the entrance and told, in charade fashion, to sit. I offer my carnet but no one is interested in looking at it. Several officers study my passport with all the other country stamps. Whenever someone walks past me I ask, "Why am I here?" Each time they hold up a hand in a *wait* motion. Either they do not understand English or are pretending not to.

After a few minutes I am escorted into an office to see another man. He does not speak English to me and eventually sends me back to the waiting area. After a dozen different officers have studied my passport, two of them record my information into their ledger. What should take a couple of minutes takes them another ten. Finally they hand me my passport and indicate that I can leave.

I breathe a silent sigh of relief and go back to my bike. Just as I start the bike the first officer of the day comes out and asks for my passport again. I give it to him and he tells me to return to my hotel. His English is not good, but he can speak a bit.

"Oh, no," I say. "I don't go anywhere without my passport." I turn off the bike and follow him back into the building. I stand rooted to a spot in front of the wicket and refuse to leave. Finally the short, stubby officer comes back in front with my passport and tells me he will follow me to my hotel.

I do not know what their game is, but I am leaving this town first thing in the morning.

The highway I take towards the Turkey border is excellent and the scenery through the mountains is spectacular. Under different circumstances I would have spent more time enjoying the beauty, but today I just want to reach the border. I admire the green hillsides and blue lakes as I ride by, stopping only for gas and lunch. Tabriz is a large city with intricate expressways. It looks like it would be a nice place to stop, but I breeze right through. I ride over five hundred kilometers before reaching the border town of Maku. I find a hotel room for thirty thousand rials, which is about five dollars and fifty cents Canadian; that includes parking for my bike in a large unused area inside locked doors. This makes me happy, as I do not want a repeat of yesterday's events.

I check my bags into my room and go down to the lobby where I meet a young couple who speak very good English. The young woman tells me that when the Shah was in office, women did not have to cover themselves from head to toe. It is the present ruler who adopted and enforced this rule. As we visit, another English-speaking man joins us. He is an English teacher here in Maku.

I ask where I can find a restaurant for dinner and Raf, the English teacher, offers to take me to one. He sits and visits with me while I eat. The custom here is to have dinner any time after 10:00, so it is much too early for him to eat. Raf does not allow me pay my bill. He says, "No, don't worry. You are our guest."

Raf has two English classes to teach this evening and invites me to sit in on them. I accept and have a wonderful time speaking with the students and answering their questions. One student asks why I do not wear socks. This question disturbs me, and I wonder if that has been the reason for some of the rude treatment I received. I am wearing my sandals, and I tell him that it is hot here and much more comfortable without socks. I explain that at home in hot weather we do not wear a lot of clothes.

The wonderful people in this small border town have eased my nervousness from the previous day. Overall, my two weeks in Iran have been a good experience. I have seen some spectacular country, visited some interesting old cities, and been treated very well by most people. The highways in this country are the best I have traveled on to date, and fuel has been ten cents a liter in most places. But accommodations have been higher than what I expected.

June 23 is my last day here. Tomorrow I will enter Turkey.

Chapter 6
Turkey

On the morning of June 24, 2003, I cross the border to Turkey. It is a cold morning and grey clouds fill the sky. Before I reach the border I am bombarded with moneychangers. I negotiate the price to exchange my last thirty-three thousand rials. The rate at borders is never as much as at the bank, but if you know what the exchange is, you can barter.

I move slowly through town behind other vehicles heading for the border. At one point in the line, I am stopped for several minutes when a man comes over and asks if I would like to take breakfast in his café. I tell him I have no Iran money left. He says, "No problem, you are our guest."

I have not had breakfast yet and have no idea how far I will have to travel to reach a restaurant once I cross the border, so I accept his invitation. Breakfast consists of bread and cheese, and the most awful coffee imaginable. I eat the bread and cheese but leave most of the coffee. I thank my host and return to my bike and rejoin the line.

The Iran border crossing goes quickly. Within ten minutes my passport and carnet are stamped for exit from the country. Departing is always easier than entering. When I reach the Turkey border I am sent back and forth to different rooms and booths to apply for my visa, pay for it, and then have it processed and stamped. I was under the impression I did not need a visa to cross into Turkey, that my passport would be sufficient. I feel positive that the government Web site indicated that Canadians could obtain a stamp in their passport at the border. Surprise, surprise! I should have applied for it at the Embassy in Tehran. This is creating a longer process for me now.

Next, I am sent to a room where an officer is signing and stamping carnets. The first thing I notice is the newspaper spread out on his desk with a bikini-clad poster girl covering a full page. This would not be permitted in Pakistan and Iran.

With my carnet and passport stamped I return to the border guard. He looks at both documents and verifies the stamps, then hands them back to me. Just as I'm about to get on my bike, he asks to see the carnet again. He turns it over and happens to notice that Turkey is not one of the countries listed. I explain to him that none of the European countries are listed because they do not require a carnet. My argument is in vain. He sends me back into the "poster girl" office where the officer makes out another paper, then sends me to the bank to pay another three dollars US. I return with the receipt of payment and am shocked to find that the officer now wants five million lira for doing the paperwork. One million Turkish Lira is equal to approximately one Canadian dollar. I should have stood my ground because this was probably pocket money for him.

You might be thinking, "That is only five dollars."

Yes, well … that's not the point. Five million in any currency feels like a lot of money!

Back I go to the border guard, who takes the final exit strip from my carnet, and sends me on my way. This exit strip is normally taken when I exit the country, not enter. Now I am sure I did not need the carnet here. There is one more gate where I have to cross and show my passport, before I leave the wonderful paved roads of Iran to travel the patched, bumpy ones of Turkey. The road winds through green hillsides and mountains with traces of snow near the peaks. The temperature is cold for riding and I wish I had my electric liner on under my jacket. I have not used it for so long I packed it at the bottom of my duffle bag. I ride for two hours before stopping for lunch and tea and a chance to warm up.

My first fuel stop is a shock. The cost is eighteen million lira for less than ten liters. I can see it is going to be expensive to travel in Turkey.

When I reach Ezurum I find a hotel and unpack my gear before going in search of a tourist information bureau. I walk several blocks, following my city map, and have no problem with directions. There are two women working at the bureau and I wait only a few minutes for my turn. The clerk I get is extremely helpful. She pulls off lists of campsites, places of interest, and much more from the computer. I leave with a handful of information.

As I walk up the street a young man who was in the tourist office steps in beside me and offers to show me the sites of Ezurum. I hesitate for a moment, and then he explains that he is a university student studying tourism and would like to help. I accept his offer and suggest we stop for coffee first. Over coffee Alper tells me he is also learning English and this gives him a chance to practice. I attempt to pay the bill but he says, "You are a guest in our country" and takes it from me.

We spend two or more hours walking to various sites. At the museum I want to pay his way but he ignores my protests and pays. By 6:30 PM I feel starved and suggest we stop for dinner. My watch shows 8:00, indicating I have come through two time zones. I am ready to call it a day. It is much too early for dinner by Turkish custom, so we go to a pastry shop. Again Alper pays and refuses the money I offer him for being my guide this afternoon.

Back at my hotel I order mashed potatoes and brown beans for dinner. It tastes delicious. This is the best meal I have had in ages!

I already love Turkey with its beautiful countryside, the wonderful people, and the good food. A typical breakfast served buffet style consists of boiled eggs, cold cuts of processed meat, tomatoes, cucumbers, fruit, and fresh rolls with butter and jam. I enjoy this immensely (omitting the processed meats).

From Ezurum I ride south towards Diyarbakir. It is a nice morning for a ride and I feel quite comfortable wearing my fleecy under my jacket along with my riding pants. For the first hundred and fifty kilometers I wind through mountains, which then open up to rolling farmland. Neatly cut rows of golden grain glisten in the sunlight—a picture perfect scene reminding me of home.

As I get closer to Diyarbakir I encounter several army check posts. Each time I must stop and show my passport and bike papers. At one check post I pull out my camera to take a picture of my bike in front of the building. One officer immediately says, "No picture!"

"I just want a picture of my bike" I reply; and quickly snap my camera and return it to my tank bag. Nothing more is said as I mount my bike and roll away.

After four more check stops, about twenty minutes apart, I begin thinking my ride today will be a long one. Fortunately, at the next stop the officers wave me through, and I arrive in Diyarbakir at about 1:00 PM. I find a room at the Kristal Hotel and bargain the price down from twenty million to fifteen million liras. It seems very strange to be handling money in the millions. Fuel at my next stop is two million per liter. What a shock, after paying ten cents per liter in Iran.

Turkish cuisine looks very inviting if you eat meat. Everywhere I go I see beef kabobs, chickens roasting on a spit, and large racks of beef on an upright spit ready to be shaved onto a donair or fresh roll. I have trouble finding fish or vegetarian meals, but vegetables and fruit, fresh rolls, and cheese are plentiful so I do not suffer. Alper had told me they eat cheese with honey on fresh rolls and that this is very healthy.

Diyarbakir is large and modern, but the attraction here is the old walled city. The walls are the second largest and best preserved in the world, second to the Great Wall of China. They measure five and one half kilometers surrounding the old city, reach twelve meters high, three to five meters wide, and have eighty-two watchtowers. Some of this construction dates back to the period before Christ.

I wander down narrow streets—too narrow for vehicles—past fruit and vegetable vendors, and shops selling a variety of goods. The tall brick buildings make the alleyways look narrower than they are. The children are very bold and follow me, asking for money. One group of kids keep grabbing at my camera so I quickly move on to another area. Mosques are busy with dedicated worshippers. There is a Christian church within the walls, Meryem Ana Kilisesi (Church of the Virgin Mary), so I walk until I find it, and pay a short visit. Then I find an area where I can climb up to the top of the wall. The view of the surrounding city is fabulous from here. Unfortunately it does not go very far as the rock is crumbling around the edges. Much of this great wall is under reconstruction.

The next morning I leave Diyarbakir at 8:00 andride about a hundred and twenty kilometers to Feribot. From here I take a short ferry ride across the water to Nemrut Dagi (Mt. Nemrut) National Park. The small ferry is loaded with two big trucks hauling cattle, eight vehicles, and my bike. That is about all the space there is.

My Magna is a big attraction for all the men on board. I snap a few pictures and in less than twenty minutes we dock on the other side. I am second off the ferry and only ride a short distance before reaching my turn to the park. The road winds its way up the mountain. The paved surface is good until the last ten-kilometer stretch where it becomes cobblestone and a considerably steeper incline. I climb the hill in first and second gear, trying to avoid some of the sharper stones. Once I reach the lodge I find a parking lot that is gravel and dirt with a sharply graded slope. I pick a spot facing the cement wall beneath the lodge, and hope I do not have trouble getting out later.

From the lodge, the trail goes higher up the mountain through a series of stairs and paths to the rock statues that make this park famous.

King Antiochus I Epiphanes built the statues between 64 and 38 BC. He claimed to be a descendant of both Darius the Great of Persia and Alexander the Great. He considered himself a God, and built the "Statues of Gods" at the summit (2,150 meters) to watch over the people. The stone figureheads of Apollo the Sun God, Tyche, Zeus, King Antiochus, and Hercules once sat on thrones, which together measured eight to ten meters high. The identical figures stand high on the east and west side of the mountain overlooking the valley below. It is said that the king's body is buried under the rock mound at the summit, but that is not yet a proven fact.

Mt. Nemrut is located one hundred kilometers from Adiyaman. A German road engineer discovered the formations at the top of the mountain in 1881. Over the next hundred years several other archaeologists organized expeditions to study the area, then in 1984 a Turkish-German team successfully carried out restoration work at the site. The heads were found toppled from their bases, most likely blown off by the strong winds that whip around the mountaintops. In 1989 Nemrut Dagi was declared a National Park. Restoration work continues for an area covering one hundred and fifty meters in diameter and fifty meters in height.

I return to my bike and carefully make my way down the cobblestone road to the park gate. The guard comes out of his little bunkhouse and strikes up a conversation. He invites me to stop for tea. There are three soldiers having tea with him so I figure it should be safe. During our visit the conversation takes a personal turn, and then the guard asks if I would like to come back later and have tea with him. I decline, bid him farewell, and continue down the mountain to find accommodation.

The next morning I ride south to Sanli Urfa, the City of Prophets. There is a lot to see here so I will stay a couple of days. I park my bike in a locked stall near my hotel and then go walking. First on my agenda is to find "Hazreti Ibrahim'in Dogum Magarasi," the birthplace of the Prophet Abraham. I enter under a row of arches that expose a huge square surrounded by arched entranceways to various shops and mosques. The ground is covered in large polished tiles, attracting hundreds of pigeons. A rectangular fountain, with very little water in it, dominates the central area. As I walk across the square I feel something drop on my head. I reach up and grasp a handful of wet bird shit. Yuk! I head for the fountain and, bending down, cup some water in my hands and attempt to wash the stuff from my hair.

I make my way to the entrance of Abraham's Cave, pay my entry fee, and go through the fancy doors into a small mosque area. The floor is covered with smooth, colored tiles, and paint covers the rock walls. Iron bars block off a rock cave, which is supposedly the birthplace of Abraham. I feel quite certain it did not look like this in his day.

Exiting the mosque, I walk to the fortress that stands high on a hill overlooking the city below. What a view from up here. I can well imagine Abraham and his followers climbing to the top of the fortress and looking down on their land and the people below. On my return trip down the hill I take the tunnel stairway through the mountain. It is pretty scary in some of the narrow places, but awesome to be walking in the steps of Abraham.

I continue on my city walking tour and get lost in a bazaar. I find myself in narrow alleyways with tall brick walls ten meters high on either side, and I begin to feel a little claustrophobic. I wonder if I will ever find my way out of this maze. When I begin to feel the panic rise in my chest, I decide to retrace my steps. Finally I come to an opening that takes me into the street, but not where I started. This exit is completely on the opposite side; that is how easy it is to become disoriented.

The next morning I ride out to the little village of Harran to see the *beehive houses*. These houses are constructed completely of mud brick (no wood), creating insulation from the extreme heat. Some are still occupied today, but most are tourist attractions. It is believed that Abraham also lived here, as well as other people from biblical times.

The old city walls, with four gates, date back to the eighth century. Inside the walls are the ruins of the Kale (citadel), a very important Islamic mosque, and the first Islamic university. Not much is left standing today, only a few upright structures of the mosque and some partial mud brick walls forming square-shaped rooms once used for learning. Harran appears to be a very poor village. When I first rode in I was bombarded with young children, as young as eight or ten years old, sporting an ID card that reads, "Hello, I am a tour guide." I shook them off at the time, but later felt guilty. After all, this is how they make money.

I return to Sanli Urfa and spend the afternoon walking through a market. I pass a man selling little chicks of all colors. At first I think they are toys, but when he holds one up it is plain to see it is alive. He has yellow, bright pink, orange, grey, blue, brown, and white chicks that still have their soft baby feathers. How on earth did he do this? Does he inject a dye into the egg before it hatches? The man does not explain.

I continue on through the food and spice stalls, where the aroma of all the different spices fills the alleys. Huge wooden barrels, open at the top, hold spices of all kinds. Birds fly above me and whip in and out from under the canopies sheltering the produce. I think about the bird that dumped on my head in the large square and wonder how many droppings have landed in a spice barrel or on other food. I enjoy the hustle and bustle of the markets. Young boys carry trays of bagels on their heads, others scurry back and forth with chai or coffee for shopkeepers, vendors are busy arranging their products, and others just sit and wait for customers or someone to talk to.

I begin to go into another courtyard to look for a restaurant, but as I step under the arches all I see are men sitting at the tables. Oh, oh, maybe I should not be here. I retreat and look for another place to eat.

On Wednesday morning, the last day of June, I leave Sanli Urfa. Today I will make it to the Mediterranean Sea. I stop at a truck stop around noon, to check my map and make sure I am still on the road to Adana. I decide to stop for lunch, and once again see only men inside. I motion to the receptionist, who is a man, if I can come in. He waves for me to enter. I order rice and beans, which is accompanied by a basket of fresh bread and butter. As I eat I enjoy watching the men checking out my bike parked outside the window, and who occasionally turn and gawk at me.

Continuing on, I arrive at Mersin around 3:00 and look for a room close to the sea. I am delighted to discover that the beach is only four blocks away. In Turkey people are actually allowed to wear bathing suits, even bikinis. I change into knee-length shorts, a t-shirt and sandals, and go for a walk on the beach.

In the city streets I find water coolers situated on sidewalks, with a glass on top. I watch people stop, take a drink, and return the glass to the top. Everyone uses the same glass. It makes me smile as I think of how germ conscious we have become in the West. Even bread here is stored unwrapped in open bins.

July 1 marks the beginning of my ride along the Mediterranean Sea. Just sixty-five kilometers west of Mersin I find a beautiful crescent-shaped beach with a hotel across the road. I stop to look around but do not plan on staying. I wonder what the price of a room at a hotel situated next to the beach would be, so decide to inquire. It is only fifteen million lira. The time is only 9:30 AM and I have been riding for less than an hour today, but the beach is so inviting I decide to stay. The owners of the hotel give me a big umbrella to take to the beach for protection from the sun. By 1:00 PM I feel the sun burning my skin, even though I have been sitting under the umbrella all this time.

Back at the hotel I shower and change into jeans and a t-shirt before going down for lunch. I have my usual tomato, cucumber, cheese, black olives, and bread—lots of bread. This is a typical Turkish breakfast but I eat it for lunch and dinner when I cannot find vegetarian meals. The Turks *do* love their meat.

I ask the owner of the hotel what there is to see nearby, and she tells me about an historical site and the Maiden Castle built out in the sea. Her fifteen-year-old daughter, Maika, offers to show me around. She hops on the back of my bike in shorts and sandals and away we go. We take a trail leading way up the hillside and walk through ruins that resemble an old city. The view of the ocean is spectacular from here. On our way down we pass a few homes, and in front of one sits a weathered old woman on a blanket by the side of the road. I want to take her picture, so Maika asks permission. She tells me this woman is one hundred years old.

A little farther down the hill we see three women in their yard sewing and weaving. The weather is so nice here, allowing them to work outside.

We stop in front of a huge arched gate and walk back to a large open theatre constructed with rock, and built into the hillside. Rows and rows of rock seats, forming a crescent shape, make their way up the slope. The weeds and small brush are slowly taking over. Maybe one day all this will be restored.

Back on the main highway we stop to see the Maiden Castle. It is situated two hundred meters from the shoreline on a tiny islet in the sea, and was once connected by a bridge to the castle Korikos. Today the bridge can be seen below the surface of the water. Both these castles date back to the second century.

When we return to the hotel I offer to pay Maika, but she says, "No, no money." I present her with a Canadian pin and she is thrilled with that. In two years she starts college and is excited about going to another country, possibly Italy, to study.

July 2 is another short riding day. I leave the hotel riding west, and very shortly thereafter, take a right turn up a mountain road to some ruins. There is a spectacular view of a deep crevice running between two mountains, and a walking trail leading down the side of the mountain to some carvings in the rocks. I take the trail and very quickly it becomes narrow, with a steep drop into the crevice on one side and the wall of the mountain on the other. Before I realize it I am standing on a sharp ledge, clinging to the side of the mountain, and am frozen in my tracks. "Okay, Doris, don't panic. You made it down this far you can make it back up." I feel the panic grip my heart and make myself take a few deep breaths. Carefully I re-trace my steps, while clinging closely to the rocks.

I make it to the top and sit for a few moments, to allow the shaking to subside, before returning to my bike. I must be more cautious. If I had fallen off that ledge, no one would ever find me.

Carrying on to Silifke, I ride up a high hill to the castle overlooking the city. There is just so much to see here in Turkey; one could explore old castles and ruins for months.

At Bozyazi I try to find a hostel or budget hotel, with no luck. I pull into a large hotel bordering the sea, to inquire about budget accommodation. I park my bike and am met by a doorman at the front of the hotel. He does not speak much English, but escorts me to the front desk. When I pose my question to the manager, he says, "You stay here."

"I can't afford this place," I reply.

"How much you want to pay?" he asks.

"I can't afford this," I repeat.

With that the bargaining begins. I end up staying in a fabulous room overlooking the ocean, with the biggest outdoor pool I have ever seen. Breakfast and dinner are included for thirty-eight million liras, or thirty-eight dollars Canadian.

It is just after 3:00 PM so I have time to go for a walk on the beach and have a swim. The pool is truly exceptional. After a relaxing three hours I go back to my room and clean up for dinner. The buffet is delicious, with several vegetarian dishes, an array of fruit, and rice pudding for dessert.

I briefly consider staying here a few days, but I've been traveling so slowly I decide to continue on. In the morning I go down for a swim before breakfast, then pack up and leave.

A few kilometers down the road stands the Mamure Castle, constructed in the third century AD. It is built on a point that juts out into the sea. I have to stop and explore again. What an amazing place. Inside the gated compound sits a mosque that has been restored and is still used by the public to this day.

By mid afternoon I reach Antalya and try to find the *centrum*, or *old city center*. With all the one-way streets I get lost and end up stopping at an Internet café. After checking my e-mail I ask directions from the owner. He tells me I am just one block off the main area, and suggests I leave my bike here and walk. I am grateful. With my bike in front of the store he can keep an eye on it.

I walk to the historic center, called Kaleiçi or Old Antalya, which surrounds the Roman harbour. Once a prosperous port, it was enclosed by thick defensive stone and cement walls with several gates that could be sealed in case of an attack. The only gate intact is Hadrian's Gate, constructed in 130 AD to commemorate Emperor Hadrian's visit to the city. I walk through this grand gate to enter the historic city. The old clock tower still stands alongside the main street. Many buildings here date from Ottoman and Roman times, with some being restored as houses, boutiques, hotels, inns, pensions, and restaurants.

The next day I ride to Kas where I check into a pension for ten million liras. I will stay here two days and do short trips to see the sights. My pension is up a steep hill from the town center, so I get my exercise several times a day. Kas is a nice little town with small shops and patio restaurants, where I relax and enjoy the sunshine.

July 6 is a full day. I head out early and ride back to Demre to see the Myra tombs and the Roman amphitheatre built in the side of the mountain. The exact date of construction of Myra is not known, but it is believed to date back to before the fifth century. The city is well known for the largest amphitheatre in the Lycian Union.

Ropes are strung along the walk leading up the mountain to the tombs, which are off limits to tourists, but I still have a grand view from the top of the amphitheatre. Twenty-nine rows of cement seats, built into the hill in a half circle, form the main seating area. Another seven rows extend above those, with a walkway running behind them. I sit in the top row and visualize what it must have been like to watch a sword duel, or a live play, or an orchestra performing on the circular stage below. The sound must have been incredible. I can almost hear the music as I close my eyes and listen.

Back on the road I notice some ruins in a field off to my right, and decide to stop. There is a bicycle parked here and by the time I have my jacket and helmet off, a young man comes walking across the field. He stops and chats, and I learn that he is the owner of the bicycle and from a city less than two hundred kilometers from Stavropol, Russia. I tell him that Stavropol is where my father was born, and ask him to tell me about the city.

"It is a big city in a mountainous region, with many factories and businesses." He says.

I ask, "Would it be safe to travel there?"

"It would be fine to travel there," he replies. "There are paved roads that would be fine to travel by motorcycle."

This has been a very special encounter. It raises my hopes of getting to that area of Russia.

On my way back to Kas I stop at the Statue of St. Nicholas, who was laid to rest in one of the Myra tombs. Then on to Kekova to see the underwater ruins of an ancient city that was buried by an earthquake in 200 BC. The road down to the docks is a narrow, rough, dirt trail. As I get closer to the parking area I am flanked by tour guides promoting their boat cruises to see the sunken city. I ward them off until I get parked, then begin negotiating. One man offers a price almost half of all the rest, so I take it.

We cruise past Simena village where the Kalekoy Castle sits on top of the mountain, then around some islands that were once part of the sunken city. Here we can view the remains below. Before returning to the dock my captain stops his small ship in a secluded bay and goes down below. I begin to wonder if I need to jump overboard and learn to swim real fast. I am his only passenger and could be in a compromising position. In a few minutes he returns with two cups of tea. It does not take long for this man to ask me to spend the night on his ship.

He says, "I have not felt this excitement in three years. I was attracted to you as soon as you rode into the parking lot. I knew this was a special meeting."

"Are you sure it was me you were attracted to, and not my bike?" I ask. As soon as the words come out of my mouth I want to bite my tongue, but it is too late now. I quickly continue, "I have a son your age."

He puts his hand on his heart and says, "I am shocked that you would say that! What does it matter when it is from the heart?"

Where have I heard that before? Here I am once again with a very attractive, much younger man and I'm afraid that it could lead to danger. As I ride back to Kas I wonder if I made a mistake in not accepting his offer.

By July 9 I have already been in Turkey for two weeks. There is so much to see and do in this country; I could quite easily live here. Maybe I lived here in another lifetime.

I ride to Bodrum and find a room early in the day. Bodrum is situated on a beautiful peninsula on the southwest coast of Turkey. Fabulous beaches lining the coast make it a popular resort for foreign and local travelers alike. Some of its main attractions are the Castle of St. Peter, the Myndos Gate, and the Roman Amphitheatre built on a hillside overlooking the city.

The most prominent feature of Bodrum is the Castle of St. Peter, dating back to the eleventh century. The castle has undergone several uses including being a military base, a prison, and a public bathhouse. It was still used in World War One to successfully fight off the enemy. Now, with extensive restoration, it is one of the finest museums in this area.

From Bodrum I ride north up the coast bordering the Aegean Sea and stop at the ancient city of Ephesus (Efes). The city was founded somewhere around the tenth century BC. Much has been uncovered to reveal what must have once been a large and elegant city. Excavation is still taking place today. During the Christian era from the 50's AD, the Apostle Paul lived here and wrote several letters recorded in the Bible, including his letter to the Ephesians (about the people of Ephesus). St. John and the Virgin Mary, as well as other biblical figures, also lived here.

The entry fee of fifteen million lira is worth every penny. I rent a walking tour tape and take my time strolling through the pathways. It is impossible to describe the feelings one has experiencing such history. I sit for several minutes on the stone seats in the Great Amphitheatre, enjoying the scenery. This open-air theatre was capable of holding twenty-four thousand spectators. Workers are busy laying new rock tile on the central ground stage.

From here I take a short ride up a mountainside to the last home of the Virgin Mary. About halfway up I stop to take a picture of the gigantic statue of her, then continue up to the buildings believed to be where she lived her last years. This road up the mountain is a major pilgrimage route for dedicated followers.

My tourist map is dotted with historic castles built along the shoreline of the sea. I continue north up the coast, enjoying the panoramic view, but do not stop until Canakkale. Here I get a room and relax for a day. On July 14 I take a ferry to Eceabat on the Gallipoli Peninsula, on the European side of Turkey. I ride through the immaculately kept *Anzac Memorial* grounds. The first sites I come to are monuments commemorating the thousands of Australians and New Zealanders who lost their lives during the Gallipoli battles of World War I.

I continue on to the Turkish memorials. The scenery in every direction on the entire peninsula is breathtaking, but haunted by the hundreds of thousands of deaths that occurred in battles over the centuries.

At Malakara I get a room for the night. The past two mornings my bike has not been starting and I had to get a boost. I think I need a new battery. At my hotel in Malakara a young university student, riding a 250cc motorcycle, spots my bike and stops to talk. His name is Paul, and he is in awe of my Magna. I tell him about having to boost my battery the past two mornings, and he immediately offers to help by contacting his friend Lon.

They pull off the seat and take the battery out. The fluid is low, so

Lon takes it to a shop and tops it up. Once the battery is replaced I go riding for an hour, following Paul on his bike. He takes me on a short tour of the area.

It always amazes me how people appear when I need them. The Universe does provide and I thank the spiritual forces that look after me.

A few days ago I contacted a Servas host in Istanbul. Tugrul offered me a place to stay and gave me directions to Mecidiyekoy, the area where he lives in Istanbul. The freeway traffic is hectic, but after riding in Bangkok, this is mild. Tugrul works until 5:00, so I spend time browsing the shops in the area until I find one that has phone service. At a small shop owned by a father and son who speak good English, I call Tugrul to tell him where I am. He instructs me to stay where I am and tells me he will meet me after work.

Tugrul arrives at about 5:30 and gives me directions to his apartment block, not far from here. He lives in a two-bedroom suite on the third floor of a walk-up apartment. Across the road is a fenced lot where I can park my motorcycle.

I feel very comfortable here. Tugrul is about thirty years old and has been a Servas host for about three years. He joined while traveling, and became a host when he returned home. "You may stay as long as you like," he says. "I am going to visit my parents in Ankara on the weekend, so just come and go as you please."

Over the next few days I get my eyes examined and buy new glasses, go to the Russian Embassy, spend some time sightseeing, inquire about motorcycle insurance, take my bike to a motorcycle shop, and meet some other Servas hosts who are friends of Tugrul's.

At the Russian Embassy the clerk tells me I need a letter of reference from the Canadian Embassy *and* an invitation letter from Russia to get a visa in my passport.

I easily obtain a letter of reference from the Canadian Embassy for fifty dollars. I search out a travel agent and find that I can get the invitation letter from Russia for a hundred dollars US. I fill out my application and am told to come back on Tuesday. Today is Friday and not much will happen over the weekend.

On Saturday I get my motorcycle into a shop that handles big bikes. They do a complete service job, including new chain and sprockets and new tires. They do not have the size of battery I need, but I have not had any problems since the fluid was topped up, so maybe it will be okay. It feels so good to have everything back in top shape.

Finding a place that will sell me insurance is not so easy. The people at the optical shop introduce me to another biker, Tansel, who helps me out. We try a couple of agencies, with no success, and then go to "Turing," a similar organization to our Canadian Automobile Association. They issue two weeks of insurance for eighty euro—that is all they can sell me. This is not good.

It is fortunate that I have met Tansel because his assistance is invaluable. When we finish at Turing we go for a ride. I follow him on his 1400 Suzuki Intruder along the Bosphorus Strait, dividing Istanbul into two continents (Europe and Asia) and connecting the Black Sea and the Sea of Marmara. I now realize why my border crossing from Iran to Turkey was a little difficult. I was entering the Asian side of Turkey, and at the time, I had no idea Turkey was part of two continents.

Back at the travel agency on Tuesday morning I find that the Russian Embassy will not give me a visa unless I have the visa for Bulgaria, Romania, and Ukraine in my passport first. They also tell me I cannot get the paperwork to take my motorcycle into Russia.

I ponder the situation for a few minutes, then decide to scrap going to Russia. By the time I wait for all these visas to be approved, and find out who will issue the paperwork for my bike, I will get to northern Russia too late in the fall. I do not want to be riding there after September or October.

I return to Tugrul's apartment and study my maps so I can plan a different route. I will go to Greece and Italy, and then make my way as far north as the season permits.

Turkey has been an amazing adventure, and a country I would love to spend a few months touring. The history is fascinating and I only touched a small part of it. Maybe I will come back one day, but for now I must continue.

On Thursday, July 24, 2003, I leave Turkey

Chapter 7
Eastern Europe

— Greece

On Thursday, July 24, 2003 I cross the border into Greece at Ipsala. This is the fastest crossing since Malaysia. The customs officer at the Turkey border stamps my passport and carnet de passage, then sends me on my way. Two kilometers farther I reach the Greece border gate where the officer stamps my passport and sends me to the next customs booth. The officer at this check post looks at my passport then hands it back.

"Don't you need paperwork for my bike?" I ask.

He waves his arm in dismissal and says, "Goodbye."

After all the hassles at previous border crossings this is great, not even a fee. I hope all of Europe is like this.

I ride the expressway until I reach Alexandroupoli. Somehow I miss the exit. My thoughts are to keep riding, but something makes me turn around and find the exit. It is 5:00 PM by the time I check into the Santa Rosa Beach Hotel and Campground. My room is thirty-five euros, a huge shock to the pocket book. One euro is equal to 1.6 Canadian dollars. I will definitely have to buy another tent and renew my Hostel International membership. I had left my tent in Australia since I was quite sure I would not camp in Asia.

When I park my bike in front of my room I see a bike with Italian license plates. Shortly thereafter I meet my neighbours Enrica and Paolo. They plan to travel for six months, and are destined for Australia. As we are enjoying ourselves over dinner, someone mentions the Servas organization. Paolo says they have made arrangements to stay with Tugrul in Istanbul.

Isn't that amazing! I just came from Tugrul's home. Now what are the chances of us meeting in Greece, not knowing each other and having this common thread? It must be destiny.

Enrica and Paolo give me some good travel information for my journey across Greece and Italy.

The next morning we say our goodbyes and continue in different directions. By noon I feel tired so I pull off the road high on a hill overlooking a beautiful valley near Thessalonika. The sun is shining and I stretch out on my bike for a short nap.

At Katarina I check for a room. The first hotel is forty euros. The clerk kindly directs me to the Hotel Elizabeth where I get a room for eighteen. That's a much better price. Since my younger sister is named Elizabeth, I figure this will be a good place to stay.

The following day I ride on to Thessaly and Meteora in the center of Greece. Enrica and Paolo stressed that I should not miss this area. The Greek word *Meteora* means *suspended in air*.

I find a room in the city of Kalampaka, and then ride up into the rocks that have eroded into majestic peaks reaching up to six hundred meters. On top of the pinnacles, medieval monks built their monasteries.

At one time over twenty monasteries crowned these rocks, today fewer remain, but six of those are still operational. One cannot drive to the top; the only way is to park and take the paths that have been carved and built around the edge, circling the rock or switching back and forth until it reaches the monastery.

I park my bike and trek the path to the top of one monastery. I cannot even imagine the work it took to haul building materials and supplies all the way up. Out of one window I see a large steel box attached to a heavy steel cable running from the monastery to the parking level far below. This is what the monks use to transport supplies today. I tour through all the open rooms and find one containing many antique items including wine barrels, large glass jugs wrapped in wicker, steel bowls, baskets of grapes, and shelves lined with skulls and bones. I wonder if these are the skulls of expired monks.

From the top I look down on the road winding through the surrounding mountains and rock pinnacles. I must ride those roads when I return to my bike. Far below is the city of Kalampaka and the view is spectacular. This is a popular place for rock climbers and I notice several people clinging to the sides of the mountain as I ride back into town.

On July 28, after only five days in Greece, I ride to Igoumenitsa on the west coast to board a ferry for Italy. This is an overnight crossing and it is 9:30 PM before I am allowed to ride my bike into the loading area. For an hour I sit and watch as big semi trucks back their trailers onto the ferry. What a skill. The most impressive display is by two drivers backing tandem trailers into their stalls. At 10:30 the attendant signals for me to ride onto the deck. My spot will allow me to be the first off tomorrow morning.

I climb to the top outer deck and find my sleeping spot on top of a ten-foot box containing emergency survival equipment. Many other passengers have secured their places on similar objects on deck. It is after midnight when I place my jacket under my upper body with the sleeves crossed for a pillow under my head, and fall sound asleep. It seems like I have just fallen asleep when I hear a voice in the distance, calling "Hello." At first I cannot comprehend, but the voice persists and becomes louder. Eventually, pulled from my sleep, I lift my head to see a young black man with tight curly hair standing by me. He asks if he can share my sleeping space.

I look around and notice many passengers are now sleeping on deck and in every available spot on boxes, containers, and the floor. My pedestal is quite large so I say, "Yes, go ahead." I pull my small backpack securely under my head and close my eyes.

My new companion keeps talking and introduces himself as Peter, from Jamaica. It seems like he wants to visit, but I have to tell him I am too tired to talk. He kindly stops chatting and I drift back to sleep.

— *Italy*

I awaken early to watch the sun rise over the sea. The air is warm and I feel comfortable in my short-sleeved t-shirt. Every muscle, bone, and joint in my body aches. I should have brought my sleeping bag up—that would have provided some cushioning on the wooden box.

Our ferry docks in the Port of Brindisi, Italy, on July 29. I watch in amazement as we sail past the walls of an old fort extending for hundreds of meters out into the sea. By 8:30 AM the large ramp opens and I ride off the ship. I watch for an Immigration and Customs booth but do not see one, and soon find myself out on the highway. Not having to deal with customs is great, but I would love to have a stamp in my passport for all the countries I travel through.

For the next twelve days I ride from Brindisi to Naples, Rome, Pisa, Florence, and Venice. The roads are great and I meet many touring bikes along the way. It is good to see people wearing helmets and proper riding gear. Finally I do not feel so conspicuous.

I take Highway E90/SS7 across the heel of Italy to Taranto, situated in the arch of the boot, on the Gulf of Taranto in the Ionian Sea. Hotel prices are very high here so I continue on to Matera and find a room for fifty euros.

The attraction in Matera is the ancient city of "Sassi di Matera," meaning "Stones of Matera." This prehistoric city was built into the rock going up the side of the mountain. Dwellings are really only caverns or caves, and as you continue higher you drive on streets built on the rooftops of houses below. Tourism has inspired the government to promote the restoration of Sassi and one is now able to walk through passageways and dwellings to see how people of that era lived. Many great movies have been made here, including Mel Gibson's *The Passion of the Christ*.

Leaving Matera I follow the SS99 to Altamura, another city that sits atop the ruins of an ancient city built into the rocks. I ride southwest on secondary roads across country until I reach Potenza and a major highway, E847. The roads I have been taking are a biker's dream— plenty of curves surrounded by hills, valleys, farms, vineyards, green trees, blue sky, and fresh air. I notice all the bicycle trails running alongside the highways in many areas, and think of my daughter and how she would love it here.

I spend one night in Potenza and hit the road early the next morning on my way to Calitri. Enrica and Paola had recommended *Il Tufello B&B* out in the countryside nearby. I find the B&B built high on a hill overlooking farmland. It is owned and operated by two wonderful women, Elizabeth and Annie, who are each around fifty-five years old.

A storm has moved in this evening and prohibits me from riding into town for dinner. Elizabeth knocks on my door around 8:00 PM carrying a tray containing a basket of freshly baked bread, cheese, and fruit. How wonderful is that! These two women are so helpful they even phone to reserve a room for me at a hostel in Naples.

There is no rush to leave the following morning, as the distance to Naples is less than one hundred and fifty kilometers. I relax and enjoy my morning over breakfast with these two great women. They make sure I take down their phone number and insist that I call if I run into any problems.

It is mid morning when I leave, riding west on the SS7 until I reach E842. My ride is very enjoyable, the road is good, and the weather is great. Upon reaching Naples I encounter the usual busy city traffic, so it takes me an hour to find the hostel. When I finally do locate it I must ride up a steep switchback road, wide enough for one vehicle, to the hostel gates. The gateposts are square brick pillars about three meters high, supporting large gates made of black wrought iron. A smaller pedestrian gate borders one side and there is an intercom mounted on one post. I buzz the reception and the large gates open for me to ride in. I appreciate the security.

The first thing on my agenda is to renew my Hostelling International membership while checking in. This will keep my accommodation costs down.

This hostel is a grand old building that looks like it could have been a school or hospital, or maybe a monastery, at one time. There are three floors consisting of a male wing, female wing, and co-ed wing. The kitchen and cafeteria are on the second floor where guests can buy meals at a reasonable price. The staircases are at least three meters wide with dark polished wood banisters. Looking at the wood finishing and decor inside the building indicates it was once a prestigious place. Maybe it was an old palace.

I haul my things up three flights of stairs and secure a bed in the room I have been assigned. Then I change into lighter clothes and go for a walk. The view from the courtyard of the hostel overlooks the sea, hills, and part of the city. I wander down and follow a street running alongside the waterfront to find a restaurant. When I pay my bill I encounter my first rude Italian. I was not given a bill so I ask the cashier how much.

She replies, "In Italy you speak Italian, in America you speak English." I am shocked! I bite back the urge to tell her maybe she is the reason this restaurant is empty.

Back at the hostel I meet Djemica Chouiref from Paris. We have a great visit and she invites me to stay with her when I reach Paris. I will certainly look her up.

I spend two nights in Naples then continue on to Rome. I follow the costal highway for over half the distance, and then take the SS7 northwest to Rome. I locate the hostel Djemica had recommended and check in. This place is extremely busy and check-in is slow. When it is finally my turn the young man tells me they don't have a bed available. If I want to wait for an hour he may have someone checking out this morning. I decide to wait, and luck is with me—I get a room.

There is so much to see in all these cities in Italy that I could stay a week or two in each, but with the exchange at the moment being approximately two Canadian dollars to one euro, the cost of traveling here is way above my budget.

I spend two days in Rome visiting a few places, but the most impressive is the Basilica di San Pietro (St. Peter's Basilica) in Vatican City. The artwork and architecture are indescribable. I stand in awe gazing at the carved pillars, arches, sculptures, paintings, and marble floors—priceless works of art. I take the tour up to the dome of the Basilica and get a bird's eye view of Piazza San Pietro below.

The "Dome," designed by Michelangelo, stretches forty-two meters in diameter and rises almost one hundred and thirty-eight meters above the street. Although Michelangelo was not the only artist/architect/ engineer who worked on the Basilica, he was the major contributor.

I walk along the canal to a large open plaza surrounded by magnificent old buildings. In the center stands a tall pillar adorned with a cross, and steps surrounding the base. Streets branch out from the circular plaza like spokes on a wheel. I relax on the steps and enjoy the amazing architecture and the activity around me.

August 4, 2003—today is my second anniversary since leaving Edmonton to begin my travels around the world. I have only been in seventeen countries and have put 75,300 kilometers on my bike. There are still so many countries I want to see. I wonder how long it will take to complete my dream.

I follow Highway E80 and SS1, which run parallel to the Mediterranean Sea, and head north to Pisa. I stop along the sea a few times to enjoy the scenery, and reach Pisa by mid afternoon. I locate a hostel out of town following a twisty road a few kilometers into the hills. It provides sleeping rooms only; there are no kitchen facilities. The luxury of having my own wheels is of great benefit here. Over the next day and a half I do a walking tour of the city of Pisa and see more of the area on my bike.

Pisa lies at the mouth of the Arno River bordering the Ligurian Sea. Canals lined with noble buildings snake their way through various parts of the city. This was the birthplace of Galileo in 1564, and today is the site of an important and busy university city.

The Leaning Tower of Pisa is definitely leaning, however I had imagined it to be much taller. It is a wonder I don't get lost traipsing through the web of narrow, medieval alleys to the Piazza dei Miracoli, *Square of Miracles*.

This evening I send an e-mail to Benka Palko in Slovenia. She is the woman who traveled for six years around the world on her F650 BMW. The stories and pictures she posted on her Web site were a big inspiration to me and played a huge part in my decision to finally live my dream. We have kept in contact via e-mail, and now I must let her know that I will be in Slovenia soon. It would be wonderful to meet her.

From Pisa I ride to Florence, a mere one hundred kilometers away, and spend the day admiring more ancient architecture surrounding the Piazza Del Duomo and San Maria Del Fiore. My camera battery is dead. I kick myself for not checking it last night. Before calling it a day I buy postcards to compensate for my lack of photographs.

The hostel I book is full but has large, six-bed tents available. I take one and have a wonderful sleep. The last few places I stayed had no air conditioning or fans and were very hot. In the tent I am able to open all the flaps and have a nice breeze blowing through all night. Fabulous!

The next morning, August 7, I ride north to Venice on the east coast. Venice is known as the *Queen of the Adriatic, City of Water, City of Bridges* and the *City of Light*. It stretches across one hundred and ten small islands in the Venetian Lagoon along the Adriatic Sea. Vehicles are not allowed on the city streets—transportation between islands is by water taxi and in the city, by foot.

I arrive at a huge parkade where I must leave my motorcycle. There is no way I can carry all my things from my bike, so I contemplate not staying. But then, I cannot bear to miss Venice when I am right here. I talk to the parking attendant, and he assures me my bike and belongings will be safe. I shed my riding gear and stuff them into one of the rolls on my back seat, exchange my riding boots for runners, rearrange clothes and toiletries into my backpack, and strap my sleeping bag to the bottom. I tie my helmet to the handle bar, place the disk lock on the front wheel, and cover my bike. Then I make one final check before I leave. Loaded down with all that I can carry, I walk, what seems like a mile, to the boat docks.

I inquire about a boat to take me to the hostel and then buy my ticket. The boat takes us across the open waters of the lagoon before entering the canals and eventually stopping right in front of the youth hostel. Wow, am I ever glad about that. Checking in early allows me to secure a top bunk right next to an open window.

There is not a moment to waste, as I will only be here two days. I make a conscious decision not to worry about my bike and trust that all will be intact when I return. I do a walking tour of the island, then spend a relaxing evening watching the water taxis cruise up and down the canal carrying tourists to and fro, and watching the sun set over the peaks of the majestic buildings across the canal. It is very peaceful. No vehicle traffic noise, just the boats as they dock along the sidewalk, and pull away again.

The next morning I take a boat across the canal to tour St. Mark's Square and St. Mark's Basilica, both built in the tenth to twelfth century. Maria, a Milanese woman who has been her before, and shares my hostel room, accompanies me. She is a wealth of information. The Basilica is spectacular. The architecture and works of art are as impressive as St. Peter's Basilica. We walk to the "Gates of Rialto"—a stone arch bridge 28.8 meters long, crossing over the Grande Canal. The "Ponte di Rialto" opened in 1591 and is the oldest of three bridges spanning the Grande Canal. After lunch Maria and I part ways and I continue poking through this beautiful part of Venice before taking a boat back to the hostel. I wish I could spend a week here, but I feel uncertain my bike would be safe for that long.

When I return to my bike the morning of August 9, I find everything just as I left it. I find my way to Highway E55 and ride northeast around the north end of the Adriatic Sea to Slovenia.

Upon leaving Italy I ask the border official if he will stamp my passport. I have to explain to him that I am traveling around the world and would like a stamp verifying that I was in Italy. He graciously obliges and leaves his booth to come and stamp my passport.

— *Slovenia*

On August 9, 2003 I cross the border into Slovenia. Once again I request a stamp in my passport and the officer grants my wish.

The scenery riding through Slovenia is spectacular with views of the Alps in the distance, grassy green hills and valleys, rivers and lakes, and forested areas. It is a very small country with forests covering half the area and twenty-six thousand kilometers of rivers and streams. It is referred to as a little *Garden of Eden*.

I have received a reply to the e-mail I sent Benka, so I will call her when I arrive in Ljubljana, the capital city of Slovenia.

When I arrive in the city I follow signs for *Centro*. After traveling into so many cities over the past two years I seem to have developed an instinct for finding my way around. When I stop I am near the center of the city. I check my map to locate the hostel I'm booked into and find that it is only three blocks away. I reach the hostel and find a long line of people waiting to check in. It is a good thing that I booked ahead. After dropping my things in my room I call Benka and arrange to meet her tomorrow. I occupy the rest of the afternoon and evening walking to the canal and the large central square.

The next morning I meet Benka for coffee and have a wonderful time sharing travel stories. She has recently completed her six-year trip around the world on an F650 BMW. Her travels took her into eighty-eight countries on seven continents, securing her a place in the *Guinness Book of World Records*. Since she returned home to Slovenia she has been compiling a coffee-table book of pictures from around the world. It will go to print in a couple of weeks.

We take a drive to Benka's apartment where I meet her sister and mother. Before I leave Benka offers me her tent—the one she used while traveling around the world. I feel honored to have it and will make good use of it.

I must try and get insurance for my bike here, so Benka gives me the names of two agencies she is sure will help me. The following day I visit both agencies, but, once again, I leave without insurance. One of the agents wants to sell me two weeks of insurance for Slovenia, but I will be leaving tomorrow and need it to cover me in Austria as well. I will try again in Austria.

I leave Ljubljana at about 8:30 the morning of August 12. The temperature is nice for riding, but a little cooler than it had been through Italy. Occasionally I notice a castle perched at the top of the rocks—what a great view they must have from there. As I travel farther north, the mountains become hills and make way for rich farmland. The ride is so enjoyable that in no time at all I have reached the border to Austria. The border guard does not even look at my passport and when I ask for a stamp he waves me on as if to say, "Don't bother me."

— Austria

By the time I reach Vienna I have covered about four hundred kilometers of a most spectacular ride. I stop at a tourist information building to pick up a city map and ask about hostels. The attendant is a man about sixty, and when I ask where the hostels are, he says, "You are taking the space from the young people. Don't you have any money?"

I want to say, "We're not all rich old bats like you." I quickly leave before I lose my cool and tell him off. I had been told that some of the European countries do not allow adults to use hostels, but so far I have encountered all ages at them. I believe times are changing. Even the name has been changed from *Youth Hostel* to *Hostelling International.*

I decide to look for a campground and find one in the city. I get a nice grassy spot near some trees for nine euros. Tonight I will use Benka's tent for the first time.

On Wednesday, August 13, I ride to the Polish Embassy just to find it closed today and tomorrow. Instead of staying two more days I decide to pack up and ride to the Czechoslovakian border. I will obtain a Polish visa at the Embassy in Praha (Prague). It is a pleasant ride through green hills of farmland, and I soon arrive at the border. I exchange one hundred euros for the equivalent in Czech koruna and have lunch before exiting Austria. The female officer is quite intrigued by the number of stamps in my passport and takes her time examining them all. She asks if I am traveling around the world before stamping it and handing it back.

A short distance farther and I arrive at the Czech Republic border. I hand over my passport and the officer asks for my visa. I state, "I am from Canada, I do not need a visa."

The officer assures me that I do. He is very kind and tells me I will have no problem entering the country when I have a visa in my passport.

How embarrassing. How could I have missed this? I feel certain the government Web site advised that I did not need a visa for the Czech Republic, just for Poland. Anyway, I am not allowed to enter so I must turn around and ride back to Vienna.

In Vienna I follow a sign to another campground located high on a hill overlooking the River Danube. The place is packed with tents and RV's, but I get a spot amongst rows and rows of others placed side-by-side and front to back. Not much room for privacy here.

The next morning I ride to the Czechoslovakian and Polish embassies. After filling out the appropriate forms at the Czech Embassy the clerk says to come back on Wednesday for my visa. I ask if it can be ready any sooner, and she says to call her on Monday. I guess that will have to do.

At the Polish embassy they keep my passport and tell me to come back on Tuesday. After a lengthy discussion I convince the clerk to have it ready for Monday. Without my passport I will not be traveling too far.

I still need to find motorcycle insurance for Europe. Other travelers had told me that I could get a green card providing insurance coverage for all of Europe. I ride to Stephansplatz and find a couple of insurance offices, but they will not insure me. One agent directs me to Donau Insurance and gives me the address. I search for the building but never do find it. I also watch for a bike shop in hopes of getting a new battery. The shops I have checked to date did not carry the right size.

Today is Thursday and since I can't get my visas until Monday I have three and a half days to tour Vienna. I visit the Schonbrunn Palace and St. Stephen's Church, spend one whole day in the Kunsthistorisches Museum (Museum of Fine Arts), relax and read in Stephen's Platz (a lovely park), ride the metro, and stroll along the River Danube. Several restaurants line sections of the river and I find one that makes excellent falafel sandwiches and where I can sit out and enjoy the surroundings. It is fortunate that I was sent back to Vienna. I would have missed all this.

At my campground I meet Bernard, from the Netherlands, who is camped two tents over and driving a beat-up old truck. He is an interesting man and we have some great conversations over coffee. I tell him about my visa episodes, my difficulty finding insurance, and my problem finding a battery for my bike.

Bernard's reply is quite profound. "Whatever you need, will come to you. If I need a radiator, one will show up."

I agree with his line of thought, but sometimes need a reminder not to worry about things.

On Monday morning I pack up my camping gear, ride to the Poland Embassy and wait for the doors to open. My passport is returned with the visa stamp filling one page. I immediately ride to the Czech Embassy to find the room full and a long line out the door. I decide not to wait and ride to McDonald's for breakfast. I am having second thoughts about going this direction. Maybe I should just ride to Germany and omit the northeast part of Europe. I would like to go to Finland, but maybe it is already too late in the season.

I must make up my mind. Instead of picking up my Czech visa I decide to stay one more night and check into the campground where I stayed upon arrival in Vienna. By the end of the day I decide to go to Germany and skip Czech Republic, Poland, and places farther north.

— *Czech Republic & Poland*

By Tuesday, August 19, I have been in Vienna a week. I am up early and packing my gear, with my mind made up that I would go directly to Germany. But when I start riding I suddenly decide to go back to the Czech Embassy and pick up my visa. I arrive at 8:00 AM, before the doors open, and am the first person in line when the key is turned at 8:30. The clerk pastes the visa into my passport, using another whole page. I guess my mind is made up. I reach the Czech border at about 11:00, have my visa stamped, and ride on towards Prague.

The countryside is pretty and very clean with rolling hills, farmland, and lots of trees. People seem calm and laid back. The food is inexpensive and good, reminding me of my mom's cooking. I ride in misty rain part of the day and by 4:30 in the afternoon am ready to call it a day. I find a campground, set up my tent, and enjoy a relaxing evening visiting with other guests.

The next morning I ride out at 7:30. Traffic is hectic riding through Prague so I keep to a main freeway through the city. I will miss seeing the historic buildings and museums but I decide to continue on. The highway goes through a lot of small towns and cities, making traveling slow today. I cross the border to Poland at about 11:00 AM. The officer smiles as he studies my passport. It is obvious they see more motorcyclists here at the borders than they do in the Asian countries.

The highway changes drastically once I cross into Poland. A lot of heavy semi trucks run these roads, leaving sunken tracks ten to twelve centimeters deep. The pavement is obviously too soft to handle the weight. Sometime mid afternoon I stop and take a picture of the lucky 7s (77777.7) on my odometer. The date is August 20, 2003.

I have been watching for a campground since about 4:00, with no luck. I end up riding until 9:00 PM before checking into a hotel. It has been a long day.

In the morning I ride into the city of Warsaw to see a bit of the architecture. I do not seem to be in the mood for sightseeing today and quickly find my way out again. In a city of 1.6 million or more, driving can be tense.

— *Lithuania*

I continue north to Lithuania. As I near the border crossing I pass a long line of big trucks pulling long trailers stopped along the side of the road. The line continues for six kilometers, moving only inches at a time. Just before reaching the border gates a female security officer stops me and asks if I have motorcycle insurance. This is just what I've been dreading.

I quickly ask, "Where do I get insurance?"

"Right here," she replies, waving to her little booth.

A flood of relief washes over me and I gladly follow her to the booth and buy insurance to travel in Lithuania. The currency here is the *lita* and at this date one Canadian dollar is equal to 2.2 litas.

I pass another six kilometers of trucks before reaching the border gates. Once into Lithuania the first noticeable difference is the flatter landscape and rundown farm buildings. Buildings are old and most are left unpainted. I can see for great distances across fields of crops and pastures. As I get closer to the cities, yards and buildings are better kept.

I reach Vilnius, the capital city of Lithuania, and look for campgrounds. When I stop at a hotel and ask, the clerk tells me they do not have campgrounds. I find a nice Guesthouse for one hundred and twenty litas, which includes breakfast. The owners are wonderful and very helpful in suggesting things to see. My bike is parked outside the front door near a pillar, which I use as a hitching post. I seldom use this chain and usually only attach my disk lock to the front wheel; but the owner suggests that I should also chain the bike to the post.

First on my agenda is to inquire about visas for Latvia and Estonia. Today is Friday and nothing is open on the weekends so I expect I will have to wait until Monday. I phone the embassies and learn that I do not need a visa for Latvia but I do for Estonia. They are closed until Tuesday and the visa will cost three hundred dollars US. The voice on the other end says, "If you want to wait an extra three days it will be forty dollars US for a transit visa."

My reason for going farther north is to get to Finland, then make my way north to Nordkapp, Norway by the end of August. That is now looking impossible. I feel I would be sacrificing the experience just to say I have reached the most northerly point of the continent. I'm not sure that is such a wise choice. I must re-evaluate.

It is already the third week of August and getting late in the season to travel into northern Finland and Norway so I decide to scrap Latvia and Estonia and take a ferry to Sweden. I check out the ferry schedules and find that one sails from Klaipeda to Sweden on Tuesday at 5:00 PM.

That gives me more than three days to see the sights of Vilnius, work on my web pages and just relax. I barter with the Guesthouse owner for a lower price since I will be staying five nights. He offers a small discount.

On Friday I do a walking tour of the old city. The Vilnius University borders a large square or courtyard and is the oldest and most famous university in northeastern Europe. It was founded in 1579 as an "Establishment of Higher Education" and developed into the most notable scientific and cultural center of the region, and the most notable scientific center of the Polish-Lithuanian Commonwealth. I spend the day touring the buildings surrounding the square.

Vilnius is a very pretty city with the Neris River running through its center. The *new* city center is built on the north side of the river and creates an impressive skyline.

The weekend is rainy and I am glad to be off the road. Light showers fall periodically during the day on Saturday, but the temperatures are still warm enough to go walking and feel comfortable. On Sunday it rains hard all morning so I spend the time working on my Web site. I walk to McDonald's for an ice cream and am joined by two men who are working in Dubai. They show a great interest in my travels and one man asks, "So when is the book coming out?"

On Tuesday morning I ride to Klaipeda on the west coast of Lithuania. My ship sails at 5:00 PM and will arrive in Sweden at 9:00 the next morning (10:00 Lithuania time).

Chapter 8

Western Europe

— Sweden

The date is August 27, when the ship docks in Karlskrona, Sweden. Seventeen hours have passed and we have crossed the Baltic Sea. I have managed to get a little sleep curled up on a lounge chair that reclines ever so slightly. The sky is laden with thick clouds and the air feels cold. I ride off the ship and follow Highway 30 north about a hundred kilometers, through scattered showers to Växjö where I stop to warm up. I appreciate my electric jacket today. Continuing on #30 to Jönköping I find the information center and hostel before going in search of hot food.

The next morning the sun is shining but I dress warmly, wearing my leggings under my jeans and riding pants, and my heated liner under my jacket. The air is like a cold spring or fall day in Canada.

Sweden has many lakes nestled amongst rolling green hills and trees. The highway is smooth with very little traffic, making for a peaceful ride. This area reminds me a little of Prince Edward Island with the rich green landscape and blues of the lakes and sky.

My Canadian dollar is worth 6.2 Swedish kronas but that does not lower my expenses. The cost of living here is very high. For example, fifty kronas only half fills my gas tank, which holds 13.5 liters. Traveling through Europe has been so expensive I have quit keeping track of my expenditures.

— *Norway*

When I reach the border to Norway I stop and follow some truckers into the office and ask where I can get my passport stamped. The clerk looks at me strangely and says, "You don't need to show your passport." That still boggles my mind.

From the border at Svinesund I ride north on E6 towards Oslo and find a nice campground on the outskirts of town for one hundred and thirty Norwegian kroners. One Canadian dollar is worth 5.3 Norwegian kroners. Norway is a spectacular country with roads winding around sparkling blue lakes and lush green hills.

On August 29 I ride to Oslo for breakfast, then head west and south through periods of rain for much of the morning. It is cloudy and very cold and I have my heated liner turned up as high as it will go. By late morning the sun peeks through the clouds and brightens up this gorgeous landscape. I continue south on Highway 41 until I reach Norway's south coast. I find a wonderful little campground at Lillesand, bordering a fiord coming off the sea. I pitch my tent with the door facing the water so I can enjoy the view as long as possible. This is a quiet little place with not too many people around. I relax and enjoy the tranquility.

The next day I ride to Horten and take the ferry to Moss, Sweden for forty Norwegian kroners. I encounter more twisty roads, great scenery, many lakes, trees, small towns, and immaculate country yards as I ride back into Sweden. The sun is shining but I still have to turn on my heated liner. I reach Göteborg late in the afternoon and find a campground only to discover I need to buy a camping card, which is needed for all campgrounds here, for ninety Swedish kronas. On top of this I pay a hundred and sixty kronas for a spot to pitch my tent. I consider looking for a hostel, but it is getting late and I want to get settled before dark. It surprises me that the campground is so crowded this late in the season, considering how cold it is.

The following morning, at my first stop for fuel, the teller points out that I am using kroners, not kronas. The money looks the same to me. It ticks me off that the campground staff didn't mention this.

Now I realize I paid even more for my camp spot since the Norwegian currency is worth more than the Swedish currency.

— *Denmark*

Today, August 31, I will cross the new bridge joining Sweden and Denmark. The bridge crosses the Oresund Strait from Malmö, Sweden to Copenhagen, Denmark, and was officially opened July 1, 2000. It has one of the longest cable stayed main spans in the world at four hundred and ninety meters, with a total length of almost eight kilometers. This stretch of the bridge bends in the shape of a quarter moon and arches up two hundred and four meters above the water, descending again onto the artificial island of Peberholm for four kilometers, then into a tunnel for another four kilometers on the Danish side. I look forward to seeing and riding over this bridge, but when I arrive, much to my disappointment, fog has obliterated all sight of it. I can barely see a meter in front of me, and am not even aware of the point at which I reach the bridge. I feel like I am riding on water in the middle of the ocean. Water crystals bead up on my windshield and face shield, making it very difficult to see. I turn my flashers on to make myself more visible to other vehicles and keep a slow but steady speed. It seems like an eternity before the bridge descends toward the island and the fog lifts and I am able to see again. I go through the tunnel and soon enter Denmark.

In the heart of Copenhagen I find a room, including breakfast, for four hundred krones. One Canadian dollar is worth 4.77 Danish krones. I spend the evening wandering through busy cobblestone streets until 9:00 PM. Normally I would not be out this late but I'm only spending one night here so I must see as much as possible.

The cool, rainy weather is a concern and I know I must not linger long in the northern part of Europe. The sun is shining when I leave Copenhagen but by the time I reach the next long bridge it is raining. This bridge is seventeen kilometers in total length and crosses the Great Belt, a strait between the main Danish islands of Zealand and Fyn. As I ride up the first arched section fog thickens and rain pours down, making visibility nil. I could be sailing out to sea on my two wheels. Visibility improves slightly as the bridge descends onto an island for about two kilometers, then worsens again as I ride over the second half, arching high over the water. It would be so wonderful to go across here in nice weather.

— Germany

When I reach Kiel, Germany I stop for the day. I'm cold and miserable from riding in rain most of the day. I find a nice room in the Hotel Zum Fritz, run a hot bath, and relax for the evening.

Next morning the sun is shining. I don't feel like riding after the last few days of rain, so I decide to stay one more day in Kiel. It is a pretty little city situated along the Baltic Sea.

Today, while visiting the aquarium, I experience a major shift in my awareness and attention to detail. I have visited other aquariums in the past and enjoyed the colorful fish and plant life, but today is different—today it seems like I am seeing all this for the very first time. I watch in wonder as the fish take in water as we do air, and as the plants swaying in the water provide food and beauty. I notice one large fish feeding on a green plant and imagine the plant saying, "Go ahead, eat lots, I will grow more." I also see sharks swim in harmony with dozens of other species, and wonder why we humans don't learn from them. A large flat fish floats down the glass to rest near another of its kind. If I listened closely I might hear it say, "Just stopped to say I love you." The whole experience leaves me wondering if I'm losing my marbles or if my travels have opened my senses to a greater level of awareness.

— Netherlands

Taking that sunny day out to enjoy the sights of Kiel has me riding in rain again. My plan was to ride to Berlin and see more of Germany, but it is very cold and miserable so I decide to head west to Amersfoort, Netherlands. I will be flying back home to Canada for a few weeks in September for a reunion with my children and grandchildren. My son Curtis and his partner Vanessa will be coming home from Australia for a visit. It will be more than four years since my children have all been together, so I must not miss this opportunity. My dear friend Jen has bought my plane ticket and contacted friends of hers in Amersfoort who will store my bike until I return. I feel so blessed!

I met Jen and her partner Martin when I was traveling in Malaysia.

We rode together for about two weeks and immediately became friends. We continue to stay in touch.

On September 9, 2003, I take the train to the Shiphole Airport in Amsterdam to catch my flight to Calgary, Alberta. In the boarding lounge I am questioned extensively about the Pakistan and Iran stamps in my Passport. They ask, "Why are you traveling alone?" and "Why are you returning to Amsterdam?"

I tell them my story about traveling around the world on my motorcycle and patiently answer all their questions. With the second anniversary of the Twin Tower disaster only two days away, there is tension in the air. I had not thought about this when I booked my flight. Finally, they allow me through the electronic security gates and I board the plane to Canada, with a connecting flight in Chicago.

I have not told anyone that I'm coming. In fact, in my e-mails to my daughter, Carey, and my sister, Liz, I told them my friend Jen was coming, and asked if one of them could please meet her at the airport.

I arrive at the airport in Calgary at 5:10 PM and wait for my backpack, which does not arrive. I go to Customer Service and put in a lost luggage claim before looking for my welcoming committee. No one! Absolutely no one has come to meet me (or my friend). My heart sinks and I want to cry. I guess this surprise thing was not such a good idea after all. I call Carey and Liz and leave a message on their machines. My plane has arrived about half an hour early so I pull myself together and walk the length of the airport. I will stop for coffee. Maybe they are on their way.

Before I reach the coffee shop I see Liz pushing a luggage cart down the corridor, squinting as she looks up at the monitors she passes along the way. I keep walking towards her, stop in front of her cart and say, "Are you looking for someone?"

She squints at me, hesitates for a moment (I'm sure she is looking for a much shorter person with long blond hair), then her face slowly changes to a mixture of surprise and delight. She is hugging me and saying, "Oh my God, Oh my God, Oh my God …" She shows me her handmade sign, "JEN FROM THE NETHERLANDS", and the description I had sent by e-mail.

As it turns out, my daughter had been at the hospital most of the day. Her partner, whom I have not yet met, has just had major back surgery. When I finally get to talk to her, she says, "I knew it, I knew it! I told my friends, I think my mom is playing a prank on me."

It is so great to be back home. I spend a wonderful six weeks visiting family and friends, and am especially grateful to see my three children and grandchildren together again. I begin to wonder if it will be difficult to return to The Netherlands and continue my journey.

It is distressing to see how much Mom's health has deteriorated over the past two years. I do not get to see some of my siblings and many of my friends, but I think of them all.

Liz's friend lends me his motorbike and I go for a ride with her, my brother, and sister-in-law. That is a special treat. My sister Liz just started riding since I left in 2001, and enjoys it as much as I do. I even have time to attend a "Women in the Wind" motorcycle meeting. I say a few words about my journey and extend an invitation to fellow members to join me on any part of my travels.

My motorcycle registration expired back in Thailand and now that I'm home I am able to renew it for eighteen months. That should be enough time for me to complete my journey around the globe and return home. Things simply have a way of working out.

On October 26 I catch my flight back to Amsterdam to resume my travels. I am excited about returning to my journey, but sad to leave my family once again. But this time I feel positive I will be home in a year.

My plane is scheduled to leave at 8:18 AM, but is delayed indefinitely due to mechanical failure. All the passengers are off-loaded and rebooked onto other flights. The second anniversary of the tragedy of 9/11 is still so real that this turn of events makes me a bit nervous. I manage to get booked onto another airline leaving at 1:10, happy that I do not have to wait another day. It is a long flight and I arrive in Amsterdam at 11:45 the next morning. I take the train to Amersfoort where my dear friends Martin and Jen are waiting for me. They have invited me to stay with them for awhile.

Over the next month I help my friends do some renovating and painting in their son's house, visit some of the sights in Holland, and take a trip to Rotterdam, the biggest seaport in the world. Jen and Martin are waiting for their BMW's to arrive at this port from Australia. We take a sightseeing boat up the canal and are amazed at the size and number of cranes working for hundreds of meters along the shoreline.

Thousands of containers stacked five or six levels high line one shore. Martin wonders which of these containers holds their bikes, and how long the processing will take before they are ready for pickup.

We visit the Euromast and take the elevator to the revolving viewing deck. What a spectacular view! This is the highest building in the Netherlands at 185 meters.

Rotterdam has some unique architecture. The Erasmus Bridge is one of the city's claim to fame. It is a cable-stay bridge stretching 808 meters across the Nieuwe Maas River, linking the north and south halves of the city. Steel cables slung over a 139-meter-high asymmetrical pylon support the bridge deck. This white pylon, with its graceful stance over the water, has earned the nickname "The Swan."

We walk through the area called Blaak to see the famous cube houses and pencil building designed by Dutch architect Piet Blom.

I spend three weeks in the Netherlands enjoying the company of my friends. I have not been riding my bike since my return from Canada, and now it won't start. I have tried everything but she just does not turn over. Is she punishing me for my thoughtless neglect? On November 21 I have Stuart, from Adventure Motor Sports, pick the bike up with his van and haul it to his shop. He has his mechanic do a complete service job and determines the fuel remaining in the carburetor was probably too stale to be of any use. With the service complete and a new front tire, she runs like new again.

I am able to get motorcycle insurance for the rest of my time in Europe—that is a relief. I find it amazing that insurance is so hard to obtain. Maybe foreign travelers pose too much of a risk.

Over these past few weeks I have been gathering information to ride into Africa. I would like to get to Cape Town, but it is impossible to ride through many of the neighboring states. I would have to ship my bike at least two times, possibly more, unless I were to fly directly to South Africa. In the end, I decide to ride into Morocco and ship my bike to South America.

Most of my gear is packed and my new maps placed in the map holder of my new tank bag. I have purchased a new inflatable mattress for tenting. Since resuming camping in Europe I have been sleeping on the ground using my jacket and riding pants for a slight cushion. It will be nice to have a proper camping mattress again. This one is not as nice as the one I left in Australia, but much better than the hard ground.

It is raining today—Saturday, November 22, 2003. I consider waiting a day, but this time of year it could rain every day. I say my goodbyes to Jen and Martin and am on the road before 9:00 AM.

— *Belgium*

Leaving Amersfoort I ride through Utrecht and Antwerpen, and stop in Brussels. It takes some scouting around to find the Bruegal Hostel, but it is worth the effort. The hostel has been recently renovated and is very clean. Parking for my bike is around back in an enclosed courtyard. To get there though, I have to wheel my bike through the lobby and out the patio doors leading to a pretty little courtyard with a cement brick patio, vines flowing down meter-high brick walls, flowering shrubs, and places to sit and enjoy the day. The scene takes me back to my favorite book from my youth: *The Secret Garden*.

After unloading my gear I take a walking tour of Brussels. Christmas decorations are already lighting the streets and providing a festive atmosphere. I stop at the "Mannekin Pis" (little boy peeing), and then continue on to the "Grand Place" which is known as one of the most beautiful town squares in Europe. The sun has gone down and it is dark. Normally I would feel uneasy, but there are so many people out walking that I do not worry. The lights in the Grand Place are spectacular.

— *France*

The following morning I leave at a leisurely pace, getting on the road at 10:00. Most of the day is cloudy, and I ride through rain off and on. By the time I reach Paris the sun is shining and the temperature is quite pleasant. I ride for about an hour in the outer rings of Paris, trying to find my way into the center of the city. At one point I see the Eiffel Tower but cannot find the road that leads towards it. Finally I stop and ask directions, but I still seem to be going in circles. By 4:30 I have still not found my way in, so I stop and ask directions for the nearest accommodations. A very kind gentleman leads me to a nearby hotel.

When I was in Italy I met Djemila, a woman from Paris who invited me to stay with her. I buy a phone card and give her a call. She is excited to hear from me and we make arrangements to meet tomorrow at her workplace in the city. She gives me some detailed directions for the city center and I study my map thoroughly this evening, in hopes of finding my way tomorrow. Paris is built with several ring roads surrounding it. I have discovered that if you make a wrong turn you could be going in circles forever. This is when a GPS would come in handy.

On the morning of November 24 I make my way into the center of Paris. Definitely not an easy task! It takes me over two hours, but I finally arrive at L'Arc de Triomphe. It stands at the center of a ten-lane roundabout with twelve streets of traffic flowing into and out of it. There are no lines indicating lanes for traffic to stay in—drivers simply estimate where they should be driving and speed their way around the monument. This famous roundabout is noted for causing a large number of accidents. Fortunately my jaunt is successful, and I come out unscathed.

Another hour passes before I find the THQ office where Djemila works. She had told me on the phone that she would arrange for me to park in the underground parking garage. This is wonderful, as it is simply impossible to find parking on the street, even for a motorcycle. The parking attendant is expecting me and directs me to an area of parking for THQ. He assures me that my gear will be safe left on the bike. I am hesitant but cannot possibly pack it around with me, so I take only my tank bag and make my way up to the lobby where I meet my friend.

What a wonderful gift it is to have a friend to show me around and give me a place to stay. Djemila suggests I leave my bike in the parkade and take the train home with her; to a little suburb several train stations outside of Paris. I express concern about leaving my gear and bike, but she assures me there is 24-hour security and it will be safe. Three days later I retrieve my bike and get completely lost once again trying to find my way out of Paris. I leave the parkade at 3:30 in the afternoon and do not make it back to Djemilas' until 7:30. I think I will leave my bike parked in her garage and travel by train.

Over the next two weeks I learn to take the train and am amazed at the underground transportation systems. There is a whole other city besides lines and lines of train tracks underground—retail shops, restaurants, fast food, cinemas, bakeries, and so much more. I cannot help but pick up fresh baguettes, cheese, and wine before catching the train home. Djemila says I make a good French woman.

I spend my days visiting the Musée du Louvre, the Eiffel Tower,

Notre Dame Cathedral, the Opera House, and L'Arc de Triomphe. I walk across interesting bridges and through fascinating neighbourhoods, go shopping, try delicious crepes from fast food kiosks, and end each day with sore, tired feet. I take the train to Versailles and visit the Chateau constructed originally as a hunting lodge by Louis XIII in 1624. King Louis XIV remodeled and added to the building and grounds in the later sixteen hundreds, creating a place for parliament and a magnificent Chateau. There are just so many things to see.

It is December 4 when I try to start my bike and find that the battery is dead again. Temperatures are dropping and I must get moving before it gets too cold. I get the battery boosted but it simply won't hold a charge for any length of time. For the next week I try every place around Paris to find a battery for my bike. No one seems to carry the right size. Finally I decide to buy a battery charger and continue to check out motorcycle shops as I travel.

On Sunday, December 14, I pack up to leave. The weather is threatening to turn cold again. I have stayed with Djemila for three weeks and offer to pay for my keep, but she will not hear of it. I leave her with a little gift and express tremendous appreciation for her hospitality.

I wake up to frost in the mornings and have to charge the battery every night. On December 16 I awaken feeling sick and begin experiencing cold chills. I rest most of the day and make some phone calls to bike shops. Finally, with the help of the hotel owner, we find a shop that has a battery to fit my bike. The next day I ride over to the shop and make my purchase for 80.85 euros. The cost is irrelevant. I install the battery and am happy to have my bike running good again.

France has beautiful countryside. I ride south through hills and valleys, vineyards, and charming cities, stopping at about 4:30 to look for accommodations. Rooms cost more here. Add to this the poor exchange on my dollar, and it's becoming very expensive. Christmas lights are up in all the cities and towns, reminding me that I still have no idea where I will spend the day. I seem to have lost track of dates and do not feel like planning for the holiday. Maybe that is because I will be alone this year.

I enjoy French cooking, especially the dessert fruit crepes. I have not gained any weight back yet, but if I keep having bread, cheese, wine, and these fabulous desserts, it will happen soon.

— *Spain*

On Friday, December 19, I cross the Pyrenees Mountains to Spain. The temperature is staying cool; I even encounter light snow for a few kilometers. More often it rains periodically throughout the day, forcing me to keep my heated jacket liner plugged in. As I head south through Spain the temperature rises some, and by the time I reach Barcelona the air feels very comfortable at about sixteen degrees Celsius.

The ride on Highway N11 along the Mediterranean Sea is beautiful but slow going. There is a lot of traffic, and built-up areas slow me down. I have booked a room at a hostel in Barcelona, but without a map of the city I get completely lost. Finally I stop at a gas station and try asking for directions. The attendants do not understand English, but suddenly a gentleman comes up to me and says, "Can I help?"

It is such a relief to hear English. This wonderful man begins to give me directions, then says, "Just follow me, I will take you there. There is so much construction going on, you will not find it." This kind gentleman leads me through city streets for twenty minutes, stopping only when we reach the hostel.

I stay two nights in Barcelona, spending one whole day seeing as much as time permits. I leave my bike parked at the hostel and take a bus to the central area of the city. I visit a famous cathedral, the Palau (Palace) Güell, designed by the architect and artist Gaudi, stroll down La Rambla to the Post, and visit the mall built out in the water. Access to the mall is via a wide pedestrian bridge that swings open to allow ships to enter the small harbour. I find another hostel located along the beach and wish I were staying there. I spend all day exploring this busy and exciting city, returning to the hostel just before dark with aching legs and feet.

I should stay longer here but have decided to continue on to Malaga for Christmas. That will put me closer to the border, and I could be in Morocco for the New Year. I will just have to come back to Barcelona another time.

On December 21 I ride the motorways to make better time. The first two tolls are each 2.2 euros. That's not too bad. At the next one

I take a ticket, and upon exiting the motorway near Valencia I am shocked when the man in the booth says, "17.80 euros."

The sun shines all day, but as I ride over the mountains the air gets a bit chilly. The landscape is hilly and treed with nice gentle curves, providing an exhilarating ride. When I reach Valencia I look for a hostel only to find the location seems to be in a seedy area. After checking out a few hotels I settle for one at forty-five euros. None of the hotels seem to have parking on site and I have to take the bike to a parkade a few blocks away. The charge for parking is eight euros.

By the time I leave the parkade my directions are all messed up. I walk for several blocks before stopping a police officer to ask directions. I cannot recall the name of my hotel and have to describe some landmarks before the officer can help me. Wow! This has given me a little wake-up call. It looks like I have become somewhat impetuous.

Valencia is a beautiful city with Christmas lights decorating the streets. My hotel is in the center of the city and my room looks out towards a large circular plaza aglow with hundreds of lights. Eight streets extend off the circle, then branch off like chicken feet scattering in all directions. It is not hard to get lost here. Today is Sunday and close to Christmas, so thousands of people are still strolling the streets after dark. I feel quite safe wandering around enjoying the festivities of the season.

The next day I ride five hundred kilometers to Almeria. I take a national highway that is non-toll all the way and make good time. This route is the long way around and goes up through small mountains, desert, and barren countryside. But by avoiding the small towns and cities on the shorter route, I make much better time. It is 4:30 when I reach Almeria and find the Hotel La Perla. My guidebook tells me it is the oldest hotel in town and located in *el centro*. I must stay here. For thirty-six euros I get a nicely kept room and can park my bike in front of the hotel's main entrance.

Christmas is a wonderful time to stay in the city center. There are so many people around that I enjoy the nightlife without feeling threatened. I walk the busy streets down to the harbour and on my way back, stop for a seafood salad and baguette. I can feel the weight coming on. It's hard to resist all these goodies.

On December 23 I only have a short ride to Malaga. Today I go along the Mediterranean coast in temperatures cool enough to warrant wearing my heated liner and nylon shell over my riding jacket. The scenery is not as pretty as I expected. The road is curvy and hilly, but the hills look barren. For long stretches I see fields of plastic covering vineyards and orchards. I surmise that this is necessary for protection from the cold, but plastic does not make for attractive architecture. The wind has caught large sheets of it, littering the landscape and leaving them flapping madly from branches on trees.

I arrive shortly after noon in Malaga and find the Hotel Sur, with a parking garage, for thirty-four euros plus five-fifty for parking. I will stay here until after Christmas. I must try to get a new rear tire on my bike before I leave Spain. It might be difficult to get one in Morocco.

Malaga is a busy little city built along the Mediterranean Sea. Streets are decorated for Christmas and entertainment is everywhere. I walk past two mimes thinking they are statues. They are very good! My hotel is near the wide pedestrian-only streets that are beautifully decorated and packed with people. I walk up to the old fort sitting at the top of a high hill overlooking the city and the sea. The view is spectacular!

I have difficulty phoning home for Christmas, but manage to leave a message for my son Brad and daughter Carey in Alberta. On December 26 I do manage to reach Brad, but the connection is so bad that I have to shout in order for him to hear me. That dampens my spirits for a short time, but I will try again in a day or two.

I get my bike into a Honda shop for a new back tire. They cannot get the Dunlop tire until January 8 or 9, so they install a Michelin for 219 euros. That seems awfully expensive but I cannot take the chance of getting one in Morocco.

On December 27 I ride to La Linea de la Concepcion, a little town across the Strait of Gibraltar. My first intention is to ride across the border onto "The Rock", but the lines of traffic are backed up for blocks. I decide to find a room, park my bike, and walk across. I try to get the border guard to stamp my passport but he tells me to get it stamped on my way out.

I head to the main building to pick up a map, and then continue on, following other tourists. There is a cable car that takes you to the top of the rock, but unfortunately it is not operational today. I wander around this touristy little town until my feet ache, then walk back to the hostel. On my way across the border I try once again to get my passport stamped, but the officer states that it is not necessary and sees no point in doing so. Oh well—that has been the case in most of Europe.

At 9:00 AM on December 28 I leave Malaga. With a new rear tire on my bike I feel confident I will be in good shape. I reach Algeciras and take a ferry to Ceuta for 33.38 euros. This fee covers my fare and that of the bike. Ceuta is still in Spain but I do not have to ride far before reaching the African border.

I have done my research about traveling in Africa and will ride only as far as Casablanca where I will make arrangements to ship my bike to South America. I look forward to visiting Morocco, but am sorry I will not be experiencing more of Africa. That will have to wait for another time.

Chapter 9

Morocco

The date is December 28, 2003. At the Spain/Morocco border I wait in a long line to obtain my vehicle registration. My turn finally comes and I am issued a permit. The guards do not ask for my carnet so I just accept their document and continue on. I am surprised at how easy the border crossing is, since I had been warned to watch out for the *touts*—hustlers who try to help you across the border for a fee. But I do not encounter any here.

I only ride as far as Tetouan before calling it a day. When I reach the city another biker rides alongside me on a 125cc Honda. When he first appears I think nothing of it, but it does not take long to realize he wants my attention. This man speaks good English and offers to find me a hotel. I decline and tell him I know where I'm going. Unfortunately this does not deter him. He continues to accompany me. Finally I relent and allow him to show me to a hotel. The first one we stop at is expensive and I explain to him that I need a budget hotel or hostel. After the third try I settle for a room at a budget hotel near the old city, or medina. The price is seventy dirhams. One Canadian dollar equals 6.806 Moroccan dirhams; one euro equals eleven dirhams.

Once again there is no parking at the hotel and I must put my bike in a parkade a few blocks away. My *guide* assures me it will be safe as there is twenty-four-hour security. I off-load my gear and haul it up twenty stairs to my room on the second floor, then ride my bike to the parkade. When I return to the hotel, my self-appointed guide is waiting for me and wants to show me around the medina. By this time I feel more appreciative and accept his offer.

My guide leads me through the old city into significant buildings, narrow alleyways, retail shops, and then a carpet factory. I tell him up front I am not interested in buying anything, since I cannot haul it on my bike, but he says it will help him if I just listen. I am some upset at this turn of events but do not have the heart to disappoint my guide. The handmade Persian carpets are so gorgeous that I am soon impressed. For an hour the salesman lays one carpet on top of another until the large warehouse floor is covered in layers upon layers of various sized carpets woven in spectacular colors and patterns. Then comes the hard push to sell me something. First the salesman asks, "Which carpet do you like?"

"I like them all, but I cannot buy any because it is impossible to carry one of these on my motorcycle," I object.

He persists and says, "Pick three that you like the best."

Once again I say, "I like many of them but I am traveling by motorcycle and do not have room to carry any."

He says, "Oh no, you do not have to buy, just pick three that you like."

Finally, after some argument I pick three carpets that are approximately three meters by four meters. This was a big mistake! Now the real pressure begins.

My salesman plays his game until I have chosen one carpet over all the rest then tells me to make an offer.

"I will not make an offer because I have no room to carry it."

"We will ship it directly to your home for no additional cost," he replies.

"No, I do not want a carpet," I exclaim, in a more forceful voice.

"Very good deal, very good deal," he says. "Make me an offer."

This continues back and forth for several minutes then I say, "You would be offended if I made an offer because I don't have enough money."

"How much do you have?" he quizzes.

I do not fall for that, and ask, "How much is the carpet?"

"Three thousand euros," he replies.

It is definite now that I can't afford this, so I say, "No, I will not make an offer. You will be offended if I make an offer!"

My salesman is not giving up. He repeats, "Make me an offer."
I finally give up and say, "two hundred euros."

As I suspected, he is offended. He makes a dramatic display of objecting to my price, but then the bargaining begins. In a few minutes of bartering I have purchased a beautiful multi-colored carpet with a deep green background for four hundred euros, which includes shipment home to Canada.

The salesman writes my name and date on the back with a felt pen and then lets me take pictures of the carpet and of him and me standing together in front of the carpet. He takes all my shipping details and I pay four hundred euros by credit card, then leave the factory quite sure that I will never see my purchase again.

My guide meets me as I exit the warehouse and continues to lead me through the medina. When he takes me into a jewelry shop I turn around and leave. I will not get caught in this high-pressure sales battle again.

The next morning I ride across the Rif Mountains on my way to Fes. It is cold but the scenery is pretty. I pass through many mountain villages and see people walking or working alongside the road. There is still a lot of manual labour out here. It is a hard life and a person's age is hard to guess by how they look. One little old lady I meet looks to be about eighty years old, with back bent and skin wrinkled and weathered. Most likely she is only fifty.

When I reach Fes a *tout* rides up beside me and tries to tag on as my guide. I quickly ditch him but before long another one has latched on. I ask him where the hostel is and he leads me there. The hostel is full so I let him find me a hotel. When we arrive he solicits his services to guide me through the medina (old city). I speak very directly to him, telling him that I do not want any high-pressure sales scenes in carpet factories, leather stores, or any other retail outlets.

The man agrees and wants one hundred and twenty dirhams to guide me for two hours. I do not feel like paying that much so I give him five dirhams for finding the hotel and he leaves. It is too late to begin a tour of the medina, so I take a short walk to a shopping area near the hotel before turning in for the night.

I notice that all the restaurants and cafés are filled with men drinking chai or juice and smoking cigarettes. The only time I see a woman is if she is accompanied by a man or with her family. Most of the women cover their heads with scarves and wear the traditional knee-length tunic or long cloak over a skirt or long pants.

Over the past two days I have encountered a lot of police checks on the highway. At most checkpoints I am waved through without stopping until just before reaching Fes. The officer's face expresses shock when he realizes that I am a woman and there is no other rider with me. He states his concern that this is a Muslim country and women do not travel alone. I appreciate his concern and assure him that I have come through Muslim countries and will be just fine.

The following morning I find my way to the medina where I join the throngs of people passing through the cement archway. Intricate carvings and tile work adorn the gate that reaches up twelve meters or more. Inside the gate I weave my way through the mob of people and past stalls selling everything from goat heads to specialty meats, to fresh fruits and vegetables, to crafts of every kind imaginable.

As I make my way farther into the medina past the open market stalls, the alleys become narrower. I look up to the top of the high cement walls and wonder if I'll find my way out. I have taken a few turns and stopped to view the inside of some interesting buildings. It would not be hard to get lost in here.

On December 31 I make my way to Sale. The sun is shining and the temperature is quite pleasant for riding. My intention was to stay in Sale for New Year's Eve, but accommodation is unavailable, so I continue on to Rabat, just a few kilometers farther. I find the Hotel Splendid for two hundred and forty dirhams. My unheated room has a sink and bidet, but I have to share the bathroom for showering. The bidet does not look all that clean so I will not be using it.

The streets of Rabat are packed tonight, so I have to push my way through the crowds. It is New Year's Eve and people are celebrating. Restaurants are full, music and noise spill out of buildings, and pedestrians jostle for space on the sidewalks. It is all too much for me tonight, so I stop for a pizza before returning to my room around 9:00 to reflect on another spectacular year of travels and adventure.

On January 2, 2004, I ride to Casablanca in the rain and check into a hotel near the center of the city. First on my agenda is to make arrangements to ship my bike to Buenos Aires. In the next four days I call and visit several freight forwarders. I do not like the information I am getting. To ship the bike by sea it will cost seven hundred and eighty

US dollars plus seven hundred dirhams for crating and eight hundred and fifty for insurance. Besides that, it will take thirty-four days to get there. To fly the bike it will cost twenty-four hundred US.

The next night there is a violent fight in the middle of the night coming from somewhere in the hotel. It begins as a yelling match then becomes what sounds like a beating. I hear a woman crying and screaming. I desperately want to go and investigate, but am too scared. In the morning I mention it to the hotel clerk but he brushes it off as though it didn't happen. Maybe he was the one doing the beating. I look for another hotel and move.

The Hotel Paris is more central and is situated on a pedestrian walkway with plenty of activity. At 6:00 PM the street comes alive with the sound of vendors bartering with customers. The window to my room is right above one such street, so I go down and join in the activity.

After inquiring with several more freight forwarders I decide to ride back to Spain and ship my bike from Barcelona. I have discovered that ships leaving from Casablanca dock in Barcelona first, before continuing on to Buenos Aires. Shipping from there will cut the time at sea in half. This makes more sense and will give me a chance to see more of Spain.

It is January 7 when I leave Casablanca. I will cross the border at Tangier and stop at Algeciras, Spain for the night. My experience in Morocco has not been the most pleasant. I seem to be in a terrible mood and catch myself sounding impatient and even rude to people. Can it be possible that I am getting tired of traveling? Maybe I am more homesick than I realize, or maybe, after traveling in Europe, I find it difficult to adjust to the constant nattering, aggressiveness, and invasion of personal space. In Asia I had become accustomed to that lifestyle, but in Morocco I find it unbearable. Regardless of the reasons, I must change my attitude so as not to ruin the rest of my journey.

This morning when leaving the Hotel de Paris I get stuck in the elevator with two other guests. The elevator stops, then drops with a thud, leaving us suspended between floors. Instantly I feel the panic rise in my chest. My face must betray my anxiety because one of my fellow passengers, a German gentleman, promptly begins assuring me that we will get help. His words are calming but this elevator is very small and

I shudder at the thought of being locked in here for any length of time. Thankfully only fifteen minutes pass before we are rescued.

My ride north from Casablanca is a pleasant and memorable one. Part of the route takes me along the sea, which I always find peaceful. Traffic on the highway is not as bad as in the cities, so I take my time and enjoy the scenery. I stop for fuel in one little town before reaching Tangier. Gas is nine dirhams per liter (approximately twice as much as in Alberta, Canada).

I leave the gas station and make my way back to the main highway, but before I have gone two blocks a police officer on a motorcycle stops me. He tells me I am speeding—ninety-eight in a forty-kilometer zone.

I plead my innocence and state, "I did not see a sign posted at forty kilometers."

"The sign is on the highway," the officer replies.

"But I just came out of that petrol station back there, not from the highway," I claim.

He asks for my license and chats awhile, asking questions unrelated to the issue. He gives me a warning and tells me that he could have given me a ticket for four hundred dirhams—then he lets me go.

I guess I'd better be a little more attentive. I don't need a ticket just before leaving the country.

At Tangier the *touts* are working in full force. Several blocks before the border crossing and ferry dock I am stopped by the first man, offering to take my passport and help me through the border procedure. I refuse to turn over my passport to him and state that I will do this myself. In less than an hour eight different people approach me offering to help with the paperwork.

I had been warned about the Tangier crossing but did not expect to be hassled this much. The line is moving slowly and time is passing quickly. I begin to fear missing my ferry booking. I can see the booths at the border crossing, but the line of traffic seems to have stopped now. Finally I give in and allow one of the *touts* to take my passport. In a few minutes he has the paperwork taken care of and instructs me to ride past the stopped vehicles to the gates. My passport is stamped and I ride to the ferry—just in time too. I am the last vehicle loaded.

On the ferry I relax and have time to reflect on my week in Morocco. I did have some interesting experiences—wandering through the old cities, pushing and shoving my way through mobs of people, visiting the massive gravesites in Sale, and purchasing a carpet I may never see again. I think about my agitated mood and wonder if this has led to the negative experiences; such as overhearing a fight in a hotel, getting stuck in an elevator, being pulled over for speeding, and having such a tough time finding acceptable shipping for my bike.

I resolve to change my attitude. This is the beginning of a new year and I still have a lot of ground to cover before returning home. I plan to make 2004 a fabulous one. Maybe I will work on my foreign language skills. I feel quite inferior speaking only one language. Along with Arabic, the Moroccans speak Spanish, French, some English, and some German. I grew up with German-speaking parents, studied French in school, yet the only language I speak is English. At this moment I find that quite appalling! How did I allow this to happen? When I reach Buenos Aires I will take Spanish lessons while I wait for my motorcycle to arrive.

— A few more days in Spain

Back in Spain I am riding highways with many tollbooths. At the fifth or sixth booth the attendant wants to chat. He speaks Spanish and French plus the odd word of English, but that does not deter him from trying to communicate. I understand a few words, enough to know that he has asked if I am married. He continues talking, appearing to have no concern about the line of traffic forming behind me. Finally he quits and says, "We talk later." I don't know when or where he thinks this will take place, but I smile and ride on. Maybe I missed the French or Spanish part of the conversation. My spirits have risen and I feel excited again. What was it about Morocco that dampened my soul?

I ride across three mountain

ranges to Cordoba and spend a couple of days exploring this wonderful old city.

Temperatures are nice when walking but riding is quite cold, especially going over mountain passes. I carry on to Madrid and spend another four days exploring the sites. I'm so glad I decided to come back to Spain. There is a tremendous amount of history to discover. I spend two days exploring Madrid with Graham, a traveler from Australia who is staying at the same hostel. We pack in as much as possible, not wasting a moment of the day.

It is a very cold ride over the mountains from Madrid to Lieda. The landscape ranges from majestic mountains to canyons of sharp cliffs and red earth. If it weren't so cold I could take more time to enjoy the scenery. My whole body is freezing by the time I check into a hotel. I soak for an hour in a hot bath. The next day begins with more of the same, warming up as I near Barcelona.

I have a small map of Barcelona this time, and having been here briefly before makes it much easier for me to get around. I find the Sea Point Hostel easily and check in. This hostel is right on the beach and offers easy access to many of the sights.

The date is January 15, and the first thing on my agenda is to arrange shipping. I contact Les Proux/Landtrans and speak to Diego. He is a great help and immediately starts the process. He sends me out to a suburb about thirty kilometers away to drop the bike off for crating. I do all the necessary things—drain the fuel, disconnect and tape the battery cables, remove the mirrors, top trunk and windshield, and strap the trunk along with some of my gear to the bike. I ask the attendant to discard the windshield. It is so marked up and cracked that I decide not to ship it. With everything complete and ready to crate, I leave my baby in the hands of strangers once again and take the metro back to the hostel.

I must meet with Diego one more time to complete all the paperwork and pay the bill. The total cost of shipping, including crating is 648 euros. The ship is to sail on January 23 and arrive in Buenos Aires February 7. That gives me more than a week to arrange my own flight and enjoy more of Barcelona.

Chapter 10

Argentina

On January 27, 2004 I take the train to the airport where I will catch my flight to Buenos Aires. I make sure I allow plenty of time to spare, just in case I get lost.

My flight takes me to Frankfurt, Germany then on to Argentina. At Frankfurt they quiz me extensively about not having an onward ticket. I explain that I will be continuing on by motorcycle once I reach Buenos Aires, but they still insist on an onward ticket. Finally, after much discussion, the ticket clerk types in a tentative booking for Canada and hands me the printout. She does not charge me for this "phantom flight"—it is simply a formality showing my intention to continue on from South America. With everyone happy I am now allowed to check in for my flight.

A few days earlier in Barcelona I met a woman from Buenos Aires who arranged for her daughter to meet me and provide a place to stay. Julia is waiting for me at the airport. She gives me a bed, some maps and brochures of things to see and do, and introduces me to more of her family.

Julia is 23 and works afternoon shifts until midnight. Her flat is in a suburb several train stops from the city center, so I learn quickly how to get around by train. I have more than a week to explore Buenos Aires before my bike arrives. I keep my promise and enroll in Spanish classes beginning on Monday. The class runs from 10:00 to 3:30, for a total of twenty hours, and costs four hundred and eighty pesos plus thirty pesos for the textbook. One Canadian dollar is equal to 2.21 Argentine pesos; and one US dollar is equal to 2.92 pesos. The course is not cheap.

Buenos Aires is a beautiful city. The streets are wide, so the pollution from vehicles is dispersed instead of left trapped in narrow alleyways. Florida Street is a pedestrian-only street that goes on for several blocks and attracts an abundance of street performers. It is wide with a brick surface, and several of the intersecting streets, although narrower, continue as pedestrian walkways. I discover Avenue 9 de Julio, known as the widest street in the world. It is sixteen lanes wide, divided by a treed boulevard. I cannot make it across in one light, no matter how fast I walk.

Street performers are everywhere—singing, dancing, and laughing. Music pours out from open shop doors. I stop and watch tango dancers perform, listen to music belting out from accordions with taped up baffles, see comic acts in the streets of San Telmo, and visit the resting place of Evita and the building where she gave her last speech from the balcony. I am enthralled! There is so much to see and do. I have fallen in love with the city and its spirited culture. Buenos Aires has captured my soul.

My Spanish classes are in the heart of the city on Florida Street. I decide to move into a hostel in the area to eliminate the daily train ride. I walk to class each morning and simply love being in the midst of all this activity. Maybe I lived here in another lifetime.

On Tuesday, February 3, I receive a call from Vanguard Logistics informing me that my shipment will arrive on Friday. I must go to their office and pay a handling fee of $189.34 US. That is the pitfall of shipping by sea; there is always a big handling charge on the receiving end. When I flew my motorcycle I took care of all the paperwork myself and went directly to air cargo to pick it up. In Singapore there was no extra charge, and in Nepal I paid a small fee (pocket money) to the agent who retrieved the crate from the warehouse.

The agent at Vanguard tells me to call on Monday and go to customs to get the shipment cleared. Customs will instruct me as to which warehouse my bike is in. Nothing is easy when shipping by sea.

Spanish classes are going well. My ability to converse is progressing very slowly. I keep thinking that by the end of the week I should be getting better. My classmates are a mixture of nationalities—Danish, Australian, British, Israeli, and Canadian. We practice our new words on each other during lunch and after class.

On Sunday I decide to contact a Servas host in hopes of getting assistance with customs. I reach Myrta, who is seventy years old. Fortunately for me, her daughter Laurie is visiting and speaks good English. Laurie offers to accompany me to the customs office and to find an agency for motorcycle insurance. It is so great to have a local friend. Laurie takes me sightseeing to places in the city I probably would not have found on my own.

On Monday and Tuesday morning I call Vanguard and am finally told to go to customs on Wednesday, February 11, to clear my shipment. Laurie meets me downtown and we proceed to customs. Having a Spanish-speaking interpreter is invaluable. It still takes an hour to complete all the paperwork, but most likely I would have been sent hither and yon without her help. When all the requests are satisfied, I am given the address of the warehouse and told to pick up my shipment tomorrow.

Laurie invites me back to her mother's home for lunch. Myrta tries speaking to me but I do not understand. I feel so helpless. Then she tries again, speaking more slowly. This time I make out enough words to put together the questions. I am convinced that if I were to stay here for a few months I could speak and understand Spanish.

My hosts show me some photos of Argentina taken in the southern regions of Patagonia and Tierra del Fuego. Once I have my bike back that is the direction I will be heading. Before I leave to walk back to my hostel, Laurie calls a taxi and arranges to have him pick me up tomorrow and take me to the warehouse. She explains everything in Spanish to the dispatcher, even that I must stop and pick up fuel to take with me. She is an angel.

The temperature has been terrific. The sun shines most days and is warm enough to cause sunburn. I must get riding soon though, if I want to make it south to Ushuaia before winter weather moves in.

On Thursday morning, February 12, my taxi arrives at 7:45. We stop at a petrol station and pick up a disposable container of fuel. It is 8:10 when we arrive at the warehouse gates. My driver drops me off and I proceed to the security booth. The security guard does not know what to do with me so he leaves me standing there for fifteen minutes.

Feeling agitated and impatient, I try harder to help him understand. Finally he makes a phone call, then asks another officer to escort me to the customs office. After standing in line for ten minutes a young woman comes out and leads me into an office to speak to an agent.

I hand my paperwork over to the agent and explain that I am here to pick up my motorcycle. After scrutinizing the papers he asks if there is another person. I assure him there is not. He then asks three times (while making a cranking motion with his wrist), "You ride moto?"

"Sí, I ride moto," I reply, pointing to myself.

The agent says something I do understand and everyone in hearing range laughs.

I silently caution myself to keep my cool. I do not want to delay things by losing my temper.

He sends me across the yard to a large warehouse to inspect my shipment. One of the boards on the crate had been damaged so the warehouse attendant instructs me to examine it carefully. The crate is very flimsy, with thin boards nailed four inches apart. As far as I can determine the only damage is to one of the boards. The contents seem to be fine.

Once I give my okay, the warehouse attendant, Remi, begins to dismantle the crate. When the bike is exposed I go to work reconnecting the battery cables, replacing the mirrors and back trunk, and strapping the roll to the back seat. Remi pours the fuel into the tank and I start the bike. At this point I expect to put on my helmet and ride out, but not so. Remi sends me back to the customs agent, who sends me to the counter to pay 347 pesos for their work.

"Take these papers across the yard to the warehouse," the clerk says.

Remi accepts the papers and sends me back to the office for more computer input, then into the custom agent's office for a signature on the final papers. Finally, I go back to the warehouse and am allowed to take my bike, but I must stop at the gate for one final inspection. The security guard takes his copy from my stack of papers and the gate opens, making way for my escape.

All this took about an hour and a half. I have really learned my lesson in patience during these past two and a half years of travel. As I ride out the gates I realize I do not even feel upset. In fact, I'm beginning to find it all quite amusing.

The odometer reads 87,232. My first stop is to get fuel and wash my bike before riding back to the hostel. I will park in the apartment parkade down the block for one night. Yesterday I met a man who spoke English and offered to let me use his parking spot in a secured building. That was very fortunate because there is no parking available at the hostel.

The morning of February 13 I leave Buenos Aires at 9:30 and head south to Mar del Plata. It rained overnight and clouds fill the sky. Mist hangs heavily in the air and the temperature has dropped considerably. I do not ride far before stopping to pull my nylon shell over my riding jacket. I curse myself for putting my heated liner at the bottom of my pack. A misty rain follows me most of the morning, finally clearing after lunch. A temperature sign in one city I ride through reads 23 degrees Celsius. It does not feel that warm—it must be the coolness from the rain.

I am riding without a windshield since I discarded mine in Spain. Riding south the wind is strong, pushing against my helmet. My neck is sore by the time I arrive in Mar del Plata at 4:30 in the afternoon. I ride through town towards the Atlantic Ocean and follow a road south until I see a campground. For sixteen pesos I pitch my tent and relax for the evening.

I have seen several motorcycles on the road. Today I saw a group of three, with one of them pulling a trailer. I think about a group from Canada who are traveling in Argentina at this time, and wonder if that might be them. Too bad they were going the opposite direction.

The morning of Valentine's Day I leave the campground at 8:00. The temperature is cool but not as bad as yesterday, and the wind has died down some—or maybe my neck is stronger. I pass fields of sunflowers with their heads hanging, ready for harvesting. Then, farther south, I notice the flowers standing tall, reaching towards the sun for heat to dry the kernels. It is a picture-perfect sight with billowy white clouds hanging over acres and acres of yellow sunflower fields.

I reach Bahia Blanca at 4:50 and search out a campground. It's not nearly as nice as the one last night, but it is beside the water. Only two other campsites are occupied. The evening is pleasant so I sit at a picnic table and write in my journal.

This year I will finish my trip around the world. I will have covered about one hundred and twenty thousand kilometers in three years and only seen a tiny part of it. I wonder how many times a person would have to go around the world to see it all—a hundred times, maybe a thousand? I think even a thousand times would not be enough. There would still be places left unseen.

We are like miniscule specks of sand in this vast Universe, undetected by the most powerful telescope. Yet, we all matter. In some small way, each one of us is important—like a tiny piece in a giant jigsaw puzzle. Where do we fit?

Riding south over the next two days I pass through San Antonio Oeste, Las Grutas, and Puerto Madryn, camping along the way. The morning of February 16 I pack up a wet tent. The rain began about 3:00 in the morning and was too much for my much-used tent. I have a few moments of reprieve as I pack up before it begins to sprinkle again. I look up towards the sky and beg, "Oh, please just give me two more minutes." Well, guess what? I got exactly two minutes before the sky opened up again. Be careful what you ask for; you just might get it.

I have ridden for three hours and by the time I reach Puerto Madryn I am soaked and cold. I decide to get a hotel room instead of camping. I find the visitor center and book a bus tour out to Punta Tombo to see the Magellanic penguins. This is the largest penguin colony in the world and I am not disappointed. There are thousands of the little creatures waddling to and from the water. They seem to have characteristics of birds, fish, and rodents all rolled into one. They can swim great lengths, and when on land, make their homes burrowing into the ground under roots and bushes. Their average height is forty-five centimeters and their average weight is four to five kilograms. Magellanic penguins mate for life, and both male and female incubate the eggs and look after the young. The female lays two eggs every spring (September). It is quite enchanting to watch them waddle around in pairs.

The ride next day is long and boring as I follow Highway 3 south. I count the mile markers to break the monotony. The terrain varies from flat, grey desert with scrub brush blowing in the wind to gentle rolling hills and red earth. I spot the occasional oil derrick off in the distance. I see several ostriches, and herds of guanacos that look like deer but are members of the camel family. The temperature begins to warm slightly over the next couple of days. This is late February and the beginning of the fall season. I hope to make it to Ushuaia, the southernmost city in South America (and the world) on the Isla Grande de Tierra del Fuego, before winter sets in.

At Piedra Buena my wrench breaks while I am adjusting my chain. There does not seem to be a shop around that sells tools, so I must wait until I reach a bigger center. I must find another one.

On February 20 I am on the road before 8:00. It is cool and the wind is at my back this morning. Good thing too, because there is no fuel for 248 kilometers. When I reach a service station at Río Gallegos I have two liters left in the tank. They do not sell wrenches here so I get the mechanic to adjust my chain, and then ask him if he will sell me his wrench. We agree on fifty pesos, which is way too much but I need it so I pay the price.

From Río Gallegos to the Chile border is all gravel. The road is hard packed so I have no problem riding on this surface until I reach a huge mud hole. I stop and size up the situation before crossing. The mud hole looks deep and is at least fifty meters long. I wait a few minutes until I see a vehicle approaching before crossing. If I dump my bike in the mud hole, at least there will be someone around to help me out. I make it across safely just as the vehicle arrives. The sad part about this is that I must return on the same road.

The border crossing goes smoothly and quickly. They must see many bikes and vehicles crossing here, so the paperwork is no issue. For a short distance the road is paved, then returns to gravel. They appear to be building a new road. Hopefully this will all be paved in the near future. It is 2:30 and the wind has picked up to a fierce gale. I have a hard time keeping the bike in a straight line. I reach the ferry crossing at 3:15 only to find out the next ferry does not run until 6:45. The last one sailed at 2:30. So I sit reading my Lonely Planet guidebook and writing in my journal.

I return to my bike at 5:30 and see I have attracted company. There is a Kawasaki KLR parked behind me. Moments later Art arrives. The first thing he says after introducing himself is, "That's not a good bike for a trip like this."

"It has served me well," I reply.

"But it can't go everywhere." He insists.

"It has gone everywhere I wanted it to go and then some," I reply, thinking this man has quite an ego.

Art is from Poland. He is about 65 years old and in very good shape. He seems to be a seasoned rider with lots to complain about. He asks if we could ride to Ushuaia together. I welcome the company, especially since the road ahead of us is mostly gravel.

We are first off the ferry to ride onto the Isla Grande de Tierra del Fuego. The road continues to be washboard and gravel until Sombrero, Chile. It is now 8:00 PM so we find a nice Hosteria and stop for the night. Had I been alone I would have found a campground, but the air is cool and it looks like it's going to rain so I spend more than I like for a very nice room.

On Saturday, February 21, we are off to a late start. We have breakfast then set off to cross the last border from Chile to Argentina—the small, most southerly peak of Tierra del Fuego. Once again the border crossing is smooth and fast. Shortly the road turns to pavement and our ride into Rio Grande is pleasant. We stop for fuel and lunch before battling the gravel and washboard road to Ushuaia.

In no time at all my bike and I are both completely covered in dust. A light sprinkle today would be welcome. The air is thick with dust, limiting visibility. I can barely see Art up ahead, so I ride with my flashers on hoping other drivers will see me. This is a treacherous ride and I am glad to stop when we reach a construction crew and must wait for oncoming traffic.

Finally we are back on pavement riding the last half hour into Ushuaia, arriving at 6:00 PM. We have covered 428 kilometers, a third of which was gravel, and have arrived at the southernmost city in the world. Ushuaia is nestled between the Martial Mountains on the north and the Beagle Channel on the south. The Earth's two largest bodies of water, the Atlantic and Pacific Oceans, lie on either side of Tierra del Fuego.

Art continues to grumble about the awful roads we have just traveled, and I wonder what advantage he has with his dual-purpose bike. My Magna did just fine on the same roads. He insists he will not ride back on them. He will ship his bike out of here. We stop for a cold drink in town before looking for accommodation. Art's budget is much richer than mine so we head off in different directions, Art looking for a nice hotel and I for a nice hostel.

I find the Hostel El Jardin high up on a hill overlooking the town, with a view of the water. It is a wonderful spot. I pick a top bunk in a co-ed room and head for the shower to get rid of the dust that has settled into every pore of my body. My riding clothes will need a good cleaning before I leave here.

I meet Art the next morning for breakfast and buy his Chilean pesos from him. He has come from Ecuador, Peru, and Chile, and gives me maps and a host of other information for my travels north. This will be very helpful, with the exception of his recommendations for accommodation. I will continue to use my guidebook to locate lower-priced lodging.

The next five days I spend exploring Ushuaia, some of the time with Art, and other times on my own. Art has checked into shipping our bikes back to Río Gallegos and it looks like we have a booking on a truck that leaves Tuesday, February 24, at midnight. The cost will be three hundred and fifty pesos each. Yes, I will send my bike and fly out to avoid those horrible gravel roads, dust, and mud holes.

Tuesday afternoon, after getting the bikes serviced, we ride to the trucking company only to find that they will not take the bikes after all. They have no way of securing them down so will not accept them unless they are crated. I decide not to send mine and, after much grumbling, Art agrees. We will ride out Thursday.

On Wednesday night we book tickets for a dinner and tango show. Art has invited two local riders, Jon and Herman who had helped him with his bike, to join us. They arrive at 11:00, after the performance is over. I guess they weren't interested in this show. I quite enjoyed the dance and musical performances. Jon and Herman were happier to get a free meal and share in three bottles of wine.

The next morning we take a few more pictures at the "Fin del Mundo" sign before leaving. Art discovers that his back wheel is rubbing against the frame and he must get it looked at. I have already checked out of my room and packed my gear on my bike, so I decide to ride out alone. I'm thinking that Art may not leave today and I am tired of waiting around just to have someone to ride the rough road with. Besides, he seems to be in a miserable mood every time he faces a challenge.

Yesterday's rain has settled the dust, making the ride to Rio Grande quite bearable. The only greasy stretch is around one mountain where construction is taking place. I ride into town about 2:00 PM and find the Hostel Argentino. The owners, Maria and Paulo, welcome me like a long lost friend and guide me down a narrow trail to park my bike on their covered patio. I could not have received a better reception.

Art arrives at the hostel by early evening, and is in a foul mood! He has a room at a hotel but no place to park his bike. Maria offers to let him park on their patio. That cheers him up some. After dinner he brings them a bottle of wine and dessert for their generosity. He can be nice when he makes an effort.

Our plan is to ride north together until I turn west. The next morning I head to the hotel at 8:30 to find that Art has still not packed his bike. By 9:30 I make a decision to continue on my own. I guess I have been riding alone for too long and have lost the patience it takes to adjust to a riding companion.

The roads are not as bad as I was anticipating. The worst mud hole has been graded over and the washboard surface is a bit smoother. I breeze through customs into Chile, then again into Argentina, and make it to Río Gallegos by mid afternoon. I get my bike washed and polished for twelve pesos. Five guys work on it as I sit and watch. This is the life!

I check into the Hotel Nevada and get a nice room for thirty pesos. The streets are busy this Friday evening. I am not sure if it is a special day or just the usual Friday night activity.

On Saturday I take Highway 5 northwest to El Calafate. After the first sixty kilometers the terrain changes, becoming hilly and green. I see the mountains in the distance and enjoy my new view and good roads most of the way, encountering only two short construction sections along the way.

My guidebook recommends Hostel Calafate, a big new log

building. I find it with no problem, but they are completely booked. That is unfortunate, as this looks like a wonderful place. I go in search of another hostel and settle for Lago Argentino for twenty pesos. Hotel rooms in this little town range from one hundred to four hundred pesos, so I am thankful for the hostels.

I unpack and go for a walk in Lagoon Park. This area is a bird sanctuary and known for the black neck swans and flamingos that converge here. I see a large flock of black neck swans on the water and many other species of birds, but no flamingos.

It rains all the next day so I spend it relaxing, reading, downloading pictures, and catching up on my Web site. The following day is March 1. I have inquired about taking an excursion to Perito Moreno Glacier Park, but the cost is 199 pesos for the day, so I decide to ride out. I pay twenty pesos for a park pass and am faced with thirty kilometers of gravel road. The attendant at the park gate tells me the road is closed for construction between 12:30 and 4:30 PM. The time I enter is 10:15 AM I figure I can ride in, take some pictures, and ride back before 12:30.

The scenery is spectacular. With a couple of picture stops it takes me an hour to reach the viewing area. I stop for lunch at the lodge before booking a spot on the boat that takes visitors to within a few meters of the face of the glacier. I am in awe! This monstrous body of ice covers an area of about 195 square kilometers, spans the width of the river about four kilometers, runs thirty kilometers in length, and rises up thirty to sixty meters. It is a windy day and very cold on the deck of the boat. The wind seems to blow harder the closer we get to the iceberg. The sun is shining, creating a kaleidoscope of blue throughout the ice. What a sensational sight!

After the boat ride I spend the remainder of the afternoon walking the trails to see the glacier from other angles. At one platform I stop to watch the glacier *calving*. This is the term used when large chunks of ice break away from the huge iceberg and fall, crashing into the water below. By the time I leave I have snapped one hundred pictures. I have seen glaciers before, but never anything quite so phenomenal as this.

It is 4:30 when I begin my ride out of the park. The road is a mess from the earlier construction. I spot a Kawasaki Classic parked alongside the road and stop. It belongs to Oscar, who is from Brazil; he has run low on fuel. We siphon two liters from my tank and pour it into his then ride together the rest of the way back to El Calafate.

I would like to take Highway 40 north from here to Bariloche, but too many people have warned me that it is a treacherous route. Oscar confirms this fact so I think I will heed the warning.

On Tuesday, March 2, I leave at 9:30 to retrace my route back to Río Gallegos. The sun is shining but the air is cold, so I plug in my jacket. I no longer carry my jerry can of extra fuel so must pay close attention to distances between gas stations. I make very good time, and when I stop for the day I have covered 656 kilometers. My body is cold and tired.

The next day I have a treacherous ride from Puerto San Julián north to Comodoro Rivadavia. I ride into a northwest wind and have trouble holding my head steady. Without a windshield the wind rips at my helmet. I am bent forward, resting the chin of my helmet on my tank bag. Even so, I have to fight to hold my head steady. Trucks that I meet create a blast of wind that tries hard to rip off my head! After four hours of battling this gale, I stop for lunch at Caleta Olivia. When I sit down I realize just how tired I am. It would be so easy to lay my head on the table and go to sleep.

I take my time over lunch, then battle the wind again for another hour north to Comodoro Rivadavia before turning onto Highway 26 heading northwest, directly into the wind. The pressure against my helmet produces tension and pain through my neck and shoulders. Several times I tuck in close behind a vehicle for protection, but their inconsistent speed makes it impossible to stay there. Finally it works. I tuck in close behind a half-ton truck traveling ninety-eight kilometers per hour and ride like this until I reach Sarmiento. Maybe these fellows are bikers and realize what I'm battling. I hope to have a chance to thank them, but they keep going when I turn into a gas station. I definitely need a windshield, although in this wind it might make things worse.

On March 4 I ride from Sarmiento to Esquel, a similar distance to yesterday's trip. I stop to rest several times. The day begins cool and I am spared the wind for the first hour. Then it begins to blow hard again. I purchase a disposable five-liter fuel container and strap it to my bike. In this stretch fuel stations are up to 270 kilometers apart.

I arrive in Esquel at about 4:30 after a long, tiring day. Hotels are expensive. There is no hostel and I am too tired to camp, so I call a Servas host. I reach the Peters family and speak to Maria. She does not speak much English but is able to relay that I should stay put and she will come meet me.

Maria arrives shortly and leads me to her home up the hills at the edge of town. The Peters live two blocks past the main road and have a magnificent view of the valley and surrounding mountains. They have five children ranging in age from ten to nineteen. The oldest daughter is in university in Buenos Aires and the second daughter will join her tomorrow. The younger daughter and two sons attend school in Esquel. It surprises me that the children do not speak English. It is not a requirement here, but the older two will study English in university.

José Peters arrives home soon after, and he makes dinner. Maria is busy getting her daughter ready for her flight to Buenos Aires tomorrow. José speaks very good English and we have a great conversation while he cooks. The family is vegetarian. Their custom is to eat late so it is 9:30 before dinner is served. We begin with a scrumptious vegetable soup and corn on the cob. Then we have two kinds of potato salad, a tomato salad, coleslaw, carrots, and pumpkin. This is a great treat for me.

José gives me a map of the area and suggests some places to visit while I am here. I make my plans for tomorrow before retiring for the night. The last few days have been long and tiring and I am ready for a good sleep.

The next morning is cloudy with periods of rain. I go shopping in Esquel and find a good pair of leather riding boots. They are a high top boot made of very thick leather, for 287 pesos. The price is not much different than what I would pay at home for something similar.

The sun has come out by the afternoon so I ride out to Trevelin and Complejo Hidroelectrico Futaleufu (hydro plant and dam) in the Parque Nacional Los Alerces. The road leading up to the top of the dam is gravel, and the wind has picked up again. After two tight switchbacks I stop to take a picture and consider turning back.

It is still a long way to the top but as I survey the situation I determine it is probably safer to keep going than to try and turn around on this gravel and rock. I carefully continue to the top and am rewarded with a fabulous view of one of many beautiful lakes in the park. Los Alerces (the "larches") is home to two- to three thousand-year-old larch trees that grow from thirty to fifty meters high, with trunks three to four meters in diameter.

The scenery is gorgeous here, but unfortunately, the roads through the park are all gravel. I make my way slowly and stop several times for pictures. The roads twist their way around mountains and alongside lakes and rivers. It would be so wonderful if they were paved. Just as I reach Esquel it begins to rain lightly. I make it back to the Peters home and park, only seconds before it starts to pour.

The date is March 6. My goal is to be in Santiago, Chile by the 13th to meet Norma at the airport the following day. Norma belongs to the Women in the Wind Chapter in Edmonton and has shipped her bike to Chile. She will be joining me for the remainder of my journey through South America and Central America, and the trip back home.

I awaken early, do my exercises, and then pack up my bike. I try to leave quietly so as not to disturb my hosts, but José comes out when I start my bike. He insists that I have breakfast with them before I leave. What wonderful people.

I ride as far as El Bolsón today, taking the route recommended by José. Much of the road is gravel with a nice hard packed track that is fairly easy to ride on. For the last twenty-seven kilometers I find myself on newly graded, loose gravel. Thick ridges left by the grader make it extremely difficult to ride. There is no packed track. Several times my bike wobbles and I fight to stay upright. The temperature is cool so I welcome the slow riding but am thankful when I finally reach pavement again.

Once I ride out of the mountains the view opens up to rolling hills and farmland. The landscape is green and the sky is blue, dotted with white puffy clouds. The feel of fall is in the air, forcing me to stop throughout the day to warm up.

I receive an e-mail from Jeff, a rider I met in Ushuaia. He took Highway 40 north from El Calafate and fell twice. He says the road was treacherous and he would not recommend it to other riders.

On March 7 I ride to San Carlos de Bariloche. This is the Lake District of Argentina in the foothills of the Andes Mountains. The scenery reminds me a lot of the foothills of the Rocky Mountains in Alberta. Today is a short ride from El Bolson, so I make an attempt at finding the waterfalls that are supposed to be nearby. I end up on more gravel and never do find the falls.

Back on Highway 258 it is a short ride north to Bariloche. I have only ridden 142 kilometers by the time I check into the Hostel La Bolsa del Deporte. The building is the size of a very large house and constructed of large logs. In the front yard there is a tree house patio with a long curved slide extending to the ground. The yard is fenced with a locked gate and I am able to park my bike under the awnings in front of the building.

It is only 2:00 in the afternoon when I check into my room so I unpack and go walking to the town center. Bariloche is a tourist town set amongst small mountains and built along the water's edge. This would be a splendid place to take a two- or three-week holiday.

I return to the hostel to make dinner and visit with other travelers, including Martin, the owner. People I meet in hostels are very interesting. Many of them are much younger than I am, but avid adventurers.

Martin is close to my age. I gather some sightseeing information from him for tomorrow's itinerary.

The next morning Marika, a Dutch woman, and I take a bus ride out to Llao Llao (pronounced jow jow, with a soft j). Llao Llao is said to be Argentina's finest resort. Accommodations here are very expensive. We are met by security at the door and are turned away when we ask to enter the restaurant. Being budget travelers I guess we are not suitably dressed. We walk around the grounds for a few minutes then try again.

I say to Marika, "We cannot come all this way and not have a coffee and dessert in the restaurant."

This time we are allowed in. Coffee and dessert is delectable! The price is more than we would normally pay for a full meal, but that's okay; we are allowed to sit by the big windows overlooking the immaculate grounds with its sensational views.

We return to Hostel La Bolsa before lunch. Martin has shown me a sixty-kilometer loop on the map that winds around lakes in the area. After lunch I take this beautiful ride, passing hosterias, hotels, cabins, bungalows, lakes, and never-ending fabulous views. I stop several times for pictures and at one point meet a couple from Windsor, Ontario. We chat for awhile and they tell me about Iguazu Falls. They strongly advise that I go there if I have time.

Iguazu Falls is north of Buenos Aires so I do not think I will make it unless Norma wants to ride in that direction. I will discuss it with her when we meet.

On March 9 I do the loop of Seven Lakes, following Highway 237 along the Nahuel Huapi River that runs through *Parque Nacional Nahuel Huapi*. Scenery changes from green to brown grey hills as I travel north and away from the lakes and rivers. My route takes me on a section of Highway 40 that is paved, then on 234 where I turn south to Junín de los Andes. The terrain becomes more mountainous and green again as I continue south to beautiful San Martin de los Andes. This little town is nestled in the mountains at the foot of a gorgeous lake. Had I known, I would have packed up my things and stayed here for a night. From San Martin I ride south to Villa La Angostura, another pretty little town in a great setting. The last fifty kilometers are gravel and dirt road, making riding treacherous for stretches. I return to

Bariloche after 456 kilometers. The loop was longer than I anticipated, but well worth it.

This evening, at dinner around the kitchen table, Martin asks about my travels and soon asks my age. He does well at masking his surprise when I tell him I am fifty-five. Then he says, "You are my idol."

Wow, how to make a girl feel special!

I have enjoyed Argentina immensely and am sorry to leave. I will probably come back one day for an extended visit, but now I must continue. Tomorrow I will cross into Chile.

Chapter 11
Chile

Today is March 10—I will cross the Andes into Chile. I retrace part of my route from yesterday heading northwest on Highway 231 to Villa La Angostura. The morning begins cool and cloudy but by the time I have ridden an hour the sun is shining and the temperature has come up enough for me to remove my outer nylon jacket. Spectacular views confront me as I ride farther into the mountains. I breeze through the Argentina border crossing, then ride about sixteen kilometers before I see a "Welcome to Chile" sign. About another twenty kilometers I reach the Chile border controls. My passport and carnet are stamped and I continue riding across the Andes to Orsono. It is mid afternoon when I arrive and I have only come 245 kilometers. It has been a tiring day so I decide to stop here for the night. I book into the Hospedaje Perez for five thousand Chilean pesos. One Canadian dollar equals 469.15 Chilean pesos. This is a great deal for a very comfortable room.

The next morning I ride north on Auto Ruta 5 before veering left toward the west coast and Valdivia. The fog is thick here so I head east, crossing Ruta 5 en route to Panquipulli. I take a road going around Lago Calafquen and battle about thirty kilometers of gravel. The scenery is incredible but the road is atrocious. I continue on to Villarrica, then to Pucón where I stop for lunch. From the streets of Pucón I have an awesome view of Volcano Villarrica.

From here I continue north to Temuco, then on to Victoria. Riding these roads is a real treat. There is no shortage of curves, and the scenery is breathtaking. I ride 480 kilometers today, making many stops for pictures, and enjoying my surroundings. I book into a nice hotel for fifteen thousand pesos. Toll roads on the Auto Ruta cost me sixteen hundred pesos today. I can see that Chile will be a bit more expensive than Argentina.

In the morning my plan is to ride off the highway west to Concepcion, but fog hangs low to the ground, creating poor visibility. There's not much to see in this weather. I stay on Ruta 5 heading north to Rancagua. About every hour I go through a tollbooth and pay another four hundred pesos. I leave the highway at Rancagua and find a good motel for the night. I guess you could say I am treating myself, as I haven't even considered pitching my tent these past few days. My room is beautiful. It has a big double bed, gas fireplace, table and chairs, TV, radio, double doors leading out to an enclosed patio and yard, and a huge bathroom. This is heaven!

Rancagua is about an hours ride south of Santiago. I consider continuing, but it is already 5:30 and I do not want to reach the city in rush hour. My plan is to arrive in Santiago in the morning, giving myself lots of time to find my way around and locate Marilu's B&B. Norma has booked the B&B, which is quite central to downtown and its sights, and the price is reasonable.

The sky is clouded over again when I leave the following morning. I find my way into Santiago with no problem and make my way to Avenue Ameneda. I have studied my map and know I will have to turn right to find Marilu's B&B. I ride in the fourth lane from the right. The first three lanes are for buses only. It is difficult to watch for street signs from this distance and I wonder how I will cross three lanes of bus traffic when I need to turn. Even though this is not the busiest time of day, traffic seems to buzz around me. I am glad I did not attempt this last night.

I know my street is coming up soon so I watch for my chance to squeeze between buses. I manage to sneak through without being hit, and when I'm safely on the side street I stop and look for signs. I am so proud of myself. I have turned onto Rafael Canas Street—the street Marilu's B&B is on. My angels were surely guiding me.

Marilu is a wonderful woman and her B&B looks cozy. Unfortunately, there is no place to park my motorcycle. Marilu calls a taxi and takes me to Tata's B&B farther out in the suburbs. Her parents just happen to be the owners and the place is wonderful, with a high fence and backyard pool. There is room to park my bike, and Norma's when it arrives, by the pool.

Marilu offers a host of information about interesting sights to see and how to use the bus system. After unpacking my gear I take a bus downtown and walk the area known for hostels. I check out several but do not find one that is as nice as Tata's. Some are cheaper but not enough to give up the comfort of a nice B&B. Getting around by bus is easy so I decide to stay put.

Sunday morning, March 14, is cloudy as I set off in a taxi to meet Norma at the airport. The plane landed twenty minutes early but getting through customs takes an hour. The airport is very busy and the halls are packed with people. I am wondering how I will possibly find her in this mob. I walk the length of the arrival hall three times, and then climb halfway up the stairs and look above the crowd. That was a brilliant idea! In a few minutes I spot her and push my way through the crowd. This is the first time we have met. We both belong to the same motorcycle group in Edmonton, but only know each other through e-mails. Norma joined the group after I left in 2001. I am excited about meeting her and happy to have a riding companion. This will be a great way to finish off my trip around the world.

Later in the afternoon I call Rafael, a contact Art gave me when I was in Ushuaia. Art said that if I needed any help while in Santiago I was to call Rafael. I would like to ask his assistance in clearing Norma's bike at customs, and also with finding a place to purchase a windshield for my bike. I talk to him for a few minutes on the phone, and then he offers to come to the B&B to meet us. We have a wonderful visit. Rafael runs a motorcycle touring company and offers to show us around and help us with the bikes.

On Monday morning we begin Spanish classes. I have found a teacher who will come out to the B&B and give us a week of private lessons on the patio. The cost is one hundred and fifty thousand pesos for twenty hours for two of us—about one hundred and sixty Canadian dollars each. I enjoy these lessons. I am getting a good review of my week studying in Buenos Aires, plus I am learning much more.

Hilde and Gus, the owners of Tata's, speak to us in Spanish each day. They are a great help. By the end of our week of lessons we are ready to have some fun.

On Saturday, March 20, we take the bus downtown and walk up the hill to Santa Lucia, then to the pedestrian mall. We go to the market and wander through the fresh fish market. Vendors try to sell us produce or try to coax us into their restaurants. We walk through a second time to find a spot to eat. A gentleman sitting at one table says, "Are you from Canada?"

We are surprised at his perfect English and stop to talk. He invites us to sit and visit. I am about to sit, when I have vivid flashbacks of the high-pressure sales people I met in other countries. I step back and ask directly, "What are you selling?"

He says with a chuckle, "Amway?"

I persist and ask what his business is. I continue to interrogate him until I'm satisfied he is not trying to sell us anything. As we chat we learn that he is in the software business and lived in Canada for twenty years. He has just moved back to Chile to expand his business here. His name is James and his wife and daughter are still in Canada. It is interesting listening to him talk about AVC (Alberta Vocational College), U of A (University of Alberta), Whyte Avenue, and many more familiar names around Edmonton.

We order lunch and continue our visit. I order eel, at Jamie's recommendation. I am a little reluctant but not disappointed once I taste it. Eel is a white meat, flaky like fish but with no fish taste. It has a more solid texture and is very good.

Later Jamie takes us to Avenue Suecia in Providencia, where you'll find all the good restaurants and pubs. We each order a pisco sour, a popular and powerful Chilean drink made from grapes, but not at all like wine. It is more like a lime margarita, but better. After a few of these the three of us take a cab to Avenue Cordoba in Vitacura to attend a wine tasting festival. One would think we should be *toast* by now with all the drinks we have had. I guess they have been spread out over a few hours and we have been doing enough walking to stay sober. Jamie, on the other hand, has had much more to drink. We end up sending him home in a cab early in the evening. Norma and I take a bus back to our B&B. It has been a wonderful day and Jamie has shown us a good time.

On Sunday morning Rafael and his friend José come by the B&B on their BMW's. Norma's bike is not here yet so she rides behind Rafael, and I take my own bike. The guys take us on a scenic ride to Con Con where José has an apartment overlooking the bay. We tour the town before buying groceries and riding to the apartment. José barbeques fresh fish and Rafael prepares a couple of tasty salads. These two men are excellent cooks and during our visit we find out that José is quite wealthy. He was in the restaurant business and the sale of one restaurant brought around two million dollars US. He has five motorbikes, several cars, four houses, and is divorced! Hmm—is it worth a try? I am told it is just as easy to love a rich man as a poor man. What is it they say about *luck*? "Luck is when opportunity meets preparedness." I guess I'm just not prepared.

We spend the next few days seeing the sights of Santiago while waiting for Norma's bike to arrive at the docks in San Antonio. On Wednesday Rafael calls to say that the ship has docked in San Antonio. He has turned the paperwork over to Carlos, a customs agent, who will handle it from here. It is Sunday before Carlos calls to request Norma's passport. She feels a little nervous about handing her passport over, so I suggest that she go with him.

Norma is on edge about all this. I remember my frustrations when I was in Australia and my bike got lost. I try to be positive and assure her that it will go well. She calls Rafael and he agrees to go with her. San Antonio is only one hundred and ten kilometers away.

On Monday morning I take my bike to a shop to check out a coolant leak and to buy a windshield. They do not have the same windshield as my original, so I settle for one that is much smaller and has a completely different mounting system. The coolant leak was just a worn gasket. Rafael will install my windshield after he and Norma return with her bike. At 1:00 PM they leave for San Antonio. I spend my time packing up things to send home. When I'm done the box is full and the cost to send it is forty-three thousand pesos—almost one hundred dollars Canadian!

At 7:30 Rafael calls to say they are almost back in Santiago. He then invites me to bring my bike to José's place where they will re-assemble Norma's bike and mount my windshield.

The sun goes down early here and when I leave the B&B it is dark. I have been to José's place a couple of times and think I know the way. After all it is only four kilometers from the B&B. Everything looks different in the dark though, and I take one wrong turn that sends me off into another area of Santiago. By the time I find my way back, an hour and a half has elapsed. When I finally reach José's, they are all worried and were about to send someone out to look for me.

Words cannot express how much I appreciate the help Rafael and José have given us. On Tuesday, March 30, Raphael leads Norma and I on a ride to Valle Nevado. It is a cloudy day but nice for riding. We are going up a mountain pass with forty-two switchbacks. It is a strenuous ride for Norma; being the first one she's done in months. When we reach the fifteenth switchback it begins to rain, so we decide to turn back. I would have loved to go right to the end but the weather is just not cooperating.

On our way back to the B&B we stop for coffee and Rafael gives us maps and contacts for our travels north of Santiago. He also gives us a contact name in La Paz, Bolivia. This is wonderful.

On March 31 we leave the B&B. It is raining off and on and Norma tries to talk me into staying until the rain stops. I know from experience that it could be like this for days. It is not that bad and I vote for starting out today. I have been here over two weeks and am anxious to resume traveling.

It is 10:00 AM by the time we start out, and traffic leaving Santiago is hectic. We take Highway 57 north to Los Andes, getting lost several times in an effort to find San Felipe and Highway 60. Once again I wish I had a GPS. On the bright side, we ride through several quaint little towns boasting stately old buildings on clean, quiet streets. We pass by grape orchards and farmland but never do find Highway 60. Somehow we are back on Highway 5 and ride along the coast to Los Vilos. The coastal route bordering the Pacific Ocean is great, winding its way around hills and through valleys. At Los Vilos we turn right on Highway 97 and ride inland sixty kilometers to Illapel (pronounced Ee-a-pell). The weather has improved all day, reinforcing my decision to leave Santiago this morning.

Before we leave the following morning Norma repacks her bags. She has brought a lot of stuff. After traveling for almost three years I have learned to pack light. I anticipate that after a couple of weeks she will be sending a box home. It is 10:00 when we finally get on the road.

We continue north on 97 through brown hills covered in small tufts of sage brush and plastered with huge cacti fringed with bright red flowers. As we ride higher the landscape becomes more barren.

We pass through Los Pozos and Combarbalá before the landscape changes again to fruit orchards and vineyards around Monte Patria and Ovalle. At Ovalle we take Highway 43 north to La Serena situated on the Pacific coast. Rafael has recommended Les Mouettes Hotel owned by the family of his friend Daniel, who is also a rider. We get a nice two-bedroom suite with a kitchenette and patio bordering the pool. We will stay two nights and tour the Pisco Elqui Valley tomorrow.

I have quit recording the money I spend. Somewhere back in Europe the cost of everything was so high I stopped entering it in my journals. I thought it would be cheaper traveling with a partner, but it seems we have just moved up to a higher class of tourist.

From La Serena we ride east on winding roads through dry brown mountains that rise up around green orchards of the Elqui Valley. Irrigation is responsible for the lush green grape orchards nestled in the valley amongst the brown hills. We ride to the end of the road to Pisco Elqui, stopping to tour the vineyard and sample Chile's famous pisco sour drink. We have lunch in Monte Grande and tour some interesting little villages before returning to La Serena.

On Saturday, April 3, at 10:30 we leave La Serena in temperatures cool enough to warrant wearing my heated liner under my jacket. Our destination is Copiapo, about three hundred and fifty kilometers north on Highway 5. At Vallenar we head west to the little fishing village of Huasco for lunch. Daniel highly recommended this place for its fresh seafood and fish. We ride through the narrow village streets built on a slope at the edge of the ocean before stopping at "Los Delicias Del Mar" restaurant. There is not much room for safe parking and as we struggle to find a spot a gentleman comes by and suggests we park on the sidewalk. What a great idea!

All eyes are on us as we enter the restaurant. People are curious about two women riding motorcycles. The menu consists of every kind of fish and seafood you can imagine, but the special today is eel. Norma and I both decide to try it and are not disappointed. It was worth the fifty-seven-kilometer ride off the highway.

From Vallenar to Copiapo the road becomes straight and boring with not much to see but dry brown earth. It is already late in the afternoon so I pick up the speed to one hundred and twenty for this last one hundred and fifty-kilometer stretch. We arrive in Copiapo early enough to wander through the central plaza and watch the street performers playing flutes, guitars, accordions, and other instruments. This evening the main attraction is a young man playing his flute accompanied by a guitarist. Fantastic entertainment. This is one of the things I love so much about South America.

The next morning, as we are leaving Copiapo, I signal to turn left at a "no left turn" sign, but quickly change my mind when an oncoming police truck throws on his lights and siren. I watch my rear view mirror for a block or two and am relieved that he did not come after me. I must pay more attention to these signs.

Continuing north on Highway 97 to Diego de Almagro is a pleasant ride. From here we turn east to El Salvador, riding through a canyon of marbled walls of pinks, grays, and greens. About twenty kilometers from El Salvador the road begins to climb around the side of the canyon wall until it reaches the plateau. Spectacular! Another great ride.

In El Salvador a good-looking man driving a car stops us and asks if we need help.

I ask, in my best Spanish, "Donde esta el restaurante?"

He replies, "Follow me."

We follow him down the hill a few blocks until he stops and motions for us to wait. He runs across the street into a yard and fires up his motorcycle. As he rides out he waves for us to follow.

Our new guide leads us on a little tour of El Salvador, then to a club at the top of a hill where they serve a set menu on Sundays. He visits with us for a few minutes and speaks with the waiter for us. Saying his goodbyes with a kiss on the cheek he leaves us to enjoy our meal. *Ooh, I could get so used to this custom.*

There are many families dining here today and the meals coming from the kitchen look wonderful. For the first course, we are served a beautifully arranged salad of one half avocado with sauce, shrimp, tomato, and lettuce. The second course is fish and veggies, and for dessert, ice cream and coffee. Our bill is 10,500 pesos, or about twenty-three dollars Canadian. Not bad for two meals like this.

We retrace our route through the canyon back to Diego de Almagro and stop for fuel. As we are leaving the gas station a dog runs out and keeps pace along the right side of my bike. I keep an eye on him expecting him to drop back, but instead he picks up speed and takes a bite at my ankle. I am startled and quickly accelerate to lose him. Good thing I'm wearing strong leather boots. When I stop later I can see his teeth marks in the leather.

We continue west on 97 to Highway 5 then turn north and head for Taltal, a nice little town along the ocean. The scenery on this stretch consists of brown and black hills, and the landscape is very dry, with not much habitation. When we leave Highway 5 and ride the last short distance towards the ocean, the road winds around mountains, which is very pleasant. In Taltal we find a charming room at the Hotel mi Tampi, a block from the ocean, for twenty thousand pesos. We are ready for some relaxation so will spend two nights here.

On April 6 we leave Taltal at 9:30 for Calama. It seems impossible to get an earlier start so I keep my cool and try hard to adjust. It will be a long day, covering about five hundred kilometers through the Atacama Desert. This desert is known to be the driest in the world. The temperature gets very hot during the day but cools off nicely in the evening. There is not much to see except dirt, sand, and crumpled cement walls depicting the ruins of villages long gone. About thirty kilometers from Antofagasta I catch sight of a large hand reaching out of the desert floor. Rudi, an avid rider from home, had told me about this and had shown me pictures of his ride through here. I stop on the side of the highway and talk to Norma. The road into the monument is gravel and sand so she decides not to ride in. I must get a picture of my bike in front of the hand, so I ride in alone.

By the time I return to the highway Norma is gone—I guess she got tired of waiting for me in this heat. I continue on to Antofagasta and spot her at a gas station.

After lunch we continue on to Calama. We are riding northeast on Highway 97, away from the Pacific coast. The landscape changes slightly with rounded hills that look like ripples of bread dough in the first kneads. We arrive in Calama at 6:30 and find a room at the Hotel Casablanca. After a shower and change of clothes we take a nice pedestrian walkway to the plaza in search of dinner.

Next morning we ride to Chuquicamata and take a tour of the copper mine. This is the largest open pit copper mine in the world. A fault line runs along one side of the terraced walls and mini earth tremors cause it to move a few millimeters each day. In February of 2003, an earthquake caused it to move five meters. Earthquake tremors occur almost daily along this fault line and the coast of Chile.

It is mid afternoon when we leave here and head to San Pedro de Atacama. As I round the crest of one hill the view takes my breath away. The mountains are marbled in shades of red, pink, gray, and brown. Jagged rocks protrude from the earth, lining the road and filling parts of the valley. Rivers of sand trail down between the rocks. The road winds through this amazing scene for about ten kilometers. A picture could not capture the beauty of it all. I wonder if this is what it would look like on the moon.

We ride into San Pedro de Atacama at around 7:00 PM. The village is small, so it does not take long to find a room. After checking a few places we settle on the Chiloe Hostel for twenty thousand pesos for two; it's very comfortable and clean.

I awaken at 4:00 AM and cannot go back to sleep, so I sit out on the patio and gaze up at the stars. The moon is almost full tonight and the stars shine brightly. What a peaceful and magical night.

After breakfast we tour the town to find a gas station. There is only one and it is tucked away in a narrow back street with no signs for directions. With our tanks full we ride out to Valle de la Luna (Valley of the Moon). We leave the pavement and ride on a road of sand and gravel to reach the park entrance. A lone attendant charges us a small entrance fee, and then we brave the road taking us higher into hills of jagged rock and sand. No vegetation exists out here.

We return to San Pedro for fuel before riding fifty-five kilometers south to Salar de Atacama, the largest salt flat in Chile and the second largest in the world. The area is surrounded by the Andes with large volcanic mountains visible to the east. The salt flat is a rough surface, due to the lack of water, and covers three thousand square kilometers. We park our bikes and walk out to Laguna Chaxa where the pink flamingos feed.

Back in San Pedro we meet Norman and Maggie, riding F650 BMW's. They are staying in the same hostel as us. We go to dinner with them and find out they are from Belfast, Ireland and are riding from Ushuaia to Alaska. Their trip has been delayed due to Maggie breaking her elbow during a fall with her bike. Norman tells us about the wonderful medical attention Maggie received in South America and how people were helpful *beyond the call of duty.*"

On Friday, April 9, we leave our little oasis in the desert and ride west to Tocopilla, then follow the Pacific coast south to Antofagasta.

It's rugged here and several areas of the road look like they were built over rockslides left behind from earthquakes. Small memorials have been erected along the way.

Over the next few days we follow Highway 5 south, retracing some of our route back to Los Andes. My bike odometer has turned over 100,000 kilometers. What a great bike—she is serving me well.

The landscape has become greener, but as we go south the clouds become heavy and the air grows cold. I plug in my electric liner to stay warm. We arrive in Los Andes late afternoon on April 12 and check into the Hotel Los Andes. It has been a tiring day and we are ready for a hot shower and nap before dinner. Tomorrow we will cross the Andes into Argentina. We have decided to ride to Iguazu Falls.

Chapter 12
Argentina

It is 9:30 on Tuesday, April 13, when Norma and I leave Los Andes, Chile (elevation 890 meters) and ride east on Highway 60 towards the Andes Mountains. The road is paved but rough for several kilometers and the scenery is incredible with the mountains in the distance. Riding higher into the mountains we encounter a steep ten-kilometer stretch where I count twenty-nine hairpin switchbacks. Trucks pulling two trailers creep along at a snail's pace, using every gear available. After a few switchbacks I stop at a pullout to take pictures and wait for Norma.

We conquer this stretch of the Andes and continue to ride around mountain curves before reaching Tunel del Cristo Rendentor, at an elevation of 3,185 meters. Chile Customs is contained within a huge carved out area inside the tunnel. Getting our passports stamped to exit the country goes smoothly. Back on our bikes we travel several more kilometers, enjoying the curves until we reach Argentina's border. Here we are instructed to fill out an entry form written in Spanish. The woman in the customs booth is not interested in helping, so between the two of us (using our limited Spanish) we manage to figure it out and return to the booth. From here we ride another twenty minutes through more beautiful scenery to another checkpoint where we present our passports and papers before continuing our ride east.

We are now on Highway 7. The road winds down along the side of the mountains with several extremely dark tunnels providing passage through the rock. We make a stop for fuel and lunch in the neat little wild-west town of Uspallata at nineteen hundred meters. Upsallata draws its fame from being the location where they filmed *Seven Years in Tibet,* starring Brad Pitt.

The road continues to decline around the mountains until we are riding in a canyon. Near Mendoza the landscape opens up to present the beautiful Mendoza Valley. Mendoza is known for its exquisite wines. We find a room at the Hotel Zamora, a quaint old building recommended by other travelers. Our room is comfortable and clean, and costs thirty-eight pesos (about seventeen dollars), including breakfast. After settling in we go for a walk through the Plaza de Independence. The Square covers a complete block and is covered with brick and tile surrounding immaculate gardens, statues, and fountains. It's a wonderful place to come and relax.

The next morning we miss the city tour we booked the previous evening. Not realizing we went through a time change, our clocks are still on Chile time. The agency kindly refunds our money. Our plan is to leave tomorrow so we do not book another tour.

Norma has to downsize her gear so she spends the morning putting a package together. I pack my journal and backup disks of pictures to send home to my daughter. We are at the post office for two hours before our parcels are stamped to go. Carlos, the young man waiting on Norma, is very friendly and informs her that he is starting a local tour company in his spare time. He offers to take us on a canyon tour for one hundred dollars US, but cannot go until Saturday. We discuss the issue over lunch and decide to stay.

Over the next two days we discover some excellent restaurants and tour a few vineyards. Mendoza has a relaxing atmosphere. It would be easy to stay here for an extended visit. People are very friendly and take time to stop and chat. Back at the hotel we meet Angel, an artist from Eastern Canada, and invite her along on our canyon tour. She is excited to go, so we confirm the extra person with Carlos and make arrangements for him to pick us up at eight Saturday morning.

Carlos arrives right on time, bringing pictures of his Virago, and of his family and friends. He is so passionate about his bike that I am surprised when he says he sold it last year to buy the Land Rover.

"I needed money to buy the Land Rover so I could start up a tour business," he says with a slight tone of regret.

We take a route used by many bus tours. The bonus of going in a Land Rover rather than a bus is that we continue farther into the canyon after the buses stop and turn around.

It is a spectacular drive through the canyon. We stop for pictures and short walks to get the best views. Carlos takes us on a different route though the canyon on our way back to Mendoza. It is late in the afternoon and the Land Rover is overheating, causing him to stop several times to let it cool down. He is concerned that we may be caught in the canyon after dark. It is advised that vehicles travel in pairs out here or have a backup plan in case of emergency. Angel, Norma, and I try not to look worried. With several cool-down stops we make it out of the canyon to a small service station where Carlos adds water to the radiator once the truck has cooled.

The sun has gone down by the time we reach Mendoza. Carlos has been an excellent guide and looks sad that the tour is over.

On Sunday, April 18, we leave Mendoza at 9:30 under blue skies and sunshine, riding west on Highway 7. The countryside becomes greener and more level. At San Luis we head off on Highway 20, a secondary road with lots of curves. At La Toma we ride north on Highway 2 experiencing very badly broken pavement with many potholes to dodge. We are now in farmland with rolling landscape, crops, cattle, fields with clumps of tall cattail, grass, and small, small trees.

At San Martin we ride thirty kilometers through a pretty canyon to Highway 20 taking us to Villa Dolores. We have had a long day and are glad to stop for the night.

The ride next morning is short and unforgettable. The road winds through Rocky Mountains, reaching up over fifteen hundred meters. We stop to enjoy the breathtaking view of the valley and road below.

At one viewpoint and rest area we stop for coffee and watch the condors flying high above the mountains.

We reach Alta Gracia early in the day and check into a beautiful room overlooking a large green, park-like yard. This lovely little city was once frequented by the wealthy. Ernesto "Che" Guevara grew up here. His childhood home is now a museum. Many articles line the walls, recounting stories of his youth, his family, and his life as a revolutionary.

From here we visit the Casa-Museo Manuel de Falla, which honors a famous musician and composer. Of course we cannot leave without buying one of his CDs.

As we stroll along the streets of Alta Gracia we take pictures of the homes occupied by upper-class families. Most are built of brick or Spanish stucco and boast several window turrets with balconies. Some are two story and some are bungalow style, all with professionally landscaped and manicured yards.

The morning is half gone by the time we pack up and begin our ride the following day. Norma and I have very different personalities—I am a morning person and she doesn't shift into gear until much, much later. It is great to have a riding companion but I do miss my early morning rides.

We continue east on Highway 13 and 19 towards Santa Fe. This is farm country and we pass many combines, big tractors, and eighteen-wheelers. The season here is fall and harvesting is in full swing. After San Francisco the wind comes up and by the time we reach Santa Fe we are tired from being battered around on the bikes.

Between Santa Fe and Paraná we cross the Rio (River) Paraná arriving in the city at 6:00 PM. Paraná is the capital city of the province of Entre Rios and offers beautiful landscapes, beaches, monuments, historical architecture, and plenty of activities. We stay an extra day to explore the sights. Moments before dinner we get caught in a downpour, so we duck into a restaurant and relax over a great meal and a bottle of wine.

Thunder rolls loudly most of the night, dumping a fair amount of rain. In the morning we pack up and continue north on Highway 12 following the east side of the Paraná River. It rains off and on all day. I would like to make it to Saladas, but somehow I take a wrong turn and we end up in Empedrado in the pouring rain. We are soaked to the skin when we arrive and Norma seems angry. *Hey, I didn't call for the rain.* A beautiful rainbow greets us as we ride into Empedrado, but even that does not cheer her up.

The only room we can find in this little town is small and dingy and costs thirty-five pesos. We hang our clothes from every spot we can find, even the ceiling fan. We have traveled over five hundred kilometers today and I begin to wonder if that is too long of a day for Norma.

Friday we stay on Highway 12, riding north to Corrientes, then northeast to Posadas in the province of Misiones. The terrain changes to rolling hills with red soil and lots of trees. At Santa Ana we turn onto Highway 14 to Oberá and San Vicente, where we get a room at the Richard Palace Hotel for thirty-six pesos. We have ridden 556 kilometers today and are ready for a rest.

I have noticed a lot of people on horseback in this area, including children of all ages going to school, men working with cattle, and others just out for a leisurely ride.

The next morning I go for breakfast alone. Norma is in a foul mood and not talking. Maybe she is just tired or maybe I'm pushing her too hard. There is just so much to see that I don't want to waste time sleeping.

We are on the road at 9:30 and have a great ride to Puerto Iguazu. It is a short trip today so we arrive by early afternoon. We check out the park entrance fee, and then ride to Iguazu to find Cabañas Leñador, recommended by Norman and Maggie. Our cabin is beautiful with two large bedrooms, kitchen, sitting room, bathroom, and a deck off the front door. The cost is ninety-five US dollars, but we splurge and book for two nights.

The following morning is Sunday and we have a leisurely breakfast at 9:00 before going out to the falls. Puerto Iguazu is at the northeast tip of Argentina bordering Paraguay on the west, Brazil on northeast, and Argentina on the south. We take a boat ride on some of the upper pools, and then walk the paths viewing the falls. What a magnificent sight! Another tourist told us the water is low this year and we might be disappointed, but we are in awe. Even with the lack of rain, the falls are spectacular. We walk for miles taking all the trails in order to capture all the views. On one trail we encounter twenty or more coati (an animal about the size of a raccoon). A park warden is standing guard and warns us that they might bite.

It has been a fabulous day and well worth the miles we had to ride to get here. Pictures cannot do justice to this sensational park.

The next morning starts out cool. This part of Argentina is very green and treed. Logging is the major export (about 70 percent), then tobacco and tea. The ride is very pleasant and by noon it has warmed up nicely. We stop at San Ignacio and tour through the Jesuit museum and ruins.

It is 6:00 PM when we arrive at Ituzaingó, a small town built along the water. We find the Hosteria Ituzaingó and secure a fabulous room for fifty pesos—down from seventy-five. The manager's name is also "Norma" and she gives us a deal when she sees our bikes. Norma rides a 1500 Kawasaki Vulcan and is excited to hear about our journey.

The following morning we visit the tourist building which houses a display of the controversial dam on the Paraná River. The display is very well done and even with our limited Spanish we can understand most of it. I inquire about riding out to the dam but am told that it is not allowed. We would have to wait an hour for the next bus tour, but we decide not to wait and continue on to Resistencia. We retrace our route west on Highway 12, following the Rio Paraná to Corrientes in the province of Chaco, where we cross the river to Resistencia.

Resistencia is popularly known as "The City of Sculptures" and an "Open Air Museum", due to the fact that over four hundred sculptures have been placed on sidewalks and in parks all over the city. Several monuments are representative of women and the family.

Sometime in the past few days I remember someone telling us not to travel in the province of Chaco because it can be dangerous. In order to avoid this province we would have to travel south, west, and north again, adding unnecessary miles. So I opt to go through.

From here we take Highway 16 northwest to 94 where we continue southwest to Highway 89 and 34 to Santiago del Estero. We make a lunch stop along the way at General Pinedo. Both Norma and I order a salad and water. When we ask for our bill the waiter says, "No, no charge."

Can you believe it! We are overwhelmed and both leave a two-dollar tip. That may not sound like much, but here it is very generous.

We arrive in Santiago del Estero, after riding 607 kilometers, and cannot find a room. After trying four establishments, the clerk in the fourth hotel phones five other places and is able to get us into the Savoy Hotel. Our bikes are drawing a lot of attention today, more so than any other day. We are sure to park them in a secure place out of sight.

It is late and we are tired, so we order a pizza and beer and relax. The pizza is large enough that we cannot eat it all. We offer the last two pieces to an old man sitting on the sidewalk and he accepts it graciously.

The next morning we ride northwest on Highway 9 towards San Miguel de Tucumán. Norma seems to be falling behind more and more each day. I am not traveling at a high speed so cannot understand why. Maybe riding five and six hundred kilometers a day is too much for her. I must remember that I have been doing this for close to three years and am more conditioned than her. I keep my cool by stopping often and taking pictures while I wait for her to catch up.

I decide to bypass Tucumán and take Ruta 307 to Cafayate. Rudy had mentioned this route, making it sound very nice. I am not disappointed. Ruta 307 takes us through rain forests along roads that cling to the side of the mountain, sometimes only wide enough for one vehicle. I am glad I'm on my bike.

As we climb higher, rain forests make way for brown mountains scattered with tall cactus. The wind picks up as we ride higher and higher. I stop more often for pictures, and a couple of times turn around and go in search of Norma to make sure she is okay.

We reach Cafayate just before 6:00 PM, covering about three hundred kilometers. It has taken us all day! Cafayate is quiet now but the population triples in tourist season, which is January and February. It is an important site in the Calchaqui Valley and known for its famous Torrontes wine. The elevation is over sixteen hundred meters, providing an exquisite combination of temperature and humidity for growing sweet and deep flavored grapes.

The next day we have a short ride to Salta via Route 68. The landscape changes to jagged red rock framed by pink and grey mountains. The road is great, with lots of curves, making the ride very enjoyable.

Before reaching Salta we take a side road around a beautiful lake. The curves are tight rounding the hills that follow alongside the lake. What a picture-perfect place.

We arrive in Salta early in the day. I suggest we look for the hotel in San Lorenzo that Norman and Maggie suggested. It is twelve kilometers out of the city, but Norma prefers to find a place in downtown Salta. We find a wonderful room at the Casa de Familia for ten pesos each. We park our bikes in a parkade around the corner for three pesos each per night. The parkade enlists twenty-four hour security, so I feel comfortable leaving the bikes there.

Today is Friday and we spend the rest of the afternoon looking for a shop to get the oil changed and a complete service job for our bikes. I need a chain and sprocket set as well. We find a shop that will service the bikes but they cannot fit them in until Monday, and we must bring all the parts. It takes a lot of walking to various shops for us to find the oil and filters. I can't find the chain and sprockets, but I do buy a chain that *seems* to be the right size. We will have to wait until Monday to see.

On Saturday evening we run into Angel and have dinner with her. It is such a small world. We had no idea she was traveling in this direction.

Salta is a lively city and a major tourist destination due to its old colonial architecture and monuments. It is situated in the Lerma Valley at almost twelve hundred meters above sea level, and is surrounded by mountains. Salta lays claim to being the nicest site ever created by nature in this region. It is also the starting point of the *Train to the Clouds*. We book a mountain/canyon excursion by jeep for Tuesday.

On Monday morning we are up early to take our bikes into the shop. We wait until the mechanic can look at the bikes, especially to make sure the chain I bought will fit. We have supplied Castrol 4T(GP) oil which costs ten pesos per liter, but the mechanic says we should have Castrol GPS oil priced at nineteen pesos per liter. Norma opts to exchange hers; I decide to use what I bought. The chain I picked up Friday will not work, so we spend at least another hour walking to various supply shops to find the right one. Unfortunately, no one has the complete chain and sprocket unit, so I purchase the chain and front sprocket only. The rear sprocket will have to do for now.

The guys at Avalon Moto Shop are wonderful. The price of parts is very high compared to labour. I am charged only a hundred and ten pesos for my oil change and for replacing the chain and front sprocket. The price of the parts is 419 pesos.

At seven o'clock Tuesday morning we are picked up for our tour. Yako is our guide. He is native to northern Argentina and speaks several languages. Our tour takes us on Ruta 51 to San Antonio de los Cobres—driving through clouds until Santa Rosa de Tastil, where we stop for a break. Locals in the village have their crafts displayed and count on tourists for income. It is cool up here so I buy a nice big shawl I can wrap around my upper body to stay warm. From here to San Antonio we drive above the clouds. What an awesome view—the mountaintops look like they are floating on clouds. The colors in the rock are spectacular. At San Antonio we are at thirty-seven hundred meters.

After lunch we drive higher and stop for pictures at 4,080 meters. From here we head north on Ruta 40 to Salinas Grandes, a large salt flat, where we are still over three thousand meters above sea level.

We begin our descent above the clouds, heading northeast on Ruta 40, and are soon driving straight into them. As we descend farther and exit the clouds, the scenery is stunning once again. The mountains in the canyon become more colorful and resemble ribbons draped across the rock. We drop lower and drive through more clouds and rain before returning to Salta at 8:30 PM. It has been a long but fabulous day.

The next morning is cloudy but we leave around ten anyway, taking Ruta 9 through the rain forest to San Salvador de Jujuy (meaning joy or happiness). Fantastic ride! By noon the sun has burned off the clouds, revealing a bright but chilly day.

We stop several times for pictures. The mountains look like they have been painted with a huge brush of many colors swiped across the face in an arch. Other formations are tall, narrow spirals looking like the peaks of a castle.

We are continually climbing. The area between Tilcara and Quebrada de Humachuaca is exceptionally beautiful and takes us over three thousand meters. When we reach Quiaca we are at 3,447 meters (11,309 feet) above sea level.

Quiaca is the border town between northwest Argentina and Bolivia. We get a very nice room at the Hosteria Munay and stay the night. Tomorrow we leave Argentina behind. It is such a diverse country. I love it all.

Chapter 13
Bolivia

It is 10:00 AM on Thursday, May 6, when we leave La Quiaca, Argentina. The temperature is so cold that my bike does not want to start. It takes a bit of coaxing before the engine turns over.

The border crossing is just outside of La Quiaca, joining the town of Villazon, Bolivia. Our paperwork goes smoothly and by 11:30 we are free to travel the roads of Bolivia. A short distance from Villazon we encounter our first road washout. The waterhole is quite large, but

easy enough to maneuver. The more treacherous part is handling the deep ridges of sand and gravel on the other side. I ride my bike through successfully then turn to coach Norma. She is too afraid to give it a try, so I walk back and ride her bike across.

The scenery is spectacular as we ride through a canyon area of multi-colored mountains, small villages, and fields with stooks of grain and a few cattle. Tupiza is set in the valley of the Rio Tupiza and is ringed by the rugged Cordillera de Chichas (a mountain range).

The road consists of gravel, rocks, sand, and dirt, making our progress slow. It is after two in the afternoon when we reach Tupiza. We have only traveled 116 kilometers.

We stop for a quick bite to eat before continuing. Norma suggests we stay here and continue tomorrow, but I feel we can make it to Atocha, just one hundred kilometers away. *If I had only known what we were facing …*

It is just after three when we set off, taking the direct route on Highway 21, and weaving around mountains that climb higher in elevation. The road is much worse here, with large rocks spread amongst the sand and gravel. I try to keep Norma in my rear view mirror but she begins to lag far behind. I travel between thirty and sixty kilometers per hour, definitely not fast, but soon lose sight of her. I ride a few curves around the mountain before I can find a relatively safe spot to pull over. This road is narrow and curves limit visibility in either direction. I am careful to pull close to the mountain edge of the road.

I wait about fifteen minutes, and then I become worried that she is in trouble. A vehicle goes by without stopping, so I figure she must be still coming. I wait another ten minutes before deciding to go back and look for her. I have almost made the U-turn when my front wheel catches a large rock and I go down. Quickly I offload my gear and try to pick up my Magna, to no avail. Is it the altitude (we are around thirty-five hundred meters), the rocks under my tires, or am I just tired? I use every ounce of energy I have, but cannot pick it up.

Now what? I desperately hope a vehicle comes along soon. My angels are with me. In a few minutes I see an old rickety bus loaded with people, and I frantically wave both arms above my head. The bus is packed. People are hanging out the windows and standing in the doorway. One man is hanging out the door. The scene looks like something out of a cartoon.

The bus comes to a stop. In seconds two or three men are at my bike, stand it upright, and jump back on the bus. Arms are waving everywhere as the bus continues up the road.

I ride back around several curves before spotting Norma. She has something in her hand and is banging on the right side of her bike near the brake pedal. When I come to a stop I ask, "Are you okay? What happened?"

"I took a really bad fall and banged up my knee and elbow," she replies. "There is a rock lodged between my brake pedal and frame. I can't go anywhere until it comes out."

I find a place to turn around, and then try to help. She is very cranky. I can't say that I blame her, but I hope her anger is not directed at me.

We get the rock out, and before continuing I suggest we let some of the air out of our tires. Rafael, in Santiago, had told us that would help when riding on dirt roads.

When we get rolling again, Norma is riding at twenty kilometers per hour. I stop many times so as to keep her in sight. The road is very bad. Some stretches are soft sand, some washboard, and others have a wide variety of rocks. She takes a few more falls. Each time we must offload her gear before picking up the bike. Our energy is zapped. I try to convince her to pick up the speed a little, even to forty kilometers per hour. It is much harder riding at twenty than forty. She is wearing herself out fighting the steering. At this rate we will never reach Atocha before dark.

The scenery is gorgeous and the road would be a biker's dream *if only* it were paved.

The sun will be setting soon and I am concerned. I decide to put Norma in the lead and she does very well. We are climbing higher around mountains, and as the sun sets, we are blinded riding around a couple of hills. We have to stop in a curve to determine which way the road goes, for fear of riding off the cliff.

At about 9:00 PM we still have about ten kilometers to go. The sun has set long ago, making riding in these conditions more difficult. We encounter more soft sand, and the black and yellow Magna wipes out again. This is slowing us down a great deal. In one of her falls the bike is in deep sand and we cannot lift it. Thankfully, a big truck comes along and we get help from the driver. He and his wife look shocked to see us, and demand, "What are you doing out here? Don't you know it is dangerous?"

Now I am really worried. I explain that we want to make it to Atocha and ask, "cuántos kilómetros?"

"Diez kilómetros," he replies. "Tenga cuidado." (Be careful)

Shortly after the truck is out of sight I hit a long, heavy section of sand. My bike fishtails two or three times, then goes down. I thought I was going to make it, but the sand was too thick. I offload my gear and we are able to get it back on its wheels.

At 10:00 PM we come to the end of the road. We have run smack dab into a riverbed! It is pitch black out and I cannot see where to go from here. I dig out a shoe to place under my kickstand, to prevent it from sinking into the sand. I try to find my flashlight. Norma suggests we put up our tents, but I disagree.

"It is way too dangerous to stay out here all night. We have no idea who will come through here. Besides, we would probably freeze to death overnight."

Norma has found her flashlight, so I take it and go for a walk. I can see vehicle tracks going in both directions in the sand and water of the riverbed. There is also a light on the other side of the river. I decide we should try to cross and see if that is Atocha.

The sand is hard packed, making riding much easier. I follow the trail leading across a train track and up a bank to a building across the road. Reluctantly, Norma follows until the bank. When I realize she is not coming, I turn around and go back. When I ask her what she is doing she says, "I'll wait for you here."

"No, we can't get separated!" I snap, in an impatient tone. "You can ride up the bank, it's not that bad."

The building turns out to be a petrol station. There is a lone attendant who does not speak English. I use my limited Spanish and ask where the road is to Atocha.

"Allá," he says as he points to the river.

"Cuántos kilómetros?" I ask

"Uno, dos kilómetros," he replies.

I ask, using sign language, if we can pitch our tent inside his locked compound.

He shakes his head vehemently. "No, Atocha esa manera," he states as he points in the direction of the river. Then he bends down and draws a map in the sand. Listening to him carefully I can understand that we must follow the "rio" to Atocha.

I guess we will be trudging on.

We fuel up our bikes and return to the river. It is now 10:30 and very dark, but we have no choice. If we stay on the hard packed track it is not so bad, but the darkness makes it hard to see. Shallow water covers some of the riverbed and ice has formed on parts of the track. I ride slowly, trying to stay in the truck tracks, and at the same time keep an eye on Norma. By now she is so played out she takes a couple more falls. My patience is wearing thin. At one point we must cross a small stream about thirty centimeters deep and two meters wide. At the opposite side is a small bank. I make it across and wait until Norma gets there. She asks me to come back and ride her bike across. I am so tired by now I just snap, "No, I'm not walking through that water. You can ride across."

She makes it across the stream just fine. We can see the lights of Atocha now and continue following the tracks, but we cannot find a road leading into town. The tracks go towards a steep bank at least a meter high. This can't be. This *cannot* be the road into town!

We ride a little farther only to find a washed out bridge. Then I notice a jeep coming down the bank, and wave him down. In my limited Spanish I ask which way into town.

"Allá," he says, pointing to the bank.

I ask if he will wait in case we need help. He shakes his head and says, "Sí."

I think he understands me, but as soon as I get back on my bike he drives away. Okay, this is it. We just have to do it. There is a meter stretch of water then the bank. I know I cannot go too slowly, so I keep a steady speed through the water then accelerate up the bank onto flat ground. Whew, I made it ... now to get Norma across. I park my bike, go to the bank and explain what to do. She hesitates for a few moments then goes for it and makes it safely up the bank. I'm so proud of her, knowing how terrifying this is.

We take a moment to catch our breath before going in search of a hotel. This little town probably only has one. We stop and ask directions and are pointed to the Residencia on the Plaza. The hotel is crappy, but we are able to park our motorcycles inside. The woman who checked us in told us there is hot water. She lied. It is so cold I cannot stand under it. I wash my hair and rinse off very quickly, then crawl into my sleeping bag. When I finally warm up I think I sleep most of the night, in spite of the horrible worn mattress and squeaky springs.

Our dinner tonight was an apple and a few peanuts. It was a very adventurous day, but not one I would like to repeat any time soon.

The altitude at Atocha is 3,715 meters.

We get up around 8:30 in an extremely cold room. There is no heat. After packing up we make an attempt to start the bikes. Norma's bike starts immediately. Mine makes a sympathetic effort but refuses to fire. Now what? I roll it out into the sun and then we go for breakfast. Maybe the sun will warm it up enough to start.

It is 10:00 when I try my bike again. To my relief, it starts. We inquire about a place to wash our bikes so we can remove the sand from the chain. We are directed to a small shop where the fellows take the bikes and do a fabulous job of cleaning them up. Norma and I relax in the sun, trying to make the best of our situation.

It is noon by the time we start riding. The men in the shop tell us to follow the riverbed. "That is the road." They do not seem to know how far, just that it will turn into a road eventually. At least this time we can see.

It is shortly after noon when we start out. Riding is not bad as long as we stay in the wet, hard-packed track. Norma is having a great deal of difficulty. I look at my clock during one stop and find that it is 1:30 and we have traveled only fifteen kilometers. If we don't pick up the pace, we will be riding in the dark again. There are not many places out here to find accommodation.

Finally we ride out of the riverbed and onto a road, battling sand for some distance, then hard packed washboard. I am not sure which is worse. We travel at twenty to thirty kilometers per hour and after forty-five kilometers come to another large river crossing. According to my map it should be Cerdas on the other side of the river. We find what looks like the best place to cross, and ride into the little village. There is one short row of small, mud brick buildings and we look for one that serves lunch. This is not Cerdas, but we cannot understand the name the villagers are calling it. I ask directions to Uyuni and they confirm that we are on the right road by pointing in the direction we will go.

By this time it is 3:30 and we still have seventy kilometers remaining. I ask Norma again if she can please pick up the speed a little so we can make it to Uyuni before dark. She grumbles that she is going as fast as she feels is safe.

The road is better now with the exception of some long, heavy, sandy stretches. In one such stretch I spin out and stop. The sand is so deep my bike ends up in an upright position. I have to get Norma to push me onto the hard packed track. In a rocky, gravel stretch Norma takes another nasty fall. She must be black and blue by now.

When I go to help she tells me her throttle is stuck.

"Maybe that has been part of your problem all along?" I ask.

She agrees that it might be, so after up-righting her bike I proceed to take her throttle lock off. I am so fed up by now that I do not even ask. I just do it. With every fall we have to offload the bike, pick it up, and then reload it. This is wasting so much time that I fear we will repeat last night's experience.

The sun is beginning to disappear behind the mountains by the time I spot Uyuni. I am so relieved that all my earlier frustrations disappear. I spot a tour bus as we ride into town and decide to follow it. I figure that bus is probably going to a hotel. Sure enough, it leads us to the Hotel Tinto where we get a very nice room, plus parking in a locked yard, for thirty Bolivian bolivianos. One Canadian dollar is equal to 6.19 bolivianos, and one US dollar is 8.11 bolivianos.

We have ridden one hundred kilometers in seven hours!

The date is Friday, May 7. Uyuni rests at an altitude of 3,670 meters. It is here where the largest salt flats in the world can be found. That was my reason for taking this route—to see the salt flats.

Hotel Tinto is only two years old and managed by Maria and Tom. Maria is Spanish and her parents own the hotel. Tom is American and is the chef. They are wonderful hosts and welcome us to their hotel and Uyuni. The beds all have fleecy sheets that are a blessing in this chilly air. Maria brings us a portable heater to warm our room. We are so tired that *even I* sleep in the next morning.

A buffet breakfast is included in the price of our room, but after looking at the menu we order pancakes with apple, banana, cinnamon, and whipped cream topping. Delicious! Tom is a great cook.

We book a jeep tour to the Salar de Uyuni for Sunday. Norma flatly refuses to ride her bike out there. Today she stated, "If we ever make it out of here, I am shipping my bike home."

What can I say? This has been way more than she bargained for.

Saturday we do laundry and walk around town a bit. I feel tired and feverish so I return to the hotel and rest. I cannot sleep so I work on my pictures and catch up on my newsletters and Web site. I hope I am not getting sick. I'm probably just tired, or reacting to the altitude.

My battery is presenting problems in this cold air, so I disconnect it, take it into our room and connect the charger. Hopefully it will start when we are ready to leave.

Sunday morning Leo, our guide, arrives to take us to the salt flat. The Salar de Uyuni covers twelve thousand square kilometers at an elevation of 3,670 meters. Our first stop is to see the train cemetery, and then off to Colchani where the salt is purified.

Leo drives out across the salt flat. It looks like one massive sheet of ice. Some places are flat for miles and miles, other places sprout cones of salt where mining or harvesting is taking place.

We drive out to the middle of the salar and stop at the huge rock island, Isla Inkawasi (or Isla Pescado), that looks like a fish. Here we have lunch. Leo has brought along a cook who prepares a wonderful lunch, and serves us at a table made from salt blocks.

Norma and I are served first, then, while Leo and the cook eat, we walk around the island and explore the few buildings located here. Houses are built of salt, rock, and cactus wood, which grow in abundance on the island. Cactus is used to build furniture, doors, and much more, and produces a beautiful lacy finish.

On our way back to town we stop at the cold geysers and the Hotel Playa Blanca, made completely from salt blocks. Visitors could once stay at the hotel but now it is open only to tours, due to the problem with sewers and hygiene.

It was a very interesting day, thanks to our excellent guide and cook.

On Monday, May 9, we leave Uyuni. There has been no fuel at the stations all weekend. I have been checking, and the word is that the fuel truck will arrive this morning. I hope this is true.

My bike will not start, even though the battery is fully charged and warm. I wheel it out into the sun and let it sit while we have breakfast. Finally it starts and we head for the petrol station where we join the line of cars, trucks, and jeeps. Most of the vehicles ahead of us have large gas containers strapped to their roofs or in their truck boxes, making me wonder how much fuel is being delivered. We soon discover that the truck has not arrived yet.

It is noon when the truck gets to the station and I wonder if there will be any fuel left by the time it is our turn. I go to the pumps and try asking if we can move ahead. We only need a small amount of gas, and I don't think it's fair that we should wait behind all these larger loads. No one seems to understand me, but I continue to make noise. Finally, one of the men motions for us to ride up. It is 1:00 PM when we leave.

Norma wants to stay another night. I opt to continue. We have two hundred and fourteen kilometers to Potosí. At the rate we are traveling it will take us two days.

We travel northeast on Highway 5 and are faced with more treacherous roads surrounded by spectacular scenery. Norma is riding so slowly it is painful for me. I cannot ride at that speed. It is much more difficult, and you are more apt to fall. There are times I want to keep on riding and not look back. I scold myself for having such nasty thoughts. After all, she is probably as agitated with me as I am with her. I focus on the beauty of the mountains, canyons, and little villages of stone and mud brick houses with their interesting fences.

It is seven o'clock, the sun has set, and it is dark. We have traveled

134 kilometers today and are still seventy-five from Potosí. We ride into a little village and stop at the first building that has a light on. It looks like a little store, so we go in and I ask, "Un habitacion por dos, por favor?"

"Sí," the clerk responds, pointing towards the back of the store, while motioning for us to come.

He takes us out the front door, through a narrow gate joining his store to the next building, and into the back courtyard. Several doors lead from the courtyard into various rooms—kitchen, bedrooms, and storage. The baño (bathroom) is a small outhouse with a big sink standing beside it. We soon find out that the sink offers only cold water.

It is a tight squeeze to get our bikes through the small gate and alleyway into the courtyard. After off-loading our gear we purchase two buns and a can of tuna from the store and serve dinner on plastic bags. We have not eaten much today since our wonderful breakfast at Hotel Tinto. After examining the beds, we pull out our sleeping bags—for more reasons than protection against the cold.

In spite of it all, we have a good sleep. There is frost on the bikes in the morning, so we do not rush to get going. Once again my bike will not start. I push it out to the edge of the village where the road slopes down, in hopes that it will start on the roll. I get Norma to push me, but after three attempts it still won't start. Now what? My battery is fairly new and should not be causing this problem. It must be the charging system.

Finally I ask Norma if we can swap batteries. We put my battery into her bike first and it starts just fine. Now, let's hope that my bike starts with her battery. I install the battery and it fires on the first try. This is very confusing. I will have to get the bike checked as soon as possible.

It is 11:00 AM when we are finally on the road. More loose sand and gravel to deal with! I try not to get impatient with Norma; after all, she has just helped me out of a bind.

For the last few kilometers into Potosí the road becomes worse, if that is possible. When I reach the pavement I stop and wait. Thirty minutes pass, and still no Norma. I am determined not to turn around and go back, but as the minutes tick by, my determination fades. Just as I am about to start back, I see her come over the last hill. I wait until she catches up and put on a cheerful face.

"We are on pavement," I exclaim. "I think this is the end of the awful roads."

She is not speaking. Oh well, all things pass.

Before I left Edmonton, Rudi had given me the name of the Hotel Molenio in Potosí. The bonus here is that we can park our bikes in the lobby. We offload our gear then go in search of a car wash. After a few minutes of riding around in circles I begin to think there is no car wash here. Norma stops a taxi and asks the driver if he will lead us to one. That was a brilliant idea.

Potosí is the highest city in South America at 4,070 meters.

In the morning we check the air in our tires and increase the pressure before starting out. We are riding northwest on Highway 1 to Oruro. It feels so good to be back on pavement. The scenery across the mountains and valleys is breathtaking. Such an array of colors! I stop often to take pictures and wait for Norma. We encounter two short, gravel diversions today, but otherwise the road is great.

Before reaching Oruro we stop for fuel. The time is 3:30. While I am filling my bike I hear a hissing noise. I check my tires and the back one is half flat. I pay for my fuel and roll the bike away from the pumps. I pull out my tire repair kit, which has never been used, and try to plug the hole. After several attempts I give up. The man running the station cannot help us, so I ask Norma if she will ride into Oruro and get help. She does not want to, but offers to let me ride her bike in. We offload her back seat and I ride about ten kilometers into town, looking for a tire repair shop.

I check a couple of shops before finding one that can help. One of the repairmen, Peter, rides as my passenger back to my bike. He looks at the situation then decides he needs a tire pump. There is no air hose at the service station and I only have two small air capsules left. Off we go again back into Oruro. When we return, Peter looks for small pieces of rubber in the yard to plug the hole, and then pumps the tire up. There is still a hissing noise. He finds another hole and plugs it. This time all is quiet. The tire should carry us back to town.

Norma does not want to carry a passenger, so we strap my gear on top of hers, and Peter rides behind me back to the shop. Two men work on the tire. It takes them all evening to repair the holes and get the tire back on the rim. It does not want to seal properly and takes several attempts before they succeed.

At about 7:00 PM the repairmen race outside and pick up all their tools and parts sitting by my bike. Both our bikes are parked along the sidewalk out front. They close the shop door and tell us not to go out and to stay away from the window.

"What is happening?" I ask.

"Protesters are coming," Peter replies, pointing up the street.

We stay put and stand along one wall away from the window. We can still see out and I notice some of the protesters stop and look at our bikes before moving on. I ask, "What are they protesting?"

Peter replies, "Who knows, everyone protests. Doctors, nurses, teachers, laborers—everyone protests."

At 8:30 the tire is finally back on my bike. My bill is seventy bolivianos, or 11 dollars Canadian.

It is already dark and we still have to find a hotel. Peter points us in the right direction, but there are not many streetlights on this road and it is difficult to see the buildings. I pull into the Paradise Hotel and ring the bell. There is no response. I ring several times, but no one answers. We pull into the next hotel where there is an attendant at the gate. I think, *this is great; it will be safe to park our bikes.*

I ask for a room for two and am told fifteen dollars US. The attendant opens the big cement gate and leads us to a courtyard lined with closed garage doors. He opens one of the doors with his remote control, hands us our keys and motions for us to enter. Wow, we get our own private garage. This is fantastic!

As soon as we walk into the room we realize this is not your typical hotel. Mirrors cover the walls and ceilings, and red and blue lights hang over the bed. We cannot stop laughing. This is a red-light hotel and rooms are rented by the hour.

We have just hauled in all our gear when the manager calls. Norma answers the phone and he tells her the room will be fifty dollars an hour, not fifteen for the night. Norma says no. Then he says, six dollars an hour. Finally we say no, we will leave. We are both beginning to wonder if there could be peepholes or cameras hidden in the room.

We pack up and leave our wonderful private garage. It is very dark out here and difficult to see where we are going. I head the opposite direction towards the city lights. We find the Monarch Hotel where we are offered two separate rooms, or one double, for eighty bolivianos. We take the separate rooms. They are very nice, and include hot water and indoor parking.

We leave Oruro around 10:00, and are only riding 227 kilometers to La Paz today. The guard at the tollbooth on the edge of town warns us that protesters may have put up road barricades. He says "Just go around them."

After about half an hour on the road we come to Caracolla and find protesters blocking access to the bridge. The deck is covered with rocks, glass, sticks, and other debris. Protesters fill the bridge so we must stop. I park my bike, take my key, and go walking to find a way around. Meanwhile, a man comes up to Norma and tells her to shut off her bike. He is the Union Agent and head of this demonstration. They are protesting the price of fuel. She talks to him about getting across and when I come back he has agreed to let us go. I express concern about riding over all that glass. He waves his arm indicating to follow him, and kicks aside debris, creating a path for us. I can hear the crunch of glass as I ride over the bridge.

For the next fifteen kilometers we face roadblocks. Some sections have burned out cars or large tree trunks placed across the road. In other areas protesters are lying on the road. Many times we ride into the ditch to get around. During one detour we have to cross a little creek and deep crevice. I get off the bike and search for a flat log or board to place across the crevice. We can see protesters watching us from the road. In places where we are able to stay on the road we elicit dirty looks from the demonstrators.

Finally we get past the roadblocks and can travel faster. Worried about my patched tire, I keep the speed between eighty and a hundred.

Riding northwest, white-capped mountains are within view. We are still at a very high altitude. The mountains look smaller and are rounded at the top. Hillsides are farmed and small rock fences divide crops and gardens. Most likely the fences also protect crops from the winds that whip through here.

We pass a man on a bicycle with a sheep tied to the back rack. I wonder if he has rescued a small lamb or if he is taking it home to slaughter. Riding through a little remote village we see two women huddled under many layers of clothing and selling produce from large burlap bags. Bolivian people in the smaller centers don't seem as receptive to tourists, and make no attempt to befriend us.

Women dress in many layers of skirts, wool stockings, and shawls. Their shoes look way too small for their stature. Perched on their head is a felt hat, usually black, with a rolled up brim completing a circle. The hat seems to sit at the very top and I wonder why it does not fall off or get blown away. A pin must keep it secure. As a child I remember thinking, as I watched my mother stick a very long pin through her church hat, *I'll never wear a hat if I have to stick a pin through my head.*

We stop for lunch about one hundred kilometers out of La Paz. Norma is very quiet, still not speaking to me. Maybe she is busy planning how she'll ship her bike home from La Paz.

It is 2:30 in the afternoon when we reach the last tollbooth before the grand entrance to La Paz. The city is built in a canyon with buildings creeping up the sides of surrounding mountains. The main highway entering La Paz emerges from the top of a mountain, giving visitors a spectacular view of the city below.

We ride down the mountain into the center of the city before looking for a hotel. We choose the Hotel Sucre Palace for forty dollars US. The room is very nice and we have secure parking at the back. Once we have unpacked our gear we go in search of a motorcycle shop. One kind gentleman at the hotel refers us to Nosiglia Sport Motorcycle Shop across town.

We take a taxi to the bike shop. Herman speaks English so we deal with him. I tell him the size of tires I need, but shortly he reports that they do not have that size, but he can order them from Brazil.

I ask all the pertinent questions, namely, what kind of tires are they, how much will they cost, how long will it take to get them, et cetera.

Herman tells me he can get Brazilian Pirellis from Santa Cruz, and thinks they could be delivered in a day or two. "Very good tires," he adds.

We will bring our bikes in for servicing tomorrow and leave them until the tires are installed. Both bikes will have a complete service job and mine will also be checked over for the starting problem. Since we exchanged batteries my bike has started every morning, and Norma hasn't had any problem with my battery in her bike.

In the morning my rear tire is almost flat again. I use the two small canisters of air and hope this will get me to the bike shop. When we arrive I ask Herman if he has heard anything about the tires. He informs me that the bus was stopped by protesters and has not arrived yet. "Today is Friday," he says. "The bus will get through on the weekend. The protesters go home on weekends."

I hope he is right.

Norma and I spend the rest of the day discovering a bit of La Paz—the huge, busy plazas, a museum, interesting shops, and crowds of people.

By Saturday my tires are still not in. I contact Carlos, a referral from Rafael in Chile. Carlos contacts the bike shop to ask about my tires and gets the same answer. He then offers to take us to the truck pull competitions on Sunday. That sounds like fun.

Saturday morning Norma and I have a discussion about a few of our differences. I comment on the sharp tone of voice she uses, and she tells me she is tired of listening to me complain about the price of the hotels we are staying in. We both agree to back off and the day goes much better.

Sunday morning Carlos and his son, Carlos Junior, pick us up for the truck pull. Norma decides not to go so I am on my own. I meet Carlos' wife Leila and second son Hugo. They live in a very nice house in the suburbs and are a lovely family. Carlos works for a large international company. He is happy with his life here. Bolivia is his home and he says, "Life is good here."

We pick up another riding buddy of Carlos' and head for the truck pull. This competition is a big event between Argentina, Chile, and Bolivia.

Bolivians greet each other differently according to gender. Women greet other women and men with a kiss on the cheek. Men greet women the same, but other men with a handshake and a shoulder hug (hands on the shoulders). Young male teens greet each other with a handshake. This is especially nice to see. It shows respect amongst the teens. I find this all very interesting as I watch the truck competitions and observe the people around me.

At nine o'clock Monday morning I call the bike shop and speak to Herman. Still no tires! He is trying to phone the bus depot, but the line has been busy all morning. He tells me that the tires have been shipped by bus and will be here today. It is 10:30 when Herman calls back to say the tires are in and our bikes will be ready by 5:30.

I feel a huge sense of relief. I did not want to keep riding on those tires.

On Tuesday, May 18, we leave La Paz. By the time we have packed up it is 11:00 AM. We have reviewed the map and our route out of the city. The streets are packed and we have to squeeze into tight spaces to make any progress. I keep watch that Norma is close behind me, but somehow, in one very crowded block I lose sight of her. I have turned the corner, but I feel certain she knows where to turn. I continue down the hill to the main intersection to find there is a protest march and the police are directing traffic. I make my turn onto the street leading out of the city and pull over to the curb. I sit and watch for several minutes but do not see her. I begin to get worried, so I park my bike and walk back to the intersection. I ask the police officer if another bike came through. He says, "No, only one."

I walk back to the block I last saw her on, two blocks past the intersection, then back to my bike and wait some more. Now what do I do? Do I continue riding? What if she has had an accident? I would never forgive myself for riding on and not checking.

I remember a discussion we had earlier in our travels together. We had agreed that if we lost each other we would go back to the last place we were together. I ride up and down the streets a couple of times, and then decide to go back to the hotel. Maybe she went back there.

Over the next three hours I send out three e-mails hoping Norma has stopped somewhere and will try to contact me. The more time that passes the more worried I become that she has had an accident, so I enlist the help of the hotel manager. We walk to the police station and the officer on duty checks to see if there have been any motorcycle accident reports. I feel relieved when he comes up with nothing.

It is now late afternoon and too late to start out for Copacabana, so I book back into the hotel. Shortly after I check into my room I receive a call from the police. The control checkpoint at El Alta said a rider fitting Norma's description went through and said she was going to Copacabana. They have notified the police to watch for her.

I'm so relieved that she has not ended up in an accident somewhere, and at the same time I am seething mad. Why did she just keep on riding? Is she that angry? If she wants to ride alone, I have no problem with that. It would have been nice if she had let me know. Over the past two months I have waited for her countless times and never rode off and left her, even though I felt like it many times.

At 6:00 PM I get an e-mail from her. The Copacabana police had stopped her and told her to contact me. I e-mail her back with the hotel phone number so we can talk. Our conversation, when she calls, is a little heated. She is crying and trying to justify her decision to keep riding. I am in no mood to hear it, and tell her I will leave for Copacabana tomorrow morning. If she would like to wait, I will meet her at the hotel where she is staying. If she wants to keep riding, that is fine by me.

The mornings are cold, but I leave the hotel at about nine. It takes half an hour to get through the busy city traffic and into the outskirts of town. The road winds up the side of the canyon to the rim, where I must make a choice of which road to take to Copacabana. The road signs are not absolutely clear, and I end up stopping in a smaller town to ask if I am on the right highway.

I have an enjoyable ride to Lake Titicaca, which lies between Bolivia and Peru at an altitude of 3,820 meters. It is the highest navigable lake in the world and contains the largest volume of water in South America.

At a pretty little town on the southeast side of the lake I board a rickety old ferry that will take me to Copacabana. A tour bus is loaded first and then I am directed to ride on. Boards are missing from the deck, so I carefully pick a wide enough space that I don't fall through the gaps when I put my feet down. The bus and my bike are the only vehicles on board. I hope we make it across this lake without sinking!

When we dock I ask one of the men to help wheel my bike off. I would hate to step back, miss a plank, and fall into a hole. I ride the short distance to Copacabana and find the hostel where Norma is staying. I am not sure how this encounter will go or what I should say to her. We discuss the issue briefly, especially the agreement we had about what to do if we get separated. Do we or don't we follow this plan? There is a lot of tension in the air. I decide to put it all behind me. We have a wonderful lunch in the hostel courtyard before continuing on to Peru.

Chapter 14

Peru

Today is May 19, 2004. We leave Copacabana by early afternoon and make our way around the west side of Lake Titicaca to Puno. The scenery is fantastic! Puno is at an elevation of 3,830 meters. We have been riding at an altitude of over thirty-five hundred meters since leaving Argentina almost three weeks ago. I think we have adjusted very well, although, I tire much quicker and do not have the strength I normally do. It dawns on me that this might be affecting Norma worse than me. I must try to be more patient.

Puno is an interesting town. The plaza is beautifully manicured with trees sculpted into many different shapes. The pedestrian mall is packed with people, and many restaurants line the street. For dinner we choose one that makes pizza in a wood-burning oven. I order pumpkin and apple soup and pizza. The food is excellent.

Finding a map of Peru is a priority on my agenda. We browse in several shops but have no luck. I will just have to track my route on my world map. It's not the greatest for detail, but it may be my only option.

The next morning I awaken early and decide to get up. My watch says 6:30, but we came through a time change yesterday so it is 7:30 here. I know Norma doesn't appreciate getting up early, but I choose not to waste my time here sleeping.

The morning air is crisp, but with our heated liners on we are fine. We get fuel at about two hundred kilometers, then a short distance farther we stop at a restaurant that seems to be in the middle of nowhere. There is a local woman, dressed very similar to the Bolivian women, selling handicrafts made from baby alpaca fur. Each of us buys a hat and a wall hanging before going in for lunch.

The road this morning has been very twisty. As we continue on to Cuzco the curves become even tighter, a joy for bikers. There is more vegetation on the mountainsides, creating hills of green and stunning landscapes.

I stop to check the little map in the *Lonely Planet* guidebook before we get too far into the city. A young American woman comes over and offers her help. She is on her way into the city for work and tells us to follow her taxi. When she exits the taxi we ask the driver to guide us to Hostel Niñas. We follow him through narrow cobblestone streets, only to find that this hostel does not have parking. From here the taxi driver leads us to Inca Peru Hostel.

We get settled in then go in search of a tour to Machu Picchu, the lost city of the Incas, situated at the top of a mountain. That is the main attraction here. There are no spots available for tomorrow so we book for Saturday. Today and tomorrow we will tour Cuzco.

The elevation here is 3,326 meters. Cuzco is a busy city with many tourists. It lies in a bowl surrounded by mountains and boasts wonderful plazas or squares with beautifully manicured gardens, and amazing architecture.

Many of the side streets are so narrow they allow only one vehicle through at a time. We wander through these alleys, in and out of shops, and then stop at one of the many great restaurants lining the Plaza de Armas. During dinner we are entertained by a five-man band, made up of two guitarists, two wind flute players, and a drummer. Then dancers in very colorful costumes perform the traditional dance of the Incas.

Friday we take a city tour of several landmarks in Cuzco, including Sacsayhuamán (Saqsaywaman), located north of the city in the Archaeological Park of Sacsayhuamán. The park embraces approximately three thousand hectares and contains many archaeological monuments along with vibrant flora and fauna from the region.

On Saturday morning we are up at five and waiting for our taxi, which we booked for 5:35. At 6:10 he finally comes and just makes it to the train station in time for our trip to Machu Picchu. We ride the train for three and a half hours, descending to the village of Aguas

Caliente, meaning *hot waters*. From here we transfer to a bus that takes us up the mountainside, switching back and forth for eight kilometers as it climbs to an altitude of twenty-four hundred meters, to the historic Inca Sanctuary.

It is believed that Machu Picchu was built around 1460 by the Incas, but abandoned as an official site for the Inca rulers one hundred years later, before the Spanish conquest of the Inca Empire. Over the centuries the surrounding jungle grew up over the site and it was not officially discovered until 1911. In 1981 it was proclaimed a Peruvian Historical Sanctuary, in 1983 a UNESCO World Heritage Site, and later, one of the New Seven Wonders of the World.

This is an amazing site, not only because it was constructed on a mountaintop, but also for the surrounding view.

Sunday morning we leave Cuzco at 8:30 and battle the traffic out of the city. The highway is nicely paved and continual curves winding around mountains of multiple colors of pinks, greys, and greens. I think of some of my riding companions back home, knowing how much they would enjoy this road.

The temperature is cool starting out this morning but soon warms up as we descend in altitude. We reach Chalhuanca at 3:30 and find a room. We have only traveled three hundred and ten kilometers, but a local man advises that it gets *frío* (cold) over the next mountain range and we should not continue this late in the day. We heed his advice even though there is not much to see in Chalhuanca.

On Monday, May 24, we hit more curves as we climb higher once again. Soon the temperature drops and the winds blast around us. I am glad we listened to the gentleman yesterday. The landscape is barren out here. We pass local people sitting by the side of the road with produce or crafts for sale. They are dressed in layers and layers of clothes with shawls and blankets wrapped around their shoulders.

Norma is riding way, way behind again today. Often she is out of sight for long periods of time. We had discussed the issue of staying in sight of each other, but that is not happening. At lunch I suggest she take the lead when we resume riding.

We are back in warmer weather again and reach some nice gentle curves. Norma is doing great but at our next stop she suggests that I take the lead again. I assure her she is doing just fine. In fact, she is taking the curves faster than I normally do. So we continue with her in the lead and me riding about three seconds behind. I keep enough space between us so she does not feel that I am pushing her.

We are about forty kilometers out of Nazca and I decide to slow down a little. The road is still continual curves and I feel we are going too fast. I lose sight of Norma in some tight bends, and when I come around one mountain curve, there she is, lying on the edge of the road.

Oh my God!

I stop my bike and run to help, asking if she is okay. By this time she is getting up and says she is fine. The front wheel of her bike is inches away from a cliff. She had gone wide in the curve and drifted out onto the gravel shoulder. I go back to my bike and get my camera. This needs to be recorded on film.

The bike is too close to the cliff edge to try and upright it here so we drag it back before lifting it. It seems to be okay except for a bent windshield. Norma has pulled muscles in her shoulder. Luckily that is the extent of the damage.

We stop at Nazca for the night. Elevation is 653 meters.

The next morning we ride north on Highway 1, the Pan American Highway. Twenty-six kilometers north of Nazca we stop to view the *Lines in the Desert*. Archaeologists are not sure what they are from, but when you fly over you can see formations of animals, plants, lizards, et cetera. We climb the tower to get a better view.

The highway is straight and boring with sand on both sides. Sometimes it consists of long, flat stretches, and other times, large hills. Occasionally we can see the ocean, but due to the fog it is not a clear view. We arrive in Lima at about 4:00 and decide to continue through to the north side. That will make our exit tomorrow much easier.

I get lost going through the city and take Norma's advice to hail a taxi and pay him to lead us out. We have done almost five hundred kilometers today and are both tired. We find an inexpensive hotel and book separate rooms. The highway noise is awful so I put my earplugs in and have a wonderful sleep.

At 7:00 the following morning I knock on Norma's door. She slams it shut in my face! When she comes out to pack her bike I ask, "Are you okay?"

"I'm fine!" She snaps.

Well, I am glad of that.

We are on the road at 7:40 and soon into heavy fog. This highway follows closely along the ocean. It does not take long for me to lose sight of Norma's light. I do not know if she has stopped or just slowed down. I stop once and wait for a few minutes, then decide to keep riding. After an hour on the road I stop for breakfast and wait for her to arrive.

The fog has lifted when we resume our ride. It seems we are riding through the sand dunes. There is not much else to see.

Norma continues to lag behind. I look back often but do not stop. I reach a tollbooth and decide to wait until I see her light. There is no charge for motorcycles at the road tolls in Peru. In Bolivia and Chile we had to pay. When we reach Casma, a police roadblock stops us. There are protesters between Casma and Chimbote. The police tell us we must wait until it is safe to go.

It is almost noon so we stop for lunch. I order a salad and fritas (fries). The food is excellent.

An hour goes by before we get word that the roadblock is lifted. We start out, but a short distance down the road we are stopped again by the police at Chimbote. Another protest is happening north of town. The police here are very helpful and want to talk.

One officer asks if we have pens.

"No," I reply. "But we do have pins."

Norma pulls out pins and key chains to give them.

Then the chatty officer asks, "You have hombres (men) in Canada?"

"No, mucho problemo," I reply.

He laughs and repeats this to his partner.

Finally they let us proceed. We are almost through Chimbote when we are stopped again. This time we are not allowed to continue, so we turn around and look for a hotel. Chimbote is a fishing town along the Pacific Ocean. The smell is awful. We would not stay if we didn't have to.

We find a room at a hostel that looks great from the outside, but inside it's not so nice. We get a very large room with a double bed, sofa, dressing room and table, and nice bathroom, for thirty sols. One Canadian dollar is worth 2.73 Peruvian Nuevo sols.

When I carry in my gear I notice the TV suspended from the wall is showing a porno flick. It is so gross I turn it off. I begin to look closer at the room and realize there are mirrors on the walls on both sides of the bed. Not again! This is another red-light hotel! When we registered we paid up front for the whole night, so at least they will not be able to change it to an hourly rate.

We are up early and leave before the protesters block the road again. There are no problems yet this morning. It's a long ride today as we go through more sand dunes. The road is good and predominantly straight. We stop in Piura after riding 561 kilometers.

The highway leading into Piura takes us past a large area of cardboard housing. My heart feels heavy for these people. We round a couple of turns and are in the town of Piura, which is quite nice. It is hard to accept the drastic difference in people's circumstances.

We find a nice hotel not far from the plaza. Norma takes a tuktuk down to the center and I go across the road to an Internet café. I phone my sister Florence, who tells me there is a family reunion the last weekend of June. Wonderful, I will make it my goal to get home for that.

The next morning, a short distance from Piura, we come to the little oasis town of Sullana. This area is green with vegetation, including palm trees and crops. Irrigation must be responsible for this because the surrounding hills and valleys are brown and grey.

We ride off the Pan American highway and take a secondary road by the ocean to Tumbes, arriving at 1:00 PM. The border crossing between Peru and Ecuador is closed from one to two, so we decide to stay. The first hotel we check wants one hundred and twenty sols for a room. It is beautiful, but we move on to the Florian Hotel near the central plaza. The room here is wonderful and only thirty-seven sols.

Tumbes is a beautiful little city and today there is a celebration and parade for the children. Young ones dressed in their finest threads are carried through the plaza in festively decorated buggies and tuktuks.

Peru is a diverse country with its majestic mountains to the east and mounds of sand dunes lining the west coast. The Pan American Highway is long and straight, but the roads through the mountains are a biker's dream, with curves that are never-ending and scenery that is phenomenal.

Tomorrow we will leave Peru and cross the border to Ecuador.

Chapter 15
Ecuador

May 29 we leave Tumbes early and are at the Peru border by 8:55. Our wait is short. In fifteen minutes an officer arrives and stamps an exit date in our passports and bike transit papers. We continue on to Ecuador Customs, and breeze through immigration and customs and one police check, but are stopped at the last control post. The officer will not accept our transit papers for the bikes because we are missing a signature on them. He sends us back to get it.

We are not sure which office we should go to so we try them all. First we try the immigration office, but they cannot help us. Then we go to the police check post, then the customs office, just to find it locked. We decide to go back to the Peru customs office. The officer photocopies our Peru transit papers and stamps and signs them. I have no idea if this will be sufficient. I have a strong feeling it won't.

We return to the last check post. The officer looks things over and shakes his head no. I try to explain which offices we went to, and after some debate he walks behind his post to the long building with a sign on top advertising *Aduanas* (Customs). He comes back shortly with a plan and says, "I will go with you."

Norma and I look at each other wondering how he will go with us. He indicates he will ride on one of our bikes.

Both our back seats are loaded down with gear. After some discussion, Norma agrees to stay at the booth and I offload my gear, taking the officer on my bike.

My passenger and I ride back through the busy market street to the first office we stopped at when entering Ecuador. They had looked at our papers the first time around and only stamped our passports. The second time around they stamped and signed the photocopied Peru transit papers. In actuality they should have made out new transit papers for Ecuador. With the help of my passenger they scurry off, and several minutes later return with two new transit papers stamped and signed as required.

I transport the officer back to his check post where Norma is patiently waiting. I reload my gear and we officially enter Ecuador. The secondary highway along the water is nicely paved in some places and rough with potholes in others. Highway signs are poor to non-existent. We are taking this route instead of the Pan American because our helpful border guard suggested that this road to Guayaquil is the better of the two.

It is 5:00 PM when we arrive in Guayaquil, a beautiful, large city built along the riverbanks of the Rio Daule. We flag down a taxi and ask him to lead us to a hotel.

We have been riding for seven days straight and Norma would like to stop for a day or two. I suggest we continue tomorrow since we will then be in Quito, where we will stay a few days to make shipping arrangements.

On Sunday, May 30, we get caught up in a detour leaving Guayaquil. Eventually I flag down a bus and ask how to get to the main highway heading north. The driver gives me directions and we are soon on a four-lane divided highway. We stop at Quevedo for lunch and I ask about the road across the mountains to Latacunga. "Is it paved or dirt road?"

Two different men tell me it is paved. They do not speak much English but they seem to understand what I am talking about.

We fuel up and head east. The first forty kilometers is broken pavement but not terrible for riding. From this point the road gets worse and eventually we are riding on rock and mud.

The tension between Norma and I has been slowly building and I just know that this will put it over the top. She is having a hard time and is riding fifteen to twenty kilometers per hour again. I ride my own speed, between forty and sixty, and every few minutes stop and wait for her to catch up. The air has become cold so I put on my heated liner.

Norma is sitting on her bike, making no movement. I ask her if she is okay and she nods her head. I suggest that she put her heated jacket on because it will be getting colder as we ride over the mountain range. She puts on her jacket and we continue. I am concerned about her.

It is getting late and the sun is going down. I ride for twenty kilometers without looking back, and then decide I had better stop. I park the bike close to the bank of a high hill and hike up. I can see for a long way, but do not spot Norma. Twenty minutes later she arrives and I ask again if she is okay. She nods her head. The road has become better in the last twenty kilometers so I continue, and shortly we are back on pavement. A few kilometers later I pull into the little village of Pijila and ask about a hotel. It is now almost dark, so we get a little room in the only hostel in town. It is positively the worst room I have stayed in during this whole journey.

Parking is on the street so I check other businesses. The owners of the library offer to let us park in their locked yard. That is a relief, and most appreciated.

Today is Sunday and Pujili has an all-day market. It is late and most of the vendors have shut down and gone home, leaving a huge mess. The whole town square looks like a garbage dump.

We leave early the next morning, reaching Latacunga in less than half an hour. If I had known we were that close, I would not have stayed in Pujili. Our bikes are filthy so we stop to wash them. The mud is caked so hard on the underside of my bike that the side stand is difficult to pull down. The chain needs a good washing and lubing before we continue.

From here we ride north on the Pan American highway to Quito. Again the signage is poor to non-existent. We reach Quito at 10:30 and end up in *el centro* (city center). What a nightmare! I would like to go to the equator before we look for a room, so I continue riding until we are back on the highway. It is now noon.

We find the monument that indicates we have reached the middle of the world and spend some time walking around the grounds and displays. A guide tells us that this spot is actually seven seconds off. The exact spot of the equator is actually on top of a mountain and was located over one thousand years ago, before the Incas. I find it amazing that this precise location (0° 0' 0"Latitude) was charted by watching the sun and without all our modern day equipment. Today the sun is shining and it is a gorgeous day—perfect for my first, and maybe only, visit to the equator.

On the ride back into Quito I take the airport exit then stop to look at my map. Norma has been questioning my directions lately, but refuses to take the lead. Her attitude and moody disposition is really getting to me. I am thinking this is worse than a bad marriage and a separation will be happening soon.

We are looking for the Hostel Andes Range which Norman and Maggie, the couple we met in Chile, recommended. They are staying here right now and it would be great if we could get a room also. We find the hostel located in a very nice neighborhood, but unfortunately it is full. We continue on and check into the Hotel Galapogas. It is an older building but our room is big, clean, and comfortable, for twenty dollars US.

It is still early in the afternoon so we go walking and stop at a couple of freight forwarding offices. The gentlemen in one office are very helpful and give us some information to think about. We can fly our bikes to Panama City Wednesday, Friday, or Saturday.

This evening Norma states, "We will ride together until we get to the United States, then you are free to leave."

"Fine, that is your choice," I reply. The tension between us is ruining the trip. We are simply two different personalities.

Tuesday we find our way to a motorcycle shop that works on big bikes. Norma's bike needs a chain and the clutch cable replaced. They do not have the correct chain for her so they take a link out of the existing one and flip it over. I feel good about having both bikes serviced before shipping them off to Panama.

The next morning we return to Agencia De Carga Aevea International, the freight forwarding office, and book our bikes in for Friday. We discuss crating versus strapping them to a pallet. I present a strong case for the latter and tell the agents I have shipped this way before with no problem. After some discussion they agree. The cost to ship two bikes is 924 dollars US. That is acceptable, and we are pleased. Friday the bikes will fly to Bogotá, Colombia, then on to Panama City the next day. We are instructed to take them to the air cargo yard Thursday afternoon.

From here we go to a travel agency and book our own flights to Panama City. Each ticket is 307 US. This will be my last flight and last shipment for my bike. From Panama City we will be able to ride all the way back to Canada.

Thursday afternoon we stop at the freight forwarding office and one of the agents accompanies us to the air cargo yard several blocks away. At the yard another man joins in to help strap the bikes onto a steel pallet. We have allowed the fuel to run low and only have a liter or two in the tank. The agent is fine with that. No one asks about the battery or instructs us to disconnect them so I remain quiet. We remove the windshields, mirrors, and top trunk, and let some of the air out of the tires to bring down the height. The agents work for an hour getting both bikes and all our gear strapped down when a woman appears from the office and asks if we have disconnected the batteries. I say, "No, but we will have to un-strap everything to do that."

The agent doing most of the packing speaks up and says, "No, it is not necessary."

He is not about to take it all apart and start again.

We pick up our waybills and say goodbye to our bikes. This time I do not feel so desperate leaving it in their hands. Maybe I have become accustomed to sending it off alone, or maybe knowing this is the last shipment eases my fears. This is a big job taken care of. We can now enjoy the rest of the evening.

Friday, June 4, is our last day in Quito. We take a bus down to the Old Town Historic Center. I love the large bricked squares (plazas) surrounded by grand old architecture. There are many plazas in the historic center providing places to stop and rest, and enjoy the activity. The streets are narrow and sidewalks are packed with people.

After lunch I take a bus back to the hotel. I still feel tired due to a recent head cold, so I relax for the rest of the day. Tomorrow we must be at the airport by 4:30 in the morning.

I do not sleep much knowing we must be up by four. My cough has started acting up again and keeps me awake most of the short night. Finally I get up at 3:45 and shower. My coughing must have kept Norma awake also, because she is up too. It is Saturday, June 5, 2004. Another birthday—today I am fifty-six.

We leave the room at 4:10 and are in the airport lineup at 4:20. The line is long and there is no movement at the counter. We stand, patiently waiting until 6:00 before it starts moving. Something is definitely wrong. When we finally reach the counter at 6:30, our departure time, we are told that the plane never arrived from Bogotá due to bad weather. We are re-booked on a 10:35 flight.

We check our luggage into a locker and go in search of a place for breakfast. The best we find, after walking several blocks, is across the road where we are served instant coffee and toast. This is not a good start to my birthday. I think about the eventful day I had last year in Pakistan, and wonder if any future birthday will be so dramatic.

Back in the airport we wait again. Finally we board and leave Quito at 11:50, arriving in Bogotá at 1:00 PM. This is a beautiful airport, much bigger than I expected, with plenty of shops and food kiosks. I order an amaretto cappuccino to celebrate my birthday.

We wait again due to another late plane. The weather is the cause of all these delays, making me a bit nervous to fly. It is 5:00 PM when we finally fly out of Bogotá and leave South America behind.

Chapter 16

Central America

— Panama

Our plane touches down in Panama City at 6:30 PM and we take a taxi to Hotel Montreal. The airport is quite a distance from the city so the taxi fare is twenty-five dollars US, plus two dollars for toll fees. The room we are given is facing a main street and the traffic noise is terrible. We are tired of street noise after Quito, so ask for another room. It is not much better. We go for a walk and find another hotel. The room is bigger and in a better location.

After we settle in I call Servas host, Maria. She is delighted to hear from us and offers to show us around tomorrow. *Wonderful!*

I check my e-mail and have several birthday wishes. It is great to hear from my family and friends. Their messages today leave me longing to be home.

We have arrived in Panama City on a Saturday and will not be able to pick up our bikes until Monday. At nine o'clock Sunday morning Maria arrives at our hotel to take us sightseeing. She drives us out to the Miraflores Locks in the Panama Canal where we tour the museum, then watch two ships pass through the locks. It takes about an hour for each ship to pass completely through.

The completion of the Panama Canal opened up major trade routes from the East Coast of the U.S. to Asia and the West Coast of South

America, and from Europe to the West Coast of the U.S and Canada. The principal commodities are containerized cargo, grains, petroleum, and petroleum products.

We drive to the four islands connected by causeways that were built when the United States Army occupied the islands. This area and the Panama Canal, with all its operations, were returned to Panama December 31, 1999.

After lunch we visit another museum, then watch the parade of one thousand women. What a colorful display of dresses and costumes on women and young girls of all ages.

Monday morning I call the airport and am told that the plane will not leave Bogotá until midnight. It will arrive in Panama at 2:00 AM.

Norma and I walk to the old city center and wander through Avenue Central, a long pedestrian street. We try to find our way to the waterfront and end up in a "seedy" looking part of town. Two tourist police officers on bicycles see us and ask where we are going. They escort us out of the area and back to Avenue Balboa. We thank them and continue walking until we can flag a taxi to take us to the Multi Center for lunch. Later in the afternoon we get caught in pouring rain while touring the old city center. The temperature is over twenty-five degrees Celsius and the rain is warm. Short bursts of rain happen often, but soon the sun shines again, and all is well.

On Tuesday, June 8, I call air cargo again only to get a person who does not speak English. The young woman at the hotel desk kindly takes the phone and interprets for me. Yes, the bikes are in and we can come pick them up. We will need twenty-five dollars US for customs.

We call a taxi to take us to the airport. Everything proceeds smoothly once we find the air cargo section. We present our waybill and pay the required fee, then follow an agent out to the warehouse. The pallet is sitting there waiting for us. We cut open the shrink wrapping and straps, fasten the mirrors and windshields, strap on the gear we sent with the shipment, and are on our way. There is no battery or gas issue this time. The bikes have enough fuel to take us to Panama City. The whole procedure takes about one hour.

It is 1:30 when we arrive back at our hotel; it's too late for checkout so we stay one more night.

We are up at 7:30 the next morning to have breakfast with Maria. She has been a wonderful host. By 8:30 we are on the road. The scenery is magnificent as we ride through hills and valleys covered in rain forest. There are thousands of different species of vegetation, and as many shades of green. Low-lying clouds hang in the valleys, creating a pleasant, mystical mood.

It is good to be on the road, heading home. I ride alone most of the day. I have quit looking back to see where Norma is. We stop at David, Panama, after 443 kilometers, and find a hotel. We are only a short distance from the border crossing to Costa Rica.

— *Costa Rica*

Checking out of Panama is fast and easy once we find the customs office. We miss the sign the first time around and have to go back. It is a small, eight-by-ten-inch yellow board on a stick about four inches from the ground.

We continue on to the Costa Rica customs office. This time it is not so fast. We are sent back and forth to different offices for everything including fumigation of the bikes. Finally, two and a half hours later, we have all our documents stamped and signed.

We ride 406 kilometers on the Pan American highway and reach San Hose just before dusk. We have no luck finding a hotel. We must seem very lost because a man and a woman in a van stop and offer to help. They lead us to the Villa Toucan, where we obtain a room for seventy dollars US. By now the time is 7:30, so we take it.

On Friday, June 11, we leave the hotel at 8:30 and ride to Alejuela, where we turn off to Volcán Poás. The entry fee into the park is thirty-four hundred colones, or seven dollars US. We park our bikes and walk the trail up to a volcano viewpoint. Fog is hanging over the trees and sections of the path. When we reach the viewpoint the whole valley is fogged in and the volcanic crater is completely behind clouds. This is disappointing, but the hike up the trail is worthwhile.

Back on the road we get lost in the curves and turns of built-up areas and have to ask directions several times to find our way back to the Pan American highway. This section of the road is full of potholes and many curves. Large trucks and old vehicles belch out black smoke from their exhausts. The smell of burning brakes is horrid, and stings my nostrils.

We reach Liberia around 4:00 PM. Norma wants to stop here but I would like to get closer to the border. We continue on for another sixty kilometers to La Cruz and stop, having ridden 328 kilometers today. Norma is not happy with me for pushing on, but that seems to be a given these days. In all fairness to her, I am much more conditioned after riding almost every day for the past three years, while her bike was put away for the winter months prior to joining me.

— *Nicaragua*

On Saturday we reach the border to Nicaragua. This is a two-hour crossing. We are required to pay seven dollars US for the visa stamp in our passports. They want us to buy insurance but I ignore the request. We are only going to be here twenty-four hours.

The highway through Nicaragua is good. This country has obviously put some money into upgrades. We stop for lunch at a little roadside restaurant and strike up a conversation with the owner. He shows us a road on the map that will cut off *a great distance*. We take it and it turns out to be full of holes and slows us down considerably. It seems I will never learn my lesson about shortcuts.

We dodge pothole after pothole until the last seventy kilometers, where we reach the main road again. The pavement is smooth and the road swept with curves. The countryside is mostly farmland and much flatter than that of Panama and Costa Rica.

It is 5:00 PM when we arrive in Somoto, after riding 353 kilometers. We check into the Hotel Panamerica. The yard looks well kept and I am expecting the rooms to be nice, but that is not the case.

We walk to the plaza in the center of Somoto and find a wonderful restaurant that serves us shrimp in a creole sauce, rice, fries, and salad. Delicious! There is a party in the plaza and a wedding in town, creating plenty of noise for the evening.

— *Honduras*

On Sunday, June 13, we cross two borders. The border crossing into Honduras takes an hour and a half. The fees are thirty dollars US for each bike and three for a stamp in each of our passport. We find staying on the Pan American highway to be a short route through Honduras. The country has become dryer with rugged hills, rock, and trees scattered amongst farmland. One hundred and forty kilometers later we are at the El Salvador border. The thirty-dollar border fee we paid this morning seems pretty expensive for a two-hour ride.

Exiting Honduras is a confusing effort. No one seems to know what to do with our bike transit papers. In the end, an officer stamps a vehicle transit form into our passports—but no one ever fills it out. We are sent to three different offices and finally leave with our original papers, and no exit stamp for the bikes.

— *El Salvador*

Entering El Salvador is even worse. We join the long line of truckers and other drivers and wait. When it is our turn we are sent back and forth to get photocopies of our vehicle registration, driver's license and passport. We find a photocopy shop and return to the wicket just to be told to wait. Two hours later we are given the official vehicle transit paper and told to get it photocopied. By the time we leave it is 3:30. We have been at the border for almost three hours and are hot and uncomfortable. Our only charge here is ten dollars US each for our tourist cards plus the cost of photocopies.

We stop for fuel and lunch, then ride fifty kilometers to San Miguel, El Salvador. We have only covered 228 kilometers today. I feel like I will never make it home for my family reunion on June 27. We get a nice room in the Hotel Madrid for twenty-two dollars. The temperature is getting warmer the farther north we go.

The following morning we ride downtown in search of a bank machine. No luck, so we continue on to San Salvador. There we find a bank machine and a fuel station, and then I check my map for the road heading south. I want to get off the Pan American and take Highway 2 so as to avoid going through Guatemala City. A kind gentleman at the gas station offers to lead us to the highway.

Nearing La Libertad I have a scary experience. I am riding along at a hundred kilometers per hour when I come up a small rise to an unmarked T intersection. I slam on my brakes, look both ways, and then shoot across the road. Traffic is coming in both directions. I look in my rear view mirror and Norma is right behind me, narrowly making it across. We stop to steady our nerves and I ask her if she saw a sign for the T. She did not see one either. We are very lucky that there was an approach on the other side.

At La Libertad we stop at a rustic hotel near the ocean and have lunch on the large outdoor patio. It is beautiful here and under other circumstances I would love to stay. Norma suggests we stay, but it is only 1:30 in the afternoon and I would like to get closer to the Guatemala border.

The road twists and turns through small seaside villages. We continue riding to Acajutla, a small seaport town. The only hotel we can find is grungy, but we stay anyway. Continuing to the border this late in the afternoon would not be wise. We have ridden 328 kilometers today. Going through many small towns prevents us from covering much distance each day.

— *Guatemala*

We are at the border by 8:00 AM on June 15. The day is promising to be a hot one. We exit El Salvador without a hitch and each obtain a stamp in our passport for Guatemala. Next, it's on to the customs office to process the bike. After going to three windows and waiting in line we are told to get photocopies of our passport, bike registration and El Salvador bike papers. When we return one kind officer invites us into the air-conditioned building to wait. It has become very hot out and waiting in that heat for over two hours is not fun. I feel privileged, and at the same time sorry for the men outside waiting in line.

By 10:30 all the paperwork is complete and we are back on the road. Our first priority is to find a bike shop. The front wheel on Norma's bike is wobbling and we must get it looked at quickly. In the next little town we find a shop. They tell us it is a bearing and are able to do the job right away.

We continue on to Antigua, a popular tourist town. It is said to be one of the oldest and prettiest places in the Americas. The streets are cobblestone and the buildings old. Central Park is a popular gathering place lively with activity. We take a tour through town and decide to stay. Before we can find a room at Casa Santa Lucia we are caught in a downpour. It lasts only a few minutes but leaves puddles in the streets.

Three volcanic mountains can be seen on the horizon surrounding Antigua. The most prominent is Volcán di Agua (Volcano of Water), 3,766 meters high, located south of the city. To the west stand

Acatenango and Volcán de Fuego (Volcano of Fire), at 3,976 and 3,763 meters, respectively. Acatenango last erupted in 1972 and Volcán de Fuego is famous for being constantly active at low levels. Smoke bellows from the top daily, but large eruptions are very rare.

Wednesday, June 16—I hope to make it across the Mexican border today. Traveling through Guatemala is slow. The road takes us up and down and around mountains green with vegetation. The scenery is stupendous, forcing us to stop several times for pictures. At a mountaintop viewpoint overlooking Lake Atitlan, we encounter a market where we stop and buy mementos to take home for family.

We are riding on secondary roads that cross back and forth over the main highway, so several times I have to stop to ask directions. It is 4:00 PM when we reach Malacatán, a small town not far from the border. It is too late to cross now so we find a room at Hotel La Estancia. We have only traveled 259 kilometers today.

Once we get settled in we go to the main lodge for dinner, and meet the owner, Ernesto—a very hospitable man. He is an artist and shows us through his studio. We meet the parrots and cockatiels that he raises and loves dearly. He tells us he enjoys life here in Guatemala.

When we return to our room Norma announces that she is going to stay here a couple of days. We have been riding for eight days straight and she needs a break. She stresses that I should keep going, that she is prepared to ride alone.

I have an agenda and still hope to make it home for my family reunion, so I will leave in the morning. One part of me feels relief that I will be traveling alone again, and another part is sorry and hesitant to leave a riding companion in a strange country.

Chapter 17
Going Home

— Mexico

I have breakfast with Ernesto, the owner of Hotel La Estancia, before leaving Malacatán. Norma is up when I get back to the room. I say goodbye, wish her a safe journey, and ask her to keep in touch. She makes no reply, so I give her a hug and leave.

The Mexican border crossing is only a few kilometers away. I pay fifteen pesos to exit Guatemala and 213 pesos for a Mexican tourist card. Payment for the tourist card is not required at this location, but is payable at any bank before exiting Mexico. To take my bike into Mexico I am required to pay $29.70 US via credit card. If I were to pay cash the charge would be an additional four hundred dollars. Go figure!

When I finally get through Customs I am welcomed by a four-lane, divided highway. I follow route 200, riding predominantly west. Mid afternoon I ride through a very hard rainstorm including thunder and lightening. It does not last too long but I am not free yet. Later in the afternoon I encounter two more small rainstorms. The last hour's ride is hot and sunny. My jacket and gloves are almost dry by the time I reach Juchitán. I have traveled 429 kilometers today.

The next morning I feel tired and weak so I take my time packing up. It's still only 7:20 when I hit the road. I stop at a service station to check the air in my tires and fuel up before riding out. The highway takes me through many small towns with large "topes" (speed bumps), making progress slow. I head north towards the east coast and the Gulf of Mexico. After three hours and two hundred kilometers I decide to take the freeway. Toll fees for the day are 213 pesos, approximately twenty dollars US, but I make better time.

I decide to stop early in Vera Cruz to get to a bank and pay the fee for my tourist card. I find a marvelous hotel with a swimming pool and parking for three hundred pesos. Wal-Mart and a large shopping plaza are across the road. I locate a bank and stand in line for forty minutes to pay my fee, then find a car wash and clean up my bike. Today has turned out to be extremely hot. I have only traveled 442 kilometers, but am glad to be off the road.

The following morning I have breakfast before heading out. I have come through a time change, so rather than 8:30 it is 7:30 when I leave. Later in the morning I ride through little towns along the Gulf of Mexico and pass by open patio restaurants. I notice many people eating seafood cocktails served in tall stem glasses. I must stop and try one of these for lunch. When I do stop for lunch, I am not disappointed. The menu is in Spanish so I guess at what to order. I believe my choice is a shrimp cocktail. The waitress brings me an eight-inch tall soda glass packed with shrimp in a delicious red sauce. This is fantastic! By the time I eat halfway down the glass the shrimp turn to oysters. I guess I missed that in my translation of the menu. Anyway, I feel full by now so I leave the rest. I *do* know that if it had been shrimp all the way to the bottom of the glass I would have devoured it all.

Traffic today is much heavier than yesterday. The road is spattered with patch jobs and topés, making travel slow. Most of the Mexicans I have met are friendly and helpful, but occasionally one will turn away when hearing English.

I stop at Tampico after about five hundred kilometers. It has been a long day and feels like much more than that. I find a comfortable room in a hotel with enclosed parking for three hundred pesos. I am tired tonight and need a good night's sleep.

On Sunday, June 20, I am up early and leave the hotel at 7:30. Getting out of the city takes time. Tampico is larger than I thought. Once I reach the highway I make good time. I arrive at the Mexican border crossing early in the afternoon and am sent through. They do not stamp my tourist card or bike papers, so I figure there must be another control booth up ahead. I pay 21 pesos to cross the bridge to Texas and find myself at US Customs and Immigration. Now what? I haven't got the exit stamps for Mexico.

— USA

There are several lanes leading to half a dozen Customs booths. All have at least six vehicles in line. When it is my turn, a female officer looks at my passport and questions me thoroughly before sending me on to the next gate. I stop here and am questioned again by two officers about all the countries in my passport. When I mention Iran the officer quickly asks about Iraq and Saudi Arabia. I tell them no, but now their suspicions are aroused, and I am told to open my trunks.

I unstrap my bags from the back seat and open all three trunks. The officers return to their air-conditioned building without looking at anything. I wait for several minutes in the blistering sun in 35-degree temperatures. Finally one officer comes back. He is about to hand my passport back when another officer stops him. The woman in the first booth, who looked at my passport, wants to check it again. Another ten minutes pass before she returns and hands it back to me. No one ever does look in my saddlebags and trunk.

With all this hassle complete, I must return to Mexico Customs to have my bike papers and passport stamped with an exit stamp. That means paying another bridge fee to cross back into Mexican territory. I must find the building marked "Banque" to obtain an exit stamp and date on my bike papers. The Banque is on the entrance side and not at all obvious to anyone leaving Mexico. Then I must walk to the entrance booth to have my tourist card stamped with an exit. Now the only way out of here is to cross back over the bridge leading to Texas, pay the toll fee again, and re-enter the lines for Customs and Immigration. The lines are longer this time around.

An officer at the first booth begins to question me again. I remind him that I was just here a short time ago and he lets me through, but I must stop at the Immigration building again. An officer comes out and asks, "Why are you still here?"

I explain what has just transpired. He laughs and sends me through.

An hour has passed and I am hot and tired. It is difficult to find the humor in this.

I ride as far as McAllen, Texas and get a room at the Pasada Anna Inn. I treat myself to dinner at the Olive Garden this evening. I have not had one of their fabulous salads in three years. This area is close to the Mexican border and mostly Spanish speaking. I can understand a few words, but the Spanish is quite different from what I learned in South America.

The closer to home I get the more anxious I am to get there. My front brake has started grinding so I must find a shop and get the brakes replaced. I contact Kay, a member of "Women in the Wind" in Temple, Texas. She invites me to stay with them and offers to make an appointment for my bike.

After another long day of riding the brake noise is getting worse. I stop at a shop on the north end of Austin just to find that they are closed today due to a family funeral. I continue on to Temple, riding through rain the latter part of the day. Kay meets me at a service station and guides me to the bike shop where I leave my bike for servicing the next day.

When we reach Kay's home, her husband Ed is in the garage working on one of their three bikes. This is a wonderful treat, to be with people who love bikes.

I e-mail my sister tonight and tell her I probably won't make it home for the family reunion on the 26th and 27th. I will have to spend a second day here waiting for my bike repair. That means leaving Temple on June 24.

My stay with Kay and Ed is fantastic. They treat me like a friend of the family. Kay and I do some shopping in a couple of motorcycle shops while my bike is being worked on. I buy riding gloves, sunglasses, a Mexico/US/Canada map, and a new helmet. My full-face modular helmet was damaged badly from a drop onto a cobblestone street in Antigua. The moveable part that flips up the front is cracked and wants to fall off. I gladly throw it away.

My bike is ready at 3:00 PM. I get everything packed up so I can leave early in the morning. This evening I treat Ed and Kay to dinner to express my thanks for keeping me and booking my bike into a good shop.

On Thursday morning, June 24, at 7:15, I leave Temple and ride northwest. There is a town in Texas called Brownfield. I grew up in the farming community of Brownfield, Alberta, so I must stop and see what Brownfield, Texas, looks like. It is mid afternoon when I arrive. I have ridden 586 kilometers and will stay here for the night.

Brownfield, Texas, has a population of 9,488 with a Wal-Mart, McDonald's, Subway, and other fast food chains. Brownfield, Alberta, has none of these. In fact, it does not have much of anything anymore. There is a school, a church, curling rink, hall, and a handful of residences. There used to be a garage, gas pumps, and a nice grocery store but I think that is all gone now.

My last few days on the road are filled with hard riding. I average close to seven hundred kilometers a day—like a horse heading for the open barn door. I ride through a corner of New Mexico, Colorado, Wyoming, then into Montana. Now that I know I won't make it home for the family reunion, I decide to ride over the Beartooth Pass. I cannot remember ever taking this route, and have heard many great stories about it, so now is a good time.

It is a spectacular ride. As I climb higher into the mountains the temperature drops, making me stop to plug in my heated liner and pull out my warm gloves. Views of snow-capped mountains and alpine lakes are phenomenal. When I reach the highest point at 10,974 feet (3,345 meters), I stop and take pictures of my bike against the snow. I ride as far as Billings, having come 622 kilometers. The date is Monday, June 28. In two more days I will be home.

I am up early the next morning. I have been through Montana several times on my bike and know that I can make good time. The highways are good with minimal traffic, and the need for sightseeing has escaped me. I stop only for fuel, water, and light snacks to keep going. I zigzag my way northwest across Montana stopping at the Sweet Grass/Coutts border. The officer looks through my passport thoroughly before sending me on.

— *Canada*

I am still carrying the carnet for my bike. Even though it expired almost a year ago, I need a stamp from Canadian Customs to prove that I have brought the bike back. This is simply a paper trail to show that the bike has not been sold in another country. It is also to make sure the governments get their import/export tax in the event that I had sold it along the way.

I am instructed to take my carnet into the customs office. I speak to three different officers and no one will stamp the carnet. I explain the procedure in as many different ways as possible, but am still refused a stamp proving that my bike is crossing back into Canada. Finally I give up and leave. I will phone the CAA office in Ottawa when I arrive home.

Note: The CAA office later advises me to have a Notary Public witness that my motorcycle is back in Alberta, and sign my carnet de passage. Then I am to mail it back to Ottawa. When it is received in their office, they will release my security letter from the bank for ten thousand dollars.

The weather has cooperated all day until late afternoon. North of Ft. McLeod on Highway 2 the wind and rain begins and lasts until High River. Half an hour later I arrive at my sister's home in Okotoks. I have traveled 877 kilometers, and it has been a very long day.

It is wonderful seeing my sister Liz. We have so much to talk about but cannot possibly catch up in one evening. That will take many more visits.

On Wednesday, June 30, 2004, I ride the last 329 kilometers back to Edmonton. I have clocked 120,608 kilometers on my Magna, visiting forty-four countries on six continents. I have achieved my goal to ride around the world. **I have lived my wildest dream!**

Epilogue

This journey has been the most incredible experience in my life. It still amazes me that I was able to gather up the courage to embark on such an adventure, *alone*. One of the most frequent questions people ask me is, "Were you ever afraid?" I find that difficult to answer because there are so many variables to feeling fear. Let me try to explain.

There were times I felt uncomfortable, or uneasy; there were times I felt anxious; and there were times I knew I must move on as quickly as possible; but these situations were minimal. I dealt with them and continued on, just as we do in our familiar environments. I did not allow myself to be fearful of what *might* happen. As we all know—*that which we fear, almost never comes to be*. I trusted my instincts, which grew stronger with each new challenge. I was cautious to stay off the roads at night and did not roam the streets in the evenings unless it felt safe. I remained keenly aware of my surroundings and listened to my intuitions.

Another question I am often asked is, "What was your favorite place?" Again, this is difficult to answer. There were so many places I loved and would go back to, or recommend to other travelers. I will list three of my favorites, each for different reasons.

First, New Zealand; these two little islands have it all—beautiful scenery, great weather, fabulous roads, wonderful people, and the opportunity to enjoy any activity you might be interested in. It would be a wonderful country to retire in.

Second, I fell in love with Argentina and the Spanish culture—the music and dancing, and the lively spirited people. The country is large and the landscape diverse—there is no end to spectacular scenery. The cost of traveling here is inexpensive and I found gorgeous resorts and explored interesting places. I wonder why more North American people don't holiday here.

Then there was Turkey; this country captured my heart, for completely different reasons. The history and the ruins throughout Turkey, which date back many centuries, fascinated me. I could have spent several more weeks, maybe months, exploring. People were welcoming and always helpful. For my female readers I might add that, if you are looking for a man, this might be the country to travel in. There was no lack of propositions, many from younger men.

There were so many other countries I enjoyed, and so many more that I never made it to. Some of the countries on my original plan were passed over due to weather or difficulty obtaining a visa. I traveled into more countries than most people ever will in their lifetime, but still only saw a tiny portion of the world. *There is just so much to see!*

One of the biggest lessons I have learned is that the world is not as dangerous as we are led to believe. People everywhere are basically the same. They work, own businesses, get married and raise families, want a good education for their children, follow their spiritual beliefs, and pray for peace in the world. We don't hear about these people, the 99 percent who are just like you and me. We only hear the bad news, which discolors reality. Adult students, to whom I taught English in Thailand, asked if it was safe to travel in the United States. That question really put things into perspective for me. They only hear our bad news and think that it is unsafe on the other side of the world.

This journey has changed my priorities in life. I live more in the present and try not to waste one precious day. Possessions are just a whole lot of *stuff* and not nearly as important to me as my experiences and relationships. Living in a few homes around the globe has made me realize that we are all connected, no matter what the distance.

Have I finished traveling? Is my spirit tamed? *Never!*

ABOUT THE AUTHOR

DORIS MARON was born June 5, 1948. At age fifty-three she sold everything she owned to live her wildest dream—to travel around the world on her motorcycle. She is the mother of three children, and her six grandchildren look up to her as their hero. From her travel journals Doris now writes and shares her adventures with the world.